CONTENTS

BOOK ONE

BOOK TWO

Publisher's Prefatory Note

The original edition of this work consists in some two thousand mimeographed pages bound in eleven volumes. The title page of the first volume reads: "Interpretation of Visions, Part I, Notes on the Seminar in Analytical Psychology given by Dr. C. G. Jung, Zürich, Autumn 1930." Each volume bears the statement: "This report is strictly for the use of members of the Seminar, with the understanding that it is not to be circulated."

This seminar was held in the English language and the visions which provide the material under discussion came from an American woman in her thirties, Christiana Morgan. The brief description of her with which Jung begins the seminar is further expanded in this edition in a postscript by Henry A. Murray, M. D., Ph. D., Professor emeritus of Harvard, printed at the end of Book Two.

The material in the original edition had been assembled and edited by Mary Foote from her notes taken during the seminars. In 1939 she undertook a revised edition of the eleven volumes, for which she had regular consultations with Jung in order to clarify the more difficult passages. Copious revisions were made of the earlier mimeographed version. These working papers, together with her other Jungian *Nachlass*, are now in the Yale University Library. (See Edward Foote, "Who was Mary Foote," *Spring 1974*, pp. 264-5.) To her and her heirs we acknowledge our thanks.

Mrs. Jane A. Pratt, acting on behalf of the Publications Board of the Analytical Psychology Club of New York, gained permission from Jung to publish a new edition of these seminars in *Spring*. These annual installments appeared between 1960 and 1969. The installments prepared by Mrs. Pratt are those which are printed here as Parts One through Ten, with only slight copy-editing changes and occasional minor additions of material from the earlier mimeographed edition. Parts Eleven through Thirteen (in Book Two of this edition) have been edited by Patricia Berry from the mimeographed edition, following the pattern of excerpting that had already been established. This edition, therefore, represents an essential account of the complete mimeographed notes of Mary Foote, i.e., Jung's Visions Seminar from beginning to end. Although the final material (Part Thirteen) comes to no dramatic conclusion, Jung turned to Nietzsche's *Zarathustra* for the subject of his next English seminar, Spring Semester, 1934.

The publication of this edition has been made possible through generous support from friends of the late Christiana Morgan; as well as from Mrs. Jane A. Pratt, Mr. and Mrs. Julius Wadsworth, Mrs. Ethel Kurth of the C.G. Jung Educational Center, Houston, the Curatorium of the C.G. Jung Institute, Zürich, and the Aion Foundation.

Daryl Sharp designed, composed, and indexed the book. Robert Hinshaw and Cornelia Schroeder assisted in the production. The cover is by Jan Luss.

C.G.JUNG

THE VISIONS SEMINARS

From the Complete Notes of Mary Foote
Postscript by Henry A. Murray

BOOK ONE
Parts One – Seven

1976

Spring Publications
c/o Postfach 190
8024 Zürich
Switzerland

IKO
J

Vol. 1

ISBN 0-88214-111-2

Spring Publications is a non-profit activity of the Analytical
Psychology Club of New York, Inc., 28 East 39th Street, New York 10016.

Manufactured in Switzerland at Spring House and Buchdruckerei
Schrumpf, 8123 Ebmatingen-Zürich, for Spring Publications, Postfach 190, 8024 Zürich.

PART ONE

Ladies and Gentlemen: I must explain to you that these lectures are about the development, one could say, of the transcendent function out of dreams, and the actual images which ultimately serve in the synthesis of the individual, the reconciliation of the pairs of opposites, and the whole process of symbol formation.

If Fate is Benevolent . . .

Our patient is a woman of about thirty years of age. She is highly educated, very intelligent, a typical intellectual, with an almost mathematical mind. She is a natural scientist by education and exceedingly rational. She has a great deal of intuition, which really ought to function, but is repressed because it yields irrational results and that is very disagreeable to the rational mind. With a mental attitude of such a character, one is likely to hurt oneself soon in life by coming up against a situation where this attitude is useless. If fate is benevolent, one will soon get into a tight hole. If fate is not benevolent, it allows one to live a long time with such an attitude, and so one loses a lot of opportunities in life. Well, this woman gets into a hole at about thirty. That is pretty decent; obviously her fate is benevolent. It has given her a chance at thirty. Other people only have their chance at forty-five or fifty. I have seen people even at sixty who finally discovered that they had seen only half the world, that they had lived only half of their life, which is, of course, a very sad discovery at such an age. Now this woman has got to the other side of the world at thirty.

People with such an extraordinarily one-sided development of their thinking function have, on the other side, an inferior feeling function, because feeling is opposite to thinking. The feeling is archaic and has all the advantages and disadvantages of an archaic function. The inferior function is generally characterized by traits of primitive psychology, above all by *participation mystique;* that is, it is peculiarly identical, or makes one identical, with other people or with other situations. She had the feelings that circumstances gave her. She could not feel hypothetically, but she could think hypothetically. As a matter of fact, her intelligence was so highly developed that she thought the things that the people in her environment did not think. . . . She

[From the lectures given between October 30 and November 5, 1930 (*Spring* 1960).]

1

was secluded, in a *tour d'ivoire,* no bridge to her, and she naturally suffered from that ice-cold isolation, as you can imagine. Now her inferior feeling is in the foundations of that *tour d'ivoire* and has some secret passages, underground ways, where it can escape from that isolation, and because it is blind like a mole one does not know where it will come out. . . . It digs underground passages and bores into other people perhaps. She is rational, married, propagating the species, everything is quite all right, yet she is completely isolated. . . . Hers is no real marriage union whatever. And so it is quite inevitable that feeling, not living in relatedness, simply cannot climb to the heights of the head, it is overwhelmed by the intellect, apparently, and disappears, but reappears projected upon a man who, of course, is not the husband. Well, that is a woman's case. There are similar cases with men.

So you see the lack of relatedness is compensated by a sudden magic relationship, a fascination, *participation mystique.* Therefore it is usually love at first sight and the most compulsory form of love. It is natural that our patient suffered from some such problems, which mean the ultimate conflict between her rational thinking and primitive nature. I omit personal details intentionally, because they matter so little to me. We are all spellbound by those external circumstances and they distract our minds from the real thing, which is that we ourselves are split inside. . . .

Quite naturally, being in such a red-hot conflict, she did not know what to do. She tried all the usual things, squashing it, insisting that she never thought of such a thing, trying to put the whole thing out of reality, and it did not work. Naturally it would not work. It became a moral conflict, conjuring up the Ten Commandments and God knows what, but nothing would work, not even the wrath of God, because she was up against a superior fact that really was not a destructive element. It was the very best thing that could happen to her, the kindness of nature that wanted to make a whole of her and not half an egg. When she had made every attempt to squash what she had understood to be the most amazing nonsense, she finally gave up and collapsed.

Then she heard of my existence and thought that I might be a fellow who knew some magic word and so she came to me, with very much the attitude of the primitive woman who comes to the medicine man and says, "Now, here is a black hen and, if you want, I will bring you a beautiful black swine as an offering, and now kindly pass your miracles upon me." Naturally, as she was a very intellectual person, I had no trouble in showing her that she had made a mistake with such an attitude. She was soon on the right track, and understood that it was entirely up to her, that no miracle could be per-

2

formed on her. I said, "*I* don't know what to do, I haven't the slightest idea how to solve such a problem. . . . The only thing I can say is that most certainly human beings have gone through the same situation millions and millions of times in untold millions of cases. It is a typical situation, you know these love situations are most banal, and in every generation the conscious answers differ. . . ."

Man's mind, his consciousness of psyche, is a system of methods of adaptation, of how to deal with these recurring facts of life. For instance, we have eyes because there is sun. Our eyes and ears are systems of adaptation and our psyche is exactly the same, adapted not only to exterior conditions but also to conflicts within. Mythological motifs contain a lot of typically human situations, such as the fairy-tale motif according to which a man gets trapped somewhere, or the dwarfs have caught him and put him into a place where he cannot escape, and then in the night a little mouse comes and talks to him and says, "If you do this, then you can get out." This is the motif of the helpful animal intervening when everything is impossible and people expect a catastrophe — help out of a tight corner. What do these animals mean? They are merely representatives of lower instinctive forces in man and helpful in the same way. For example, when I do not know where water is, then I may observe the flight of birds and that shows me where it is, or I may say to my horse, "I don't know where the water is but you may smell the water." Or if there are no helpful animals around, a man . . . may take a rod and try it over the ground and maybe his unconscious will tell him where the water is. These are facts.

Now I say, if the unconscious can help in such a case, why not in this woman's situation? I am pretty sure that the unconscious contains a solution, so I propose to my patient to watch its activity as given through dreams, because we do not make dreams, they simply come up from the unconscious. We do not know whether they are true or not, and it is a matter of experience to see if they are merely nonsense. She agreed to this idea and so we started in with analysis. At first, as is usually the case, the dreams contained more personal stuff, all sorts of little resistances and wrong attitudes, but when all that was settled, then they began to come to the fundamental things and to prepare very carefully the attitude most favorable for the production of the symbols which brought about the solution of her problem. We will begin now with a dream which happened when the first part of the analysis, all that personal part, was practically over.

3

The Interrupted Music

DREAM: I was trying to play some music and all the different members of my family tried to interfere. I was on a terrace looking out over the sea and still playing, when a rich Jew at the next table began to play also. The music that he played was so beautiful that I stopped playing for a minute myself to listen to him.

Have you an idea what this dream means: It is very simple. What is music? Of course, it is feeling. She is very intellectual and has very inferior feeling, so it is probable that we will encounter most of her feeling in the unconscious. The dream brings up that problem. So playing music means giving play to her feelings, compensating her chiefly intellectual attitude. For even in analysis she takes the whole thing chiefly from an intellectual viewpoint and uses her feelings very little because they are not manageable, not disposable in reality. Therefore she uses them in the dream.

As an example, there was a very rational man in antiquity and that was old Socrates. . . . He had a sort of humorous daemon that whispered very wise advice to him. . . . On one occasion, probably after a very strenuous night of rational talking, the daemon said: "Thou shouldst make more music, Socrates." He couldn't get it. He thought a great deal about it and finally he bought a flute! But it is quite obvious that music in those days meant, of course, the Dionysian element, which was very much a feeling affair, quite opposite to the general rational attitude of Socrates.

So you see my patient, one could say, was admonished to play music. . . . But when she tries to play her feelings, use her own feelings, then it suddenly becomes evident that every member of the family is against it. "Such a terrible thing must not happen in our family!" She insists that, despite the members of this "holy" family, she will continue to play her feelings; but there is a rich Jew who plays very much better than she and therefore she gives up. Yet how can these feelings develop if she cannot use them? She must pathetically admit that she is going to exercise them just in order to get them alive, and naturally everything in her surroundings — all the members of her family — will be dead against it, will advise her not to have her feelings. But then something subtle happens: namely, the opposition of the family does not kill her, but the fact that somebody plays better music, *that* kills her. Now what does the rich Jew mean? That is a bit cryptic.

First Suggestion: The Jew stands for authority.

Dr. Jung: But anyone who plays better than she would have authority. He might be a great artist, for instance.

4

Second Suggestion: He stands for beauty and love of art.

Third Suggestion: Love of power?

Dr. Jung: Well, there is a far more immediate connection. His religion is not the religion of the New Testament. And this woman is a Protestant of Puritan extraction. We must go a little more deeply into the psychology of the Protestant religion. He knows little or nothing of St. Paul. You see the Protestant is like a Jew: in his unconscious one finds a Jew. . . . For instance, my great-grandfather on my mother's side was a very pious Protestant and he believed that the language spoken in heaven was Hebrew and therefore he was a professor of the Hebrew language. You see, he wanted to make ready, to be a sort of guardian angel who understood the language of the heavenly company. One could say that he was on the other side an Old Testament Jew. And that is the reason, too, why they gave the children Jewish names in those days. That had nothing to do with the New Testament whatever. That was the Jew in them. Indeed the whole mental make-up of the Protestant showed that he believed in authority, he was absolutely convinced of the Law, he worshipped the Law. Often he does not really worship the God of Love, does not believe in a God of Tolerance. . . .

That Jew simply means this woman's unconscious mind, the unconscious man in her. Now what is the unconscious man? I suppose nearly everyone here knows about it. It is the animus. So the animus is a figure personifying the opinionating of a woman. I cannot put it better. Unrealized ready-made opinions, and spoken with authority. I know women who have an opinion about everything, they know it all, but when I say "Yes, that is so," they are disappointed. They want me to say no. But if I said no, that unconscious man would come up and have a terrible row with me, because such opinion in a woman is a man who wants to fight, this thing in a woman makes enemies, and very often a woman is a victim of this unconscious figure. It is the animus.

Now the rich Jew is an animus of great wealth, great power, great authority, and he is in possession of her feelings. Naturally everything that falls into the unconscious is possessed by the animus. He is there with open mouth and catches everything that falls down from the table of consciousness, and the more she is unaware of the other side, the more powerful he is. For instance, it is practically a rule of thumb in my analysis that when I have gotten along quite smoothly with a woman in my treatment for a while, then suddenly everything is wrong. She begins to argue and everything has capsized apparently, and you don't know what is head and what is tail and it is all the work of the animus. Suddenly the animus has overriden her and made a complete mess of the whole thing. One asks, "Why is all this? " and she does not know. So I say, "Well, your animus has been starved for a while and gotten very hungry and he then becomes particularly attentive; you were apparently not conscious enough and you didn't watch your treasures; you didn't watch your feeling, let us say, for a while; some infinitesimal part of yourself has been left unconscious and instantly the animus takes it, he has eaten and is strong again and begins to argue."

For instance, it sometimes happens that a woman shows me her feelings in a particularly nice way — gives me some flowers or something of the sort. But then again when she has a temptation to do so, up comes the thought, "Dr. Jung knows so many women who are all nice to him, all women have transferences and send flowers, so why should I do so? " and she lets it go. That is food for the animus. It can be a very inconsiderable thing, a *quantité négligeable*, but she should have said something, *expressed* a feeling, thanked me for something for instance. Instantly the feeling turns away, it goes into the unconscious, and the neglect of that little feeling duty develops into a most murderous discussion if one is fool enough to allow it. The only thing a man can do is to say yes, and punish her by disappointment. Then she suddenly discovers that she has been the victim of an evil spirit.

There is a very nice German poem, a folk-song really, of a little hunchback who follows a girl; everywhere she goes there he is, and says something evil which spoils the pleasure, a sort of whispering ghost who puts in his poison. That is the animus.

In this dream, then, the very subtle thing that happens is that she is not stopped in her music by actual obstruction through her relatives, or her own ideas as expressed by them, but by a factor in herself — that figure of the animus who turns up playing far more wonderful music than she ever could. This comes from the fact that psychologically she is not master of her inferior function. In the same way a person with differentiated feeling is never completely in possession of his thinking, but is suddenly possessed by a thought, a thought sits upon his brain like a bird and does not go away when he wants it to go away, and does not come when he wants it to come.

The inferior function is just nature. It does not obey us, though it may partially obey us. For instance, I may talk to that lady of her child, of everything that interests her, of her books, and she has an identical feeling tone. There the feeling is allowed, inasmuch as it is guided by the intellect and feels in the right way. But the feeling which is allowed in the conscious you could compare to that part of nature cultivated in your garden. It is nature, but nature chosen by you, by no means the unrestrained, uncontrollable

6

force of nature in a primeval forest. The rest of the function, which is by far the most wonderful **part really**, is not under your guidance, not under your control. It belongs to nature, to the nature of the soul, to all those realms which you cannot possibly control because they are unconscious. It is as if they were under the control of that powerful mysterious figure.

Now such a figure, the animus or the anima figure, is felt by the primitive, or by an unprejudiced man who does not think intellectually, as a most powerful presence — like a daemon or a God. One might say that a God began to play in her and then she had to stop. But in using the word "God" I may arouse prejudice. I do not use that word in a particularly favorable sense, as one might say, "Isn't it marvelous? A God began to play in her and naturally she stopped." For if you understand the word rightly, in the antique sense, it means a *power*, and she must make the attempt to use it herself, and nothing should discourage her, even if the Gods are doing it better. And if the God, the power, takes the form of the animus, then especially she must not allow herself to be stopped, inasmuch as, if the animus interferes here, he is negative. So if I am allowed to use the word "God" at all, naturally I use it in the antique sense which can be quite negative. The Gods had too many scandalous love-affairs and so they made themselves ridiculous and lost their authority with later men. The primitive man could stand it because he just naively marvels, just watches what the Gods are going to do next. He does that with the white man, too; if the white man gets into a tight corner, he just sits about and wonders what the white man is going to do next. And so the primitive man watched his Gods, and if they did something frightfully immoral, it was still admirable; the greatest obscenity was marvelous.

So for the relatively primitive level of consciousness it does not matter how the Gods behave. But for a higher civilization, if they became disreputable, then they were ridiculous, and that depreciated them so much that they finally collapsed and new Gods entered the scene. So the new attitude of the patient ought to be that of later men. She should criticize her animus and say that it is outrageous that when she begins to play he should interrupt her. She should not allow him to stop her. That is what I told her.

The Doctor Who Lived by the Sea

DREAM: I was going to see a doctor who lived in a house beside the sea. I lost my way and desperately asked people to put me on the right path so that I could get to him.

Naturally when she dreams of the doctor, everybody is inclined to think he is myself. She is under my treatment and so that refers to me. Now it is only funny that the unconscious does not say so more definitely. Naturally anybody who analyzed dreams according to Freud's point of view would say that it was I, but I am not so sure. If the unconscious wanted to convey the idea that this was Dr. Jung, it would say so; then the dream itself, which we cannot criticize, would have brought me in. But the dream says "the doctor by the sea," and the Lake of Zürich is not a sea. Therefore there is some change in the whole situation and we see that behind the impressions of the daily life — behind the scenes — another picture looms up, covered by a thin veil of actual facts. In order to understand dreams, we must learn to think like that. We should not judge dreams from realities because in the long run that leads nowhere.

The dream lives in an atmosphere which is not our atmosphere in this conscious world, where it is hard and there are no veils and, if you do not pay attention to realities as such, they will simply drag you under. But on the other side, such realities mean little; they are sometimes veils so thin that you perceive at once the greater picture behind the veil of facts. So you see what we call important here, that stupendous fact that she is now actually under my treatment, that I have a house on the bank of a lake where she comes almost daily to hear disagreeable news, all that becomes like a mist. We can look through it to another picture to that dream doctor whose house is by the sea, a different, big, sort of heroic landscape by the sea. In the dream is the vastness of the ocean, an extraordinary view. Here, we have a view of a few miles, no view at all, but there, is a tremendous horizon. Also a house placed on the shore of the sea is quite different from a villa here on the bank of the Lake of Zürich, you get an entirely different atmosphere. Moreover there is no question in reality of her losing her way. She does not lose her way in finding my house. She has been two months under my treatment and even if she lost her way there would be no desperate asking for it. But if that house is a strange house, if that doctor is a strange doctor, then she may lose her way; it is vast country and she has to fight almost desperately to find the way to that place.

Now you see that is the sort of archetypal image that puts one right back into prehistoric ages. There is terrible trouble. . . . She feels cheated by a daemon or, say, by a hostile God. In such an archetypal situation . . . she does not know what to do, so she seeks the help of the medicine man who has been there since eternity. Usually he lives alone and in an inaccessible place. . . . You see the place chosen is expressive of his own psychology, so the medicine man chooses an extraordinary place and the more difficult to find the better, for of course the medicine man is never here, he is always in some strange corner of the world beyond the seas. . . . So to find the medicine man, this woman must travel far, she must toil, she must ask her way desperately to that far and unknown place. . . .

You see this dreamer, who now speaks of the quest to seek the great healer, would make a great mistake to see the great healer in me. Naturally her first leap was at me. But I said, "No, thank you." Because otherwise she would hang me later on when things go wrong, for that doctor will most certainly be hard, very difficult. Those primitive medicine men do terrible things, they torture you! And then she will cry out and say, "You said you were the great medicine man — you led me on that way." So I don't take all that. Right from the beginning I decline with thanks the great honor of being called the medicine man. If a dream should say that somebody is going to Dr. C. G. Jung living at Seestrasse, Küsnacht, then I admit that is myself. . . . But here the problem is much greater than I and it is wise to keep to the words the dream gives you because one cannot expect to be wiser than nature.

Freud would say, "Wish-fulfillment — a resistance; she wishes not to find her way to you because things are getting disagreeable." And that is truth, too, sure enough. There are doubts in her. It is such a novelty to her that the unconscious should find a solution where she does not. For we are bored by the unconscious. We have tremendous pride and imagination about ourselves and the power of our consciousness because we are so efficient. Who built such powerful machines? Our consciousness, of course! And so we believe in it and we think of that unconscious self as nothing, a more or less disreputable appendix to the wonderful light we have up here in our heads!

So if one said to her, "Apparently you have great difficulty in getting to that doctor — what are your resistances to me? " one would be on the wrong track, because she would gladly accept that personal aspect, she would see a loop-hole, she would say to herself, "This man likes to assume the role of the Great Healer. I will hand out my whole stuff to him and if he does not succeed, woe to him!" She would have somebody to make responsible if things do not turn out as they should. So I have learned from painful experience to interpret dreams correctly.

The healer is the animus again, only this time he no longer plays music, he appears in the disguise of the doctor, and later on you will see that he again takes on different forms. Now on this occasion I explained to the lady what I understood about the animus, and the relation between the animus and the unconscious.

9

[At this point the patient has been introduced and her situation explained. It was immediately after this session of analysis that her first visions began. As Dr. Jung says: *She felt very sleepy and lay down, thinking she would fall asleep. Instead, she merely got into a very drowsy condition and saw with her inner eyes a hypnagogic vision.* Unfortunately, space does not permit us to give the material which follows in full. Her initial visions are predominantly of an introductory character, and we will have to limit ourselves to the first one only. – Ed.]

The Peacock on the Back of a Man

VISION: She saw a beautiful peacock perched on the back of a man, and the beak of the peacock was pointed at the neck of the man. . . .

Naturally, she could not understand this picture. But as it was exceedingly symbolic, I asked her associations about the peacock. She said that it is a most beautiful bird when it opens up its tail; it has blue eyes, gorgeous colors, and all that. I felt what she meant. This is again an experience difficult to describe but, if you have a feeling heart, you will understand it. When that marvelous beauty of color and form and light appears, then you have a feeling of things unfolding. That is what the peacock stands for in the history of symbolism. The spring and the sunrise. The idea was that his flesh was incorruptible. In the early Christian church and in the sermons of St. Augustine and St. Anthony of Padua, for instance, the peacock was used as a symbol of resurrection. That was because with the approach of winter, he loses his feathers and regains them again with the sun, with the spring. So he is the symbol of regeneration, and as such you see him in the early church as a symbol of the resurrection of the soul. He is also a symbol of the Redeemer, because he brings back the divine childhood, by rebirth. Now all this material was, of course, not conscious to her. She was vaguely aware that it had some religious meaning, but what it was she did not know.

In the symbolism of the East the peacock also plays a certain role, but more unfavorable. There, it is a proud Luciferian kind of a bird, self-produced and disobedient to the creator of things. In the Kurd tribes there were so-called devil-worshippers who worshipped the peacock as their symbol of creative power. . . .

Now in the phantasy, the peacock is perched on the back of a man, and the back of a man is always a symbol for the unconscious side. Our unconscious bounds our field of vision and that is the reason why the shadow becomes the symbol of the unconscious of man. The primitive man is always haunted by the feeling of a presence, as if somebody were following him. We observe the same in ourselves. In the silence of the night on a lonely

10

path one feels that somebody is surely following and one looks behind to see. If one is quite alone in a house, after a while one hears a noise, as if something was said, and one gets the feeling of a presence. The primitives sought for the cause of that feeling and expressed it as a living shadow. The shadow is the one that is behind us, and it became a precious idea — this power behind us. The Greeks have a beautiful word for it, *synopados*, meaning "the one that comes with me and is behind me." But that shadow is by no means what we would call shadow — a lack of light — rather, it is a living thing of great mana, great power. Therefore if a person treads on it, it is most dangerous, and it is a terrible thing when a shadow falls on somebody. If you are sitting somewhere in the sun and a medicine man walks past and his shadow falls on you — in a fortnight you are dead. . . . So you see the shadow is full of mana to the primitive. . . .

Often the shadow has the simplest causes, yet it is mysterious, it does not do what we do, it has different qualities. For instance, it can stretch very far, sometimes for miles back, and sometimes it disappears altogether in a ghost-like way. You cannot touch it. They describe it as a cool wind and say that ghosts are shadows. Hades is the shadow world and the shadows dwell there. It is often symbolized as a bird that flies away. The idea is that when one dies one becomes a shadow and puts on wings, a feathered garment. You can read in the Gilgamesh epic about the sad place where souls wear feathered garments.

So here the peacock assumes the role of a sort of ghost that possesses the man. But we must cling to our original hypothesis that this is the animus again, that this is the man in her, and now this vision says that behind her man, behind the animus, is a new principle that possesses him. It is his genius that sits behind him like the king's hawk, or the eagle of Zeus. This is the peacock-ghost of unfolding, of beauty, of spring — of everything that is symbolized by the peacock. It is an almost prophetic vision and it is very difficult to translate. Therefore I prefer to keep quite naively to the picture itself.

There is still one detail to which I want to call your attention and that is that the peacock is holding his beak to the man's neck. There is a slight menace in it. One thinks that if that man is doing something he ought not, the peacock is likely to kill him. In such a position, one thinks of the peacock stabbing a vital place, breaking the man's neck. It suggests that this man is controlled from the unconscious by that powerful being. If one tries to translate such a vision into psychological language, one must say that the animus which we saw expressed as the rich Jew, or the doctor, or anybody else, is not only the animus, really; he is himself controlled in turn by a much

11

greater thing – by the spirit of creation, of sunrise, of rebirth. And this means, too, that if she maintains the right relationship to the man, she may attain to magic rebirth through the realization of this spirit that controls her, this *daimonion.*

Details in Dreams and the Independence of the Unconscious

In analyzing dreams it is always advisable to enter into the details of the symbolism – it is by no means indifferent what kind of symbol the dream chooses. Here I take a different standpoint from the Freudian school to which the symbolism is absolutely indifferent. Ten thousand things can have the same meaning, say the genitals or something of the sort. But I say it is all-important what the dream says, and not what we interpret into it. We may go astray with our interpretation but the dream is a natural fruit and we have not organized or produced it. It is like a strange bird. We may say, this bird should not be. . . . Our attitude may be that it is a thing which should not even be born, but that is surely not a scientific attitude. We must take the dream for what it is. We must not say, "This is merely a symbol for such and such a thing," as if we had control of the sources of the dream. We must be grateful if we discover what the sources of the dream are, but we have absolutely no control over those sources.

Question: Is it true that a patient chooses in the dream the symbol of which he has had an experience in reality? If she had had an experience of earthquake, would the dream in that case choose an earthquake?

Dr. Jung: Well, provided that the earthquake or the fire is the apt symbol to express what actually is meant. For instance, I have experienced fire, earthquake, floods, and bombardment. Now if my unconscious should choose to demonstrate the insufficiency of a certain general attitude of mine, then it would have a choice; but if an earthquake destroys my house and the unconscious chooses the symbol of a flood instead, from that I know that it is a very specific danger and not simply a question of destruction. For instance, I may dream that a house tumbles down on account of either fire or of earthquake. The earthquake would convey just as much the idea of destruction as the fire; but if I want to know something about the real nature of the thing that besets me, then I must know about the specific destructive agent.

Comment: But I think if you had had only one experience in real life, for instance, that of fire, then the dream would choose fire.

Dr. Jung: One can dream of all those things even if one has never had an experience of them. We know that. For instance, one dreams of amazing

12

animals, tremendous serpents that one never has seen, horrible monsters which do not exist. One has all the emotions of seeing a real dragon when surely one never saw a dragon, and yet people are afraid of them. I remember dreams of patients, people in Switzerland who never were in the war and who surely never had seen a bombardment from the air, yet a number of them dreamed of bombs coming down and killing people. They had read vivid descriptions and seen photos in the illustrated papers, and so naturally they could use that material. All this has shown me that the unconscious has the most amazing faculty for picking its own material. For instance, when I was in Africa, I never dreamed of Africa. Only once a Negro appeared in my dreams and I thought, "Now at last Africa has gotten under my skin," and then it dawned upon me that that Negro was my barber in Chattanooga, in the United States, not an African Negro at all. That is what the unconscious can do.

People in the most amazing situations can dream the most obvious banalities, with not a trace of all the powerful experiences they may be living through during the daytime; and people who are living very simple normal lives have dreams that are full of horrible things. So we can establish from all this that the unconscious is most amazingly independent. There is absolutely no rule. The only rule is that extraordinary independence of anything to do with the conscious. You can be certain that you have no possible chance to influence the unconscious from the conscious. If the unconscious chooses to say something else, it will most certainly say something else, despite all your efforts. If you should succeed in suggesting to yourself to have a certain dream, I should say it was because it suited the unconscious – there was really something behind it.

Suppose you want to experiment and you say, "Now tonight when I go to sleep I shall concentrate upon a certain image which must appear in my dream." Then you begin to consider upon what image you will concentrate and you come to the conclusion that it shall be the idea of fire. You have the expectation and the will that it shall appear in the dream, and it does appear, and you say, "Ah, now we have it!" But you do not question how you came to choose that particular symbol in the daytime. For instance, sometimes when we are talking, a certain word leaps up and inserts itself into our sentence, or we forget a name already on our lips. Now from these disturbances we could almost reconstruct the dream that is going on all the time in the unconscious and the minute we are alone, we instantly sink down into that fabric of dreams.

If you go down a little more, have an *abaissement du niveau mental*, so that the clear light of consciousness is lowered and there is a sort of twilight, then you find yourself in that stratum of yourself where you are in the immediate neighborhood of dreams. When you are very tired, it often happens that your perception of reality becomes dream-like. . . . And it happens also, when you are so tired as to be nearly unconscious, that autonomous phenomena come up – you see people that don't exist, you hear voices, you hear your name called, you are simply in the neighborhood of dreams where your whole psychical life begins to be objectified.

This happens in your experiment too. So when you choose a symbolism, you never know whether your unconscious has not chosen it for you. You say you have chosen fire but you are never sure that the unconscious will not say, "No, I say water!" And if the dream repeats fire, the only safe conclusion which I know of in that case is that the dream has chosen to say so. How the devil do you know it has *not* chosen it? My respect for dreams goes very far, and I am impressed again and again by the extraordinary independence of the unconscious, the most extraordinary mental independence I know. The independence of the conscious is ridiculous in comparison. The conscious is tremendously dependent but the unconscious not at all.

For instance, in any conscious matter, you can say you got it from such and such source, read it in the newspaper perhaps, but when it comes to the unconscious, there you are safe only when you assume that it is a genuine production which grows out of the soil like a plant, and you cannot say of that plant (as you can of a conscious production) that it is only because a certain poet made a poem about such a flower growing in such a place. This flower is not here on account of the poet. Any kind of wind may have blown the seed here, and so it is with dreams.

The dreams and visions are the products of nature and they are most amazingly uninfluenced even if it looks quite otherwise. I insist on that point, because Freud's point of view is just the contrary. He thinks that the unconscious is tremendously influenced and certain dreams only come from the fact that one has seen this or that. But I bet anything, if you see a street accident, perhaps a most horrible and impressive scene, that you will dream nothing about it, or if you do, that it will be distorted. Then it is most certainly not only a mere accident, but a symbol that expresses some psychological problem in yourself. The real accident has simply been used as a sort of language. . . . The unconscious can use it if it suits its purpose, or not at all if it is not symbolic.

So you see I have little confidence in the theory that impressions of the day are respected. I have too often seen cases when people thought they

14

were deeply impressed, but the next dream would be of the old aunts and cousins as before, no lasting impression whatever. They say, "Now I see it! Now I realize it!" Then the next reaction is just the contrary, everything the other way round. So we see that the unconscious is not yet reached, it is not touched. The reactions of the unconscious are still the same as if nothing whatever had happened. The great importance of dreams and the reason why we have to analyze them is to see where we are in our unconscious. We can be God knows where in our conscious, on top of Mount Everest in our intuition — and in our unconscious, not even out of the cradle.

Question: You would agree, would you not, that the character of the dreams is dependent upon the general intensity of the attitude — that their character after analysis is different from before, so the change of the conscious standpoint is a determining factor?

Dr. Jung: My point is really the insistence upon the fact that no matter what your conscious attitude is, the unconscious has an absolutely free hand and can do what it pleases. Naturally if you assimilate large parts of the unconscious to the conscious, then it changes. All people in practical analysis know that usually before analysis patients have nice and ordinary dreams, perfectly presentable, but no sooner have they taken to analysis than the whole thing is smashed up and they get terrible dreams, all the beauty gone. That comes from the fact that people who come for analysis are dissociated. They are disorientated in every way, and then from the first lesson they get a sort of order in their conscious chaos. They see a line. Then instantly the chaos is in the unconscious.

A Music Lesson

DREAM: I kept a Swiss boy waiting a long time whilst I was dressing and I was not quite dressed when I went into the next room where he was waiting. I say, "Now I will play the tune which I have learned." The boy says, "No, you have kept me waiting so long that now you will learn what I have to teach."

This is one of those scenes that belong to that layer of her unconscious from which her visions later on will start. In this dream, however, there is nothing that would let us see or divine what is coming. It is only a very modest beginning, symbolized by music lessons. You remember that this woman is highly intellectual and anybody with differentiated intellect has to pay for such an accomplishment, usually with inferior feeling, as people with a very refined, differentiated feeling function pay with lack of development of the mind. For feeling excludes thinking, and thinking excludes feeling. People say, why should it? Of course, we should all be angels and have golden wings. It would be much nicer.

When the plant grows up it is wise enough to develop leaves on each side, but we are in the unhappy position that if we develop one side, we do not develop the other; we cannot develop everything at the same time. This differentiation of a function is one of the miracles of culture, of consciousness. Consciousness says, this is very useful, now use your clever mind and you will have power. That is true. The deeper the differentiated thinking goes, the more you will use it and the more it works and yields success. But the more you do so, the less you will consider feeling. You see we are not like plants exactly in that respect. Only as long as we are unconscious are we like plants, like very primitive man, or a child that has practically no consciousness or only the very objective consciousness that is identical with things that happen. But our actual willful consciousness, which claims to have a free will or free choice, is a very disturbing factor; it can choose things, it can say, this is useful and I shall build it up. As long as we are like nature, we grow like plants, we develop thinking as well as feeling, but all in an unconscious way.

Inasmuch as it is not distorted by consciousness, the primitive has a nature-like *naïveté*. But as soon as there is consciousness, the conscious chooses, it is the beginning of differentiation, and differentiation is one-sidedness necessarily. But when such a one-sidedness of development reaches a certain culmination, then comes a break, then comes a sort of collapse, what you call in America a break-down. Then the differentiated function collapses because, in the case of an intellectual person, feeling was wanted and could not be produced, either in an extraverted situation or a situation within. Usually if one studies the history of such a collapse, one finds that the situation has evolved in the years previous to it, where things have become so entangled that only the inferior function could have brought order, if it had not been too inferior. People often think when I speak of inferior feeling that I mean weak in intensity. That is by no means true. It is something fearfully strong but primitive, barbarous, animal-like, and you cannot control it. It controls you. And whenever a situation demands the inferior function, then you are in for trouble.

This woman collapsed. She came to an end with her brain-box, and her feeling only said awkward unacceptable things which she did not like to hear — things that were too evil, too foolish — and so she had to reject the feeling because she could not apply it. Moreover there was no question of applying it because the feeling would not obey her which is always true of the inferior function. . . . The assumption is, now I will use my feeling. But touch it, and

16

the feeling uses you. It can't be used. It is too hot. Then you drop it, you withdraw, and then you are at a complete standstill and nothing moves. You are on the side of the mind again, completely dry, sterile. Again you have to take up the feeling and with it comes the whole problem. That is the problem with which the patient came to me, and it is quite logical that after a while the unconscious would suggest music lessons. It is like the story of Socrates and his flute. It is the same situation here, and now the Swiss boy comes to teach her music, the art of feeling, and it would not be a very exalted type of music, it is a peasant type, played on the accordion, by no means classical. But it would be sufficient if she only could possess that much, quite a primitive way of expressing herself, for she is absolutely inarticulate. Now I wonder how you would interpret that Swiss boy. Oh, don't laugh! You don't know. I know what you think but you are all wrong.

Suggestion: It is her new mind in Switzerland here.

Dr. Jung: Yes, you are perfectly right. That is true. But you see the orthodox explanation would be that it was myself under a disguise. I have already explained to you that I would be a great fool if I accepted such an interpretation. I get sugar in one case but I get pepper in another.

Suggestion: It is a new attitude, is it not?

Dr. Jung: It is a new animus, but that is not an attitude, it is a function. The boy is a figure in herself. The best thing technically is to handle it as it is presented by the dream. The dream says *a* Swiss boy, a more or less unimportant figure. She doesn't even know how he looks, any sort of Swiss person, a youngish man. So it would be a great mistake to say that that figure was myself for then we would be forced to the conclusion that her unconscious was belittling me which would mean that she overvalues me in the conscious. Such things happen, but then the dream would probably say, "Dr. Jung comes in to teach you the accordion and in so doing he behaves in a very foolish way for, as a matter of fact, he does not know how to play the accordion; I play much better than he does and would have to show him." That is what the dream would say if the unconscious wanted to belittle me. It would use my name or my personality, because it is quite free to dream of me or anybody else. So that Swiss boy is a subjective figure in herself that has been created in her recently, because she had not been to Switzerland before nor known any Swiss people. Therefore we are quite safe in assuming that this figure originated just now, that it is a specific Swiss creation. Now what is the thing that has been created in her in Switzerland?

Answer: That she learned to think in a new way?

Dr. Jung: Learning to think analytically is the impressive thing to her.

17

That is the Swiss boy in her, who has recently been created. . . . That Swiss boy is a sort of spirit, a sort of mental visioning, a system of views, a kind of thinking, that originated in Switzerland and that advises music. That is the way the dream expresses itself. One could say, the analytical procedure so far has yielded the impression that it would be an advisable thing to pay more attention to her feeling. That is all. And if I interpret it like that, I leave the honor to her function — leave it to *her* merit. I do not reduce her function to *my* merit so that she entirely forgets that she has a function of her own, because with such a procedure I would teach her to make projections. People already project enough. I am scared of too many projections. So the dream thus far says it is the result of her own thinking process that she should learn to play the accordion.

Now she keeps him waiting. That means that it is a long time before she can make up her mind to accept the fact that she should function with her feeling. She is scared of it but she does not realize that she is scared. The inferior function is always in a state of repression or unconsciousness so we can never realize to the full what it really means or what its power is. So it takes her a long time to get dressed and when she enters the room she has not even finished dressing, which means that her attitude is not yet what it ought to be, not quite adapted. That is quite evident because she enters saying, "I will play the tune that I have learned." She touches feeling with the attitude, "Now I will show you what I want" — and she forgets entirely that when she touches feeling, she does what *it* wants. You remember the boy says, "Nothing of the kind, you do what *I* want." That is the inferior function. She can say to her thinking, "I will sit down and think over a certain matter," and behold the miracle — she can produce thought! That is the differentiated function. But she has the same attitude to her feeling. She says, "Now I am going to feel," and then nothing happens, or if something happens, it takes her by the hand and puts her into a pot of boiling oil.

That is exactly what happens here. She approaches the feeling problem represented by the music teacher with the attitude, "I can do it" — and then the boy says, "No, you can't, I am going to teach you." He takes the lead instantly, which shows that this Swiss boy was the kind of thought or spirit — one could use the word "spirit" aptly — which is by no means under her control, to be put in her pocket and taken out and played with. It is a living factor in her psychology that takes the lead. Now we don't know whether it always has had the leadership or control over her, or whether it is just at this moment, or whether it will be forever. We only know that for the time being something is going to take her hand, to force her hand. She has to obey something which is in herself, you can call it an idea or a phantasy, it does not matter; the result is the same, her hand is forced. The problem now begins to work by itself, spontaneously. She can run away yet it will reach her from within. For the fire is kindled and the process of disintegration is on the way.

Now the next dream came the next night.

To the End of the Lake Where Four Valleys Converge

DREAM: I was in a boat with some man. He said, "We must go to the very end of the lake, where the four valleys converge, where they bring down the flocks of sheep to the water." When we got there, he found a lame sheep in the flock, and I found a little lamb that was pregnant. It surprised me because it seemed too young to be pregnant. We tenderly took those two sheep in our arms and carried them to the boat. I kept wrapping them up. The man said, "They may die, they are shivering so." So I wrapped them up once more.

Now this dream is of an entirely new character. She is on the move already. She is in the boat with a man. The situation in the dream refers to a lake which obviously is the Lake of Zürich, as the boy is Swiss. The situation then, is located here — the actual situation, no memory situation and that unknown man with her is the music teacher. It is the same function but this time he shows a new quality. He is the man who sails the boat, he is the man at the tiller who takes the lead, and he says, "We must go to the very end of the lake." It is a higher necessity, a *must*, we must go to the end of the thing, the whole length of the lake. It is a sort of enterprise, an undertaking, and it must be done thoroughly, to the very end. And now there comes something most amazing: the dream says, "where the four valleys converge." Here things are getting quite mythological. What do you think about this? Traveling with an unknown man in a boat has a mythological connotation. It could be a metaphor. One is in the same boat with somebody — it is the same enterprise. Now we know the man is the teacher. He is the new spirit she has learned or created in Switzerland, and that spirit now takes her along. He is taking her by the hand, saying, "You go where I go, you follow me," and she accepts it, and the next enterprise is an adventure, traveling on the lake and going to the very end of it. What would that be in mythology?

Answer: The Quest of the Golden Fleece.

Dr. Jung: Yes, the Argonauts, the seeking of the Golden Fleece. Well I am afraid that at the other end there is no fleece, but there are sheep. In the adventures of the Argonauts you read, for instance, of their having to pass through the rocks where the pigeon loses its tail, and all that. They take an exceedingly psychological trip. Under what general name would you speak of it? It is the night sea journey. The lake is the unconscious if you take it as a symbol; the sea is a symbol for that, of course. Why? It is because when you try to look into the unconscious you see nothing — you only see your ego, nothing else, because it is dark underneath and light above and you see only yourself. Yet you know thousands of things are sunken there, monsters are there, eternal night down there. The world of our ancestors, even the world of our childhood, is still going on down in those depths. It is like the shining surface of a sheet of water which at the same time is deep and dark. We may assume that the whole world is sunk in the depths of the sea — like Atlantis — and we see nothing but our own image reflected in that shining surface. That is the reason the unconscious is expressed by the sea or by any body of water, even stagnant water.

Now that trip to the end of the lake is a serious experience, not just an amusing excursion. It is really a trip that takes you to the very end and there you would expect to find something definite, something new. And this thing that is so new and definite is symbolized by four valleys that converge, that come together, and flocks of sheep are coming down to drink the water of life. This is almost a Biblical image. It is not to be met with in reality. I cannot remember a place where four valleys converge, and when I asked the patient, she was completely stumped. . . . Well, one thinks of the four directions; in the Indian Pueblos one hears of the four cardinal points of the horizon, one thinks of the orientation of temples according to the four cardinal points. Also there is a peculiar thing about this image, there is a dynamic element in it; it is not only a static figure, because flocks of sheep are travelling down from all the four corners in order to come to the center, to drink from the water. Where do you see something similar, something within the knowledge of any civilized person to-day?

Answer: When Jesus was born.

Dr. Jung: There exists a legend that when Jesus was born and the three wise men are supposed to have come together from the four corners of the world, there were not three men, but four, but the fourth did not come in time. Jesus is the source of life and his followers are the sheep. This is the place of the waters of life where people will seek their salvation. That is one analogy. I know of two within your reach — you were taught them. It is the reverse picture, the center, and the waters of life coming out in four rivers. Where is that?

20

Answer: The Garden of Eden?

Dr. Jung: The Garden of Eden, of course. The four streams flowing out from Paradise. Then another picture, flocks of humanity streaming in. Where do you find that?

Answer: In the City of the Four Gates.

Dr. Jung: Yes, you find it in Revelation, the Last Judgment, where all the peoples of the earth stream together, like sheep. They separate the sheep from the goats. And the center of the whole performance is the Heavenly Jerusalem where the judgment is rendered. You have seen such pictures in illustrated editions of the Bible, all those flocks of sheep coming to the Last Judgment. Now you see the unconscious contains such pictures. You will say it is the influence of our Christian teaching but people from all over the world who have not received that teaching will have the same basic symbol in their unconscious. You find it in the Pueblos, in India, in China — the four-fold symbol. You find it even in the *tetraktys* of Pythagoras, a principle which must refer to the same basic orientation symbol; it is always the four cardinal points. Now the four cardinal points do not exist in reality. They are an entirely man-made projection. They are simply the projection of an inner sense of orientation that consists of four points, and why that is so, I do not know.

Special Character of Big Dreams

Whenever something turns up in a dream that has little or no connection with ordinary life, in which there are no railroads or street-cars or houses, no parents or relations, but where there are dragons or temples or something that does not exist in one's usual surroundings, then you can be sure that the unconscious is tending to convey the idea of something extraordinary, something uncommon, and it depends upon the nature of the symbolism to tell us what particular kind of extraordinary thing it is. If you dream of a dragon, it would be most obviously a mythological idea. And in our patient's dream of four valleys that come together where those flocks of sheep are brought down to the water, one feels right away that it must be a quite particular symbolism.

One does well to contemplate such a picture. That is one of the reasons why I let people make drawings, because it helps their imagination. As long as one merely looks at the picture in the dream, one has rather a fleeting impression which soon vanishes, but when you make a drawing of it, then it remains in your imagination, it remains in your field of vision; and that gives you a chance at more associations, more context. It is sometimes quite

21

surprising to see how much associative material comes out in that way. Sometimes people who cannot really paint at all make a funny kind of picture which is peculiarly stimulating to their imagination on account of the many mistakes they make. It looks like something entirely different and then they suddenly are aware of what the thing really meant, just from the fact that through their very mistakes, the unconscious contents are associated with the picture. A drawing of a dream content does not mean art, it means aid, it is like making a diagram as a method to explain a subject. Such a diagram has no claim to be art, it is just a visualization of your thoughts.

I did not suggest to the patient to make a drawing in this case. It was not necessary because she is a woman of vivid imagination and high intelligence, and she felt at once that here was something significant. In comparison with the dream before, you see that we are on a decidedly deeper level here. Such a meaningful dream takes on an epic form. To be with an unknown man in a boat is perhaps not an uncommon thing, but one must go to the very end of the lake, it is a sort of quest, an adventure, it sounds like a hieratic text. Then you come to the place where the four valleys meet, and there something exceedingly symbolic happens, the man finds a lame sheep and she finds a little lamb that is pregnant. That again shows such a symmetry of vision that one sees at once that it is highly symbolic.

When dreams have that symmetrical character, one can be sure they are referring to an archetypal pattern. Ordinary dreams are just dynamic, a sort of wavy line, while those dreams that refer back to an archetypal pattern have a sort of static structure. Just look at this dream with the four converging lines and the water in the center. . . . The primitives know these dreams and don't call them by the ordinary word for dreams — they would not even speak of ordinary dreams — they call them big visions, and assume that only big men have big visions. The ancients also believed that. So if one hears of a great dream, one assumes that a great personage has dreamed it, and if a child has such a dream, then sure enough that child has a great destiny. The mere citizen has no dreams, his dreams don't count.

Now, you see, this would be such a big dream, it conveys the idea of greatness, it is super-personal. Small people are personal. Big people are more than personal, they are representatives, they are exponents, they reach beyond. This dream would mean that greatness has been touched. Here is size and width of horizon. One could assume that here could be destiny. When such an archetypal pattern comes to the foreground, you can be sure that fate is on the way. And fate is power, an instinctive power in man, because he creates his own fate. It is often quite difficult to understand

22

such dreams because they have a far-reaching meaning, far-reaching in the sense of time. A dream may anticipate something that lies in the far future and then one would say it was prophetic, but that is not necessarily so. It does not anticipate the future *just* literally; it simply shows the apparent line or pattern of the future. It is a signpost, as when one sees a signpost on a road saying that it is four hundred miles to Paris which means that a potential Paris is there, it is seen ahead. Such a dream, therefore, means that something is anticipated, whatever it is.

The Sheep

Let us speak first of the lame sheep that the man has picked up. Have you an idea about that?

Answer: The sheep could be the Christian attitude.

Dr. Jung: You associate the sheep and flocks with the Christian attitude. But now to deal with that one sheep, why one out of many? Well, if we think of the idea of symmetry, that is the old philosophical idea of *correspondentia*, as between above and below, for instance; or the old *correspondentia* between right and left. So the lame sheep would correspond to that man's figure, as the pregnant lamb would correspond to the woman's figure. When the man picks up the lame sheep, he is picking up something that is in correspondence with himself, which expresses himself in a way, because these figures in the archetypal pattern are acting symbolically, you know, exactly as the prophets in the Old Testament acted prophetically or symbolically. You find that those Old Testament prophets did the most astonishing things to catch the eye, so to speak, to express an idea symbolically. The worst case was the prophet Hosea who symbolically married a prostitute because the Lord ordered him to do so, expressing in that way that the people had prostituted themselves to the heathen — he showed the people what they were by marrying a prostitute by divine command. That is symbolical doing or acting, and in a dream of this order such actions or gestures are equally symbolical. When the dream figures take up those animals, it is as if they were speaking through their action, as if they would convey a certain idea, as if they said, for instance, "This I do to show you that one should feel compassion" — or something like that.

I told you that these sheep might be of Christian origin, because sheep, particularly the lamb, play a very great role in Christian symbolism, and it is quite certain that Christian symbols would come up somewhere with our patient. Her inherited Christian attitude is responsible for the standstill in which this woman found herself, when her development came to an end.

23

She simply could not solve her problems with the typical Protestant point
of view. In natural conditions there would be no standstill and life would
simply flow on, and only if consciousness interfered by imposing a certain
attitude would life be stopped. So naturally it is our most developed attitude that accounts for our breakdowns.

I have often been asked why I bother about religion, because people cannot understand how a neurosis could have to do with religion. Surely it has
nothing to do with religion as it is usually understood, as an affair of the
church. Nowadays we have such a foolish conception of religion. One is a
Catholic, or a Jew, or some other denomination, and people think that is
religion, but that is only a sort of specialization of a certain creed which has
nothing to do with the religious attitude. The religious attitude is quite
different and above all it is not conscious. You can profess whatever you
like in your consciousness but your unconscious attitude is perhaps quite
different. . . . It was quite unconscious to this patient what sheep could mean,
because sheep meant nothing to her — just sheep, though of course she knows
that in church hymns Christ is called a lamb. . . . This is not taken seriously
in these days but formerly the lamb played a tremendous role, which accounts
for the widespread lamb symbolism in early Christian art. This lamb symbolism is a piece of Catholicism in our patient which is quite unexpected.
Now do you see an analogy in speaking of this Christian symbolism?

Answer: The shepherd.

Dr. Jung: Yes, of course. The figure of the shepherd who picks up a
little lamb and carries it. You see here the man assumes the role of the good
shepherd. Already, he is a guide — he guides the dreamer to the place of
the four valleys and when he comes to his flock picks up a lame sheep. He
is a figure that can be likened to a very interesting figure of the primitive
church, called the *Poimen*, which has now vanished from ecclesiastical ter-
minology. The good shepherd has remained, but the other figure has vanished with a certain book that was almost canonical at the time called *The
Shepherd of Hermas*. When the New Testament writings were gathered
together, that was omitted. I must use the Greek word *Poimen* here because
this *Poimen* is a pre-Christian figure. It is not a Christian invention, it is a
pagan invention, and has a direct historical relation to Orpheus. And Orpheus
is another figure related to Christ; he was understood to be an anticipation
of Christ because he tamed wild passions in the form of wild animals by his
delicate music. He is also like a shepherd, and moreover he is called "the
Fisher," and as such he played a great role in the Dionysian mysteries which
were of course pre-Christian. So we see the Christ figure in heathen cults.

24

We even find in certain inscriptions Christ almost identical with Bacchus, absolutely on the same level. And you know Caligula, that famous perverted Emperor, had a sanctuary where he kept the images of the great Gods, and Christ was one of them; for of course in the early days the figure of Christ was quite hazy, our idea of him is an absolutely new invention.

In very early times he was not a person at all, and so he was always handled in that way — symbolized accordingly. So for instance, the form of the *Poimen* was a sort of tremendous big angel, of more than human size, a great invisible spirit, a good God, and that very impersonal figure was never called Christ. That name was taboo. He was called the Shepherd of Men — Poimandres, the great leader of men, a mystery man, but directly related to *The Shepherd of Hermas*, which is decidedly Christian and part of the early Christian literature until the fifth or sixth century. We have the pagan form in a very interesting Greek text, and the best idea I can give you of that is that it is a book which might have been written by an analytical patient about his or her visions, about how the *Poimen* appeared to him or to her. It was a man who wrote it because the mysteries were then chiefly a man's business. To-day they are a woman's business. In that text you find a description of how the *Poimen* appeared to him, what his teaching was, and how he received guidance through the *Poimen*, the leader or shepherd of men.

Now our good lady has of course not the least idea of what she is dreaming. It is just that unknown man who picks up the sheep, but you see as a matter of fact she returns here to the archetypal pattern really of the spirit-like leader of men. It goes right back to the spirit-leaders of primitive tribes — where certain men called medicine men are at times possessed by spirits, chiefly ancestral spirits, who lead them and tell what is good for the people.

There is a marvellous example in that book by Rasmussen about his experiences among the Polar Eskimos in the north of Greenland. He gives there a striking case where part of those Polar Eskimos, foreseeing starvation, were led by a medicine man who had had a vision, across by Baffin's Bay to the North American continent where they reached food. Now that man never had been there and nobody knew that they could get across the sea, yet he succeeded in convincing the tribe. He had a vision that the Happy Land was there. In the winter when Baffin's Bay was frozen over, they started to travel across. Half way over, part of the tribe began to doubt, they said there was nothing ahead and decided to return, and they died of starvation. The other half he led safely across. This describes exactly what the shepherd or medicine man means under primitive circumstances. It is an intuitive mind possessed by a vision, clairvoyance, because that is the only function by which the life of a tribe can be safely led, for, of course, there are no other possibilities or sources of guidance. They cannot do it by thinking because thinking is not differentiated, so it has to be clairvoyance to let the people know, for instance, when there will be war and where the flocks are.

When we met the medicine man of the Elgonyis, he told us that he had no more dreams since the English were in the country. I said, "But how is that? " and he said it was because the chief man in power knew everything. He was in charge of the whole country and knew exactly what to do, and since then, his own political function, the foresight or spirit-leading of the tribe, had come to an end. You know all our *raisonnement* is done in a way by the primitive but only in his unconscious, because his functions are not yet developed out of his unconscious, so it manifests, of course, in the form of a revelation. It is as if a voice told them in the night what should be done. There are count-less examples of that in the Old Testament. The prophets were *Poimenes,* spirit-leaders.

Now such an archetype still exists in us in the form of dream-pictures. We can dream of the spirit-teacher in many different forms. We might dream of an important kind of person, a doctor or a professor or a managing direc-tor, or a board of directors even – invisible directors. For instance, those of you who know about the psychology of mediums, know that a medium is very often controlled by a so-called "control," who is the spiritual guide. . . . In normal circumstances people don't know of the existence of the spiritual leader, but in the analysis of their dreams they come across them. That man in the boat is one case of it; he says she must go through with it and reveals himself as some sort of good shepherd. You can't see it from this dream exactly. You only get a hint, but I can tell you that he is the one. He comes in later on and you will see that he is the figure. He slowly develops into the primitive spirit-leader, a seer, who sees ahead all the things which she is meant to go through later on, exactly like that Eskimo seer who saw the way across to the mainland, who was there in spirit, experiencing the whole journey across the ice before it actually came off, although only afterwards, when he had succeeded in convincing his fellow-beings, did the actual exper-ience come. That is the way it goes, it will develop that the spirit-leader who has turned up beforehand in the dream will take the lead, will foresee and experience by anticipation, and she will go the same way and will experience it in her own life.

Now picking up one of the lame sheep denotes his quality as a good shep-herd. There is something wrong with both of these sheep; one is lame and the one she picks up is pregnant which is an abnormality, a thing that should not be actually, and so both may die as the shepherd intimates. He says that they may die because they shiver so much; they are already quite cold. Now if we take that sheep symbolism as indicating a specific Christian way of solving the great problem of how to live, then we could say that it is demonstrated here in a twofold way, that that attitude won't live any longer in her despite the fact that she hugs the lamb and keeps it warm. It is very doubtful — quite possibly this specific Christian inheritance may die. Yet, of course, animals always denote instinctive forces and it really would be bad for her if they died, so there is a possibility of their living, but in that case those instinctive forces at all events would need a different kind of formula, or rather, a new spiritual guide.

For a formula is like a word of power, like the Christian Creed, or the *mantra* in India, a word of power that symbolizes the spiritual guidance, a word that will help you on your way. Therefore we sometimes speak of the Word that has brought salvation to us instead of the actual spiritual leader. A leader appears once and leaves the Word behind, and so the function of spiritual guidance is often conveyed over to a word, a *mantra*. It is a form instead of the living spirit itself. Such a Word is symbolic and of such a form that it can express the tendencies of blind instinct. The instinct goes to it and puts on that form. The spirit fits into it.

For instance, the medieval Christian formula was satisfactory to all the instincts of medieval man, it appealed to him, he was indubitably caught by that formula, and very little of him went off on sidetracks. Therefore there was one universal Catholic Church with the same form, the same style, from Norway down to Sicily. Practically the whole known Western World was then one and the same civilization, one and the same mind, and in the church one and the same language was spoken. It is an extraordinary confirmation of the fact that all the instinctual cravings of the human beings at that time were sufficiently expressed in that form. But of course such a word, or such a formula, will last only for a while and then it will no longer serve; so when one compares the Christian of the seventeenth or eighteenth centuries with the Christian of the second century, there is all the difference in the world. One would not recognize the identity.

If one had confronted Pope Pius I (d. circ. 154) with Professor Ritschl (Albrecht Ritschl 1822-1889), the modern theologian, it would be impossible for them to understand one another because they speak of entirely different things. Professor Ritschl is one of the originators of the idea that Jesus was a person, while the primitive Christian had no such idea. To them he was the *Poimen*, a living presence, a spiritual leader, who was invisible but he was there. But Professor Ritschl said that Christianity was like an enormously long railroad train and an engine suddenly pushes against the last car; then that push goes through the whole chain of cars until it reaches the very first, the present. Is it not terrible to think that God has been irresponsible for two thousand years? . . . He might just as well be locked up. Or retired — quite satisfied that He once gave a kick to that train of cars and that we still feel the faint repercussion. . . . Now how could a man like Hermas, who knew of the great presence, of the great spirit-leader, how could he understand such a hellish mistake as this jerk of a train? . . . To the early Christians, the life of the spirit was the main thing. To Professor Ritschl it is all the phenomena of the depot — pushing trains and so on. So from that example you can see that the formula changes from century to century, and now it needs a new formulation. Of course the Christian formula is still functioning, but there are an unusual number of people now-a-days who cannot or do not follow it. There are many people *ex ecclesia* and they naturally follow a new way; they are seeking a new formula and the question is what it may be.

Now here in the dream, this woman is with the sheep inasmuch as she is still an instinctual member of the Christian church. Her mind is lame and she is pregnant. She is still too young to carry and yet she is pregnant with the future. That means that she is too young as a person, not ripe, not mature, she is pregnant with the future but she cannot carry it. That is an almost general truth for the whole present epoch. Most people can't stand it. Their minds are too lame and they get neurotic, they cannot get up and bring it about, and that is expressed by these two symbolical sheep — inasmuch as the dreamer's mind or psychology is still part of the Christian flock.

After this dream, the patient was attacked by an extraordinary feeling of lassitude and weariness. This was perfectly inexplicable to her but the reason is quite obvious from the dream. The lameness and illness of the sheep is a living fact in her. One has such a feeling of weariness, a sort of resignation, of despair, when one has lost a hope — a form in which one could live, for instance. When that possibility is gone, one is overcome by this kind of psychogenic fatigue. It is a direct consequence of the dream, or of the realization that has taken place in the dream. And, mind you, this reaction came before we had analyzed it. She did not know what the dream conveyed but she felt the effect of it, which is often the case.

28

The Head with a Halo

VISION: Now she sees another figure — a human head which is dark like a shadow, and around it is a halo with spokes like a wheel.

> *Question*: What is that?
> *Answer*: An early Christian nimbus.
> *Dr. Jung*: Yes, the early Christian nimbus. You find it in the early Christian basilicas. It is like the sun halo of the old God of the Mithraic cult. The nimbus of the Emperors played a great role in the mystery cults — and that includes Christianity. . . . One encounters this particular wheel-like form of the cross in Christian archeology. I had not said a word to this woman as yet about the *Poimen*, but this is a head that one would find in the catacombs. The style would be late Roman or early Norman. That the *Poimen* interpretation is right seems to be confirmed by the visions that followed. The patient did not even recognize it as a halo. She was astonished, she thought it was a wheel, a man's head with a wheel. She did not know that it was a sun wheel, which is one of the earliest forms of the sun symbol. And, of course, the sun symbol behind the head of an emperor or a God means that his head is like the sun.

The Road Home

DREAM: I was motoring to my native town, terribly anxious for fear I had not enough oil or petrol. I had great difficulty in finding the road. At last, when I found it, a man said, "You should have known this was the way for there are other cars on this road, and you have been going along lonely lanes."

This dream was repeated in the same night in exactly the same form, meaning that it expressed something that was particularly important for the dreamer. For instance, when one is in doubt whether somebody has understood a thing, one says it twice, and in the same way the unconscious repeats it a second time to make it more impressive so that the dreamer will not forget it.

Now the dream says that she is on the road to her native town, the place where she came from and where she is at home. That is symbolical. She is returning to the home place. That is right, and one immediately associates to it the place where the four valleys meet. Of course, that is not particularly indicated in the dream, but you will remember the association of the four valleys, which we spoke of before, to the town built on the number four, the Heavenly Jerusalem in Revelation which is of course the home town

29

for everybody. In this case it is her individual town where she belongs, not just the Heavenly Jerusalem which belongs to all. This is a symbol for herself, her symbol of individuation — for her — going home to herself. That explains why she is so terribly anxious about getting there, it is because it is a goal.

But she is in doubt whether she has enough oil and petrol, which is the means by which the car moves. Oil and petrol are absolutely necessary for the life of the car, and if you translate that into psychological language then it means pretty much the same for her. If she has not enough oil, sure enough, the machine will get too hot and be destroyed and if there is no petrol, it will not go at all. Petrol is a condensation of energy. It is liquid energy, and there naturally might be doubt in her mind whether she will have enough patience, or realization, or will-power, or energy to get there, whether her supply will be sufficient for this long road to herself.

And besides the doubt as to whether she can complete the journey, there was great difficulty in finding the road. Apparently it is very difficult to find the road to the native town. She is inclined to lose her way, either because there are many opportunities to go the wrong way, or because she *likes* to go the wrong way and avoid the main road to herself. If you feel yourself into her situation, you will understand right away what her difficulty is, that the way to yourself is the longest way and the hardest way. Everybody would pay anything, his whole fortune, to avoid going to himself. Most people hate themselves, despise themselves, and for nothing in the world would they go where they are, where their native town is, because it is just hell!

And mind you, it is Christian teaching that man is bad from the beginning and the place of his origin is hell, so why should he care to go there? . . . We think we are not influenced by that kind of teaching but it is still our creed. Even if a man thinks the whole New Testament is bunk, it seems to him that it is quite bad and morbid to be alone with himself. If I ask him to spend even one hour to himself daily, he thinks I am crazy, for he considers himself a sort of dungheap, a waste paper basket, inside, and why spend time on such nonsense? That is the Christian teaching. The origin of man is bad and he needs the intercession of the saints and the grace of God to get anywhere. If left to himself he is a miserable worm just ready to go down to the eternal fires where he came from. A terrible punishment in hell does not appeal to us, but for seventeen or eighteen hundred years our life has been a part of that formula and we naturally suffer from the psychological effect of such an education. There is no escape. We can be quite liberal in our

30

point of view, atheists perhaps, but we cannot get away from it because it is in our blood. In our heads we are liberated from it but go a little farther down and we are right in the Middle Ages.

And so the way to the self is a most painful and shocking thing and one does not wonder at all these difficulties in the road of my dreamer, so many desires not to find the road. Therefore she hears the voice of that man, the spiritual guide — the animus — admonishing her, "You should have known this was the way." She half knows that, yet she would so much have preferred not to know. He tells her that there are other cars on the road, she could have seen that other people were traveling the same way so she had no excuse for going off on lonely lanes. She has taken to all sorts of other possibilities — bypaths — instead of sticking to the main road. Here you see that voice appearing in its true form, as a spirit, guide, shepherd.

The Mole and the Canary

DREAM: I was with a mole and a canary bird. I had cut their nails and was afraid I had cut them too short and caused them pain. Someone said, "The mole goes deep down into the earth." I took the canary out of its cage. It did not fly away. I had expected that it would.

Now here are two animals, one a mole. The mole is a nocturnal sort of animal that lives under the ground — that digs in the ground. The other is a bird, an inhabitant of the kingdom of the air. So these two animals are exceedingly symbolical. One would typify a sort of instinctive tendency, an unconscious tendency, to move underground, below; and the other a similar instinctive movement above, in the air, which is a spiritual or a thought symbol.

You see everything that appertains to thought or spirit is air. Spirit is air. The very word *spiritus* means breath. *Animus*, mind, is wind. *Pneuma* in Greek is wind and spirit. So birds are the usual symbols for thoughts, inspirations, enthusiasm, anything that lifts up or is light; and the dark animals like snakes, moles, mice, and the aquatic animals, symbolize the heavy dark things. They can denote sexuality, and all sorts of earthly desires or instincts or emotions, because usually the emotions are supposed to be located in a sphere below the brain, either in the heart, or still lower in the abdomen. . . .

When man was less developed than he is today, the psychical process was located in different centers, and we still bear the traces of those centers. The head with us is chiefly the seat of thought and reasoning processes, while our emotional processes have a center between above and below, here in the heart. And we still have a feeling of a psychical center in the abdomen

31

because certain things show quite clearly in the abdominal processes – for instance, upsets of the stomach are quite frequent in cases of neurosis, and there is practically no case of hysteria without symptoms in the abdomen. The stomach functions as if it were a psychical organ that expresses certain thoughts or emotions through certain disturbances.

So you see the mole represents a vital psychical function that moves down below, below consciousness, while the bird, as it were, goes above. He is in the brain sphere or above it, since a thought leaves the head like a bird; and if we follow the bird, then we lift ourselves up above ourselves and leave behind, say, our body, or the corresponding part of our psychology, our earth psychology. It is interesting that the mole is a wild animal, and the canary is most decidedly domesticated, always kept in a cage. The dreamer is cutting the nails of those two. You know that a canary bird kept in a cage has always a tendency to grow nails that are too long because it cannot use them properly and therefore they have to be cut artificially. But the mole never needs to have its nails cut because it uses them all the time for digging, so it is perfectly useless and ridiculous to cut the claws or the nails of that wild animal; obviously she makes a mistake to handle the mole as if it were a caged animal, a canary bird.

Now the conclusion that we can draw is that, as the bird symbolized the mind, so the thought function is with her the caged function. You see the unconscious is quite free to speak of an eagle, or any other wild uncaged bird, but in her case the mind is thoroughly domesticated, it is her differentiated function over which she has complete control. It is absolutely at her mercy. It is a wild thing that has lost its wildness, its freedom, and is left at her disposition in a cage. But down below are the emotional things, or whatever the inferior function may be. I use the word inferior for the function – in her case feeling – that is lower, and the farthest from the one that is differentiated. And inasmuch as her mind is of the scientific type, the function following her thinking could be sensation which would give her an empirical mind. The thinking, then, would be up here in the head; the sensation about on the level of the mouth; the intuition in the region of the heart; and then down below in the abdomen would be the feeling. She would feel with the abdomen and not with the heart.

That of course is a quite particular kind of feeling. It is a peculiar thing that the lower down you go in these psychical centers, the more you lose the consciousness of a separate Self, the more you become collective, the more you are in a state of *participation mystique*; and when you arrive at the lowest center, then you have lost your consciousness of Self altogether –

you have no Self any more and the ego is a name only. There is no real will power, one functions by tribal influences, one is simply part of a clan with the herd instinct only, and has lost one's individual consciousness. Any function that is on the lowest level will share these qualities, absolutely collective and undifferentiated in character, not discriminated at all from the functions of other people, and therefore always in a state of complete projection. The feelings of that woman, for instance, would be as absolutely in *participation mystique* with her surroundings as those of very primitive people. She never would realize a feeling that is clearly her own, because it is not her own, it is the feeling that is prevailing in other people. She is absolutely dependent upon the feeling atmosphere; if that is blue, then she is blue, and she cannot hinder it. It is ungovernable, it is explosive, it is and is not. One can have quite a nice feeling in one moment, and in the next it is hopelessly lost and one doesn't know why; it is completely lost. These are qualities of the inferior function.

This woman, for instance, is full of tremendous emotion, fearfully strong, and she is completely possessed by it, or she is just as much possessed by the lack of it. She cannot pull it up by will, neither can she chase it away by will. The inferior function is like a wild animal with superior strength; and you cannot kick about a lion or something like that because it might eat you. Now in this dream she handles those instinctual tendencies in the same way. In the case of the canary bird, being an entirely domesticated function, the signs of autonomous growth shown in the nails can be cut to advantage, but if you catch the mole and cut his nails, that is a mistake, because that thing is a wild animal. In other words, the function that is wild should not be curtailed, it should not be cut down, because then it cannot function properly any more. That means that her undomesticated, inferior function works best when left alone, and if she interferes, it is a mistake. She can blame her thinking function for thinking illogically, she can do what she pleases with her mind, but she can not do the same with her inferior feeling function. If you want to establish any kind of connection with a wild animal you must adapt yourself to it, you must study its habits, and it is the same with the inferior function; you must study its own laws, its own habits, and you ought to realize that it functions best when you leave it alone. Since it has to do with you, you should establish a connection with it, but the connection should be along the lines of the function.

In the dream, this woman realizes that she might have done something wrong to the animals, that she might have cut the nails too short and caused pain. This is the fact to which the dream calls her attention, that she must

33

be careful about this, and then somebody makes the remark that the mole goes *deep* down in the ground. Now that is rather a banal truth, yet if the dream insists on such a thing, it must have its particular merit. Evidently she is almost being taught in the dream what the mole means, that it is the function which goes very deep down into the ground is emphasized. Now this seems to be news to the patient. Obviously, she has not realized it, because she has cut the nails of the mole which would hinder it from doing its job.

The idea is evidently that something ought to get underground, because up above nothing moves. She opens the cage of the canary and it does not fly away. That is the trouble with our differentiated function, it remains within our reach, it is sterilized by domestication. Such birds do not soar away, they just remain with us, they never would function like Noah's dove or Wotan's raven, which would fly abroad and bring us information from parts where we cannot go to, hear or see. That is what such a function can do when it is wild. So you see she cannot expect anything to come out of her mind because her mind is domesticated and sterilized through differen- tiation, but she can hope for something to come from her wild function, a primitive and inferior function that reaches into the darkness where she cannot see. It needs the instinct of a mole to find anything there.

The meaning of the dream is quite obvious, the intention is to lay stress upon the function of the mole, and also upon the fact that she cannot expect anything of her mind. Hitherto, she has been under the impression that analysis and similar things are all done through the mind, that the main job is a mental one. Therefore my particular reluctance to explain things to her. She always wanted things explained and then they were put aside in a drawer — sort of killed — and nothing happened any more.

We misuse our differentiated function in order to protect ourselves, very often in a wrong way, we use it to kill life when it threatens to become awkward. Up to a certain point this protection is quite valuable, but when you come to that place in your life where the development of your person- ality becomes an inevitable problem, then you are no longer allowed to kill life. Then you must accept life.

In Hindu philosophy, there is the idea of karma, *your* fate. To a certain extent, you work against karma, against, for instance, the family fate. Other- wise the child would be absolutely overcome by inherited fate, the family curse, it would never begin to live, it would be suffocated from the very be- ginning. So young people have to work away from karma, they must differ- entiate themselves in order to live, they must free themselves from the spell

34

and be able to tear away all the veils of unconsciousness. But then having liberated yourself from the evil family fate — inherited sin — the moment will come in the middle of life where your task becomes difficult. For the ultimate task of life, according to the Hindu teaching, is that you should take up your karma, that you work it out, because if you do not, a wrong karma accumulates, and then you have it in the next existence — a hell of a time. But now fortunately you can do something about it, you can take it up, accept it. And as a rule people — particularly those who are in analysis — are simply forced through the logical development of analysis to take up their individual fates, their particular situation with all its disadvantages and shortcomings. You could call it "individuation."

Now in this great pursuit of the working out of karma, you simply come to a dead end if you try to do it through your differentiated function. That has served you well in liberating you from the original unconsciousness — from the past — so that you can establish yourself as a separate social figure or unit. But when the question arises about the totality, the rounding out of your personality, or the taking up of karma, then you must listen to other functions as well and particularly to the inferior function, because then you discover that there are situations in life with which one cannot possibly deal with one function only. Generally, in human life, a person with a differentiated thinking function will encounter a situation which he cannot solve by his mind alone, he will need feeling. An intuitive will come to an impasse where his intuition serves him not at all; he needs sensation, the function of reality, in order to be able to continue his life, because he has left too many situations unsolved, and finally he is overcome by them, nailed down by the unsolved problems behind, and only his reality function can be a help. And in sensation types you see how they get into a hole that is just nothing but reality and they need intuition very badly in order to crawl out of it, to have the feeling that life is really lived.

Our patient was in such a hole. Her scientific mind was good for nothing. Differentiated feeling would have guided her, but she had none, only the feeling of a very primitive man, and naturally that was not up to the situation either. So the necessity has arisen of following the inferior function into its own realms, into the depths, down into the abdominal seat of the inferior function. That is the motive of going down. We shall come to it presently again. And that is the thing that seems to promise life — her solution. For the canary bird is perfectly hopeless.

35

PART TWO

The Saint and the Bull

DREAM: I found myself in a graveyard in the devastated area in France. The graves were made of red sandstone. I saw people walking over a large grave where many soldiers were buried. Someone said, "Look at this gravestone." I looked and saw carved on it a statue of a saint. A bull was eating one of the saint's fingers. (The patient's account is a bit short here. It was a large tombstone and upon it was carved the figure of a saint and beside it the figure of a bull and, in spite of the fact that both figures were carved in stone, they were alive — half dead and half alive.) Seeing that the bull was gnawing the fingers of the saint, I felt nauseated with horror and walked away, shaking my own hand as though to free it from the bull (as if her own hand had been gnawed by the bull).

Now this place is very specific, it is a graveyard in France. . . . When the dream refers to a graveyard of the war of 1914, it means more than the lives wasted there, or the destruction of northern France, or the economic devastation; it also means the spiritual devastation — the spiritual after-effects of the war . . . (therefore) the backwash of the great war is the setting in which this particular thought is presented, and the thought is the figure of the saint with the bull. Now what is the connection between the bull and the saint?

Answer: Mithraism and Christianity.

Dr. Jung: Yes . . . because the central figure of the Mithraic cult was the bull. The bull plays very much the role of the lamb in Christian mythology, but more than that. You see the lamb is merely the cult of the sacrificial victim, the lamb was simply led to the sacrificial stone and slaughtered, and so it does not mean much, but the Mithraic bull means a great deal. It is the creative power, the great world bull, it is the bull of the beginning, it is the bull God, most powerful and admirable. And its death is the immediate cause of rebirth, of natural rebirth. . . . The idea in the Mithraic cult was that the God was sacrificing the divine bull, his own libido, his own life power and fertility, in order to increase the fertility of the earth, as a sort of blessing to the earth. So you see the Mithraic idea, from the standpoint of symbology, is very similar to the Christian dogma, and as a matter of fact the early Christian cult took over quite a lot from the Mithraic ritual. . . .

[From the lectures given between November 12 and December 9, 1930 (*Spring* 1961).]

But when somebody dreams of a bull it does not (necessarily) mean that this derives from Mithras by some unknown channel; it is merely the same natural thought that was naturally expressed in the Mithras cult originally. I repeat, it is not a derivation from the Mithras cult when somebody in our days dreams of bulls. As in this dream, for instance, it is an autochthonous reproduction of the same thought; our mind thinks in the same way and we think the same things that man has thought before, that man will always think. Therefore you find bull-worship, or the worship of similar animals, in all the most remote corners of the earth, at the most different times, because it is archetypal. The archetype is eternal, outside of time. . . .

In this dream we see that the bull, with this background of Mithraic ideas behind him, is eating the saint's fingers which means that, in a friendly way, it is beginning to devour the Christian saint. And our patient, naturally, is all on the side of the Christian saint — a fact of which she is entirely unconscious. If you questioned her, she would say that it was shocking to ask her such a thing, that she loathed such an idea; yet secretly she likes to be a Christian saint, she flirts with the idea without knowing it. "But how is that possible? " she says, "I am not a Christian." She does not sing Christian hymns, she does not go to church, and she holds blasphemous views about clergymen, so she is sure she is not a Christian. But the point is that her attitude to her own problems, to her own world, is thoroughly Christian, and she cannot help feeling herself a sort of saint, because she is dealing with her own psychology in the way of a saint. Now what would you call a saintly attitude? . . .

Answers: Renunciation? Martyrdom? Perfection?

Dr. Jung: Now do you get the picture? You see everybody has said a truth. [It is doing whatever we do with "perfection," the attitude of sacrificing ourselves to a "cause," no matter what "cause."] One can do the most absurd things with a saintly attitude. . . .

I tell you it is with the greatest difficulty that we extract ourselves from the illusion or delusion of saintliness. You would not believe it, but if you want to learn something you can catch yourself time and again thinking, is it not a great spiritual merit that you do such and such a thing, feeling terribly good, and naturally there is a God in heaven who keeps records of what you do and naturally you will have such and such a reward. Of course you do not think all that consciously, but you feel the accumulation of grace when you do things in the right way, and that is such a lure that you can hardly bear to resist it. I see it with people in analysis; it is the most difficult thing to educate them out of the illusion of saintliness. It is a sort of prejudice, an ancestral effect of early Christian ideas. It has nothing to do with conscious convictions, but is the foundation of our whole mental atmosphere. . . . We overvalue the conscious tremendously. . . . But in certain spheres of psychology, we see that consciousness means nothing. You can convince somebody of a psychological truth, for instance, and he will say, "Oh yes, I see. . . ." It is as if I said to him, "You have a young cobra in your pocket," and he had replied, "Is that so, how interesting." Such a man thinks he is perfectly convinced, he thinks he is aware, but in reality he never would put his hand in his pocket if he realized what the cobra in his pocket meant. And so it is in psychology, when it comes to a basic attitude. For instance, our dreamer would most certainly have said, "Oh, I see exactly what you mean," yet she would exactly not have seen it because that prejudice is too strong, that prejudice which reaches back one thousand years or more beyond her own individual existence. That is not easily removed, it is something formidable, it is a long work until you get to the bottom of such an attitude, until you have really done with it. . . .

And the important thing about saintliness is that it is *not* a thing that happens of itself, it is not just there; it is a matter of training, or self-education; it is a cultural product, it is an ideal. With the primitive, however, it is not an ideal. For instance, the medicine man doesn't want to be a medicine man; he will do everything in order to avoid it. . . . The ways in which saintliness is realized are quite different, of course. . . . The Christian saint has an entirely different face, a different figure, from a Hindu or Chinese sage, but naturally the point they have in common is the intentional differentiation of the type. They even work out the most complicated systems, like yoga or the Christian rites, to bring about the type chosen. . . . The saint is supposed to be a more perfect individual . . . and the education of a saint, the technique by which a saint is produced, is really a technique that excludes the collective unconscious very carefully. . . .

In this dream it is a matter of that Christian product, that ideal of saintliness, which is peculiarly upset by the war, apparently. Because the central idea of the graveyard seems to be represented on that gravestone, namely, the idea of Christian saintliness being devoured by the bull, by the animal. Now that is a very profound idea really, because when you boil down the psychology of war and ask yourself, "What is the thing that has produced the war, what is the psychological idea that helped people to continue the war? " it was merely their idealism, their extraordinary devotion to their own cause; for when two are fighting, each one equally devoted to his own side, then they go on fighting. They did it with the greatest faith, the greatest conviction on either side and so they continued it. If several of those powers, or only one even, had had a less Christian attitude, which means a less ideal attitude, that thing would have crumbled away. . . . It would have collapsed after a few months as it does with primitives. . . . These terrible things only come about when people have been whipped into form, when they have an ideal and extraordinary devotion.

Now all this shows you what that dream symbolism means — the bull eating the saint, the fingers of his hand. For example, there is a saying, Don't give the devil a finger or he will take the whole hand. The hand also symbolizes the activity of man, what he is doing. Without hands, man is ineffective, he cannot create, he cannot do anything more; so when the saint's hands are eaten, he can no longer apply himself. . . .

Now obviously (this bull) is not just the animal in man, it must be something more. I mean, it is not, say, animal consciousness versus the spiritual consciousness of the Western man. You see there must be something special about this animal, it is not an ordinary bull. The patient herself instantly associated it with Mithra, so we cannot assume that it is just like other cattle. It is a divine bull, as the saint is divine. So it is a divine principle set against another divine principle, which, of course, makes a great difference. . . .

The divine bull is an abstract bull. Therefore when you speak of the force of instincts or the instinctual attitude, it would not be merely an individual animal unconsciousness in somebody, a slip. It must be something on principle . . . something universal. It is just as good or as efficient as saintliness, because the bull can eat the saint. Thus an instinctual attitude must be meant that is equivalent to the Christian attitude. . . . We must try to understand this instinctual attitude — and I add, an instinctual attitude *on principle.* Can you imagine what I mean when I speak of an instinctual attitude on principle?

Answer: Fecundity.

Dr. Jung: We hope it will be a principle of fecundity but for the time being it eats the saint — an attitude that obviously undermines the Christian idea of saintliness. Now how do you understand that? . . .

It is spring symbolism. The bull is Taurus, the sign of May. It is not the summer, it is really the full blossoming of spring in astrology and we can take it as such. Why are we justified in that assumption? We have had it before in these dreams, we have already had spring symbolism [in these seminars].

Suggestions: The spring lamb. The peacock.

Dr. Jung: You are right, it is the Christian lamb. And the peacock is a spring symbol in Eastern rites. I did not invent the peacock as a spring symbol, it was regarded as such in antiquity. So this bull could be understood as a sort of spring, a new manifestation, a natural power. But what about it being something on principle — that always involves a creed. You see, you cannot make a saint by just saying, "Now you get effective." You must tell him what for; in a case like that you must always make the *point d'honneur* first. . . . There is always some idea or standard connected with it. . . .

Over against that attitude, the bull would be the instinctual attitude on principle, and it is very difficult for us to understand what that means, because the Christian attitude will always say it is *laisser faire, laisser aller,* a system of individual disorganization. And there you see we stumble in our Christian mentality. We forget that the animal is the most pious thing that exists. It is the one thing except plants that really fulfills its destiny or the superior will — the will of God, if you want to put it into religious language. We are of the devil because we are always deviating, because we are always living something of our own, not fulfilling the divine will. Animals are pious; they live exactly as they were meant to. . . .

Apparently the attitude of saintliness is to be repressed by an actual factor symbolized by the bull, which is a creative force still undifferentiated. It is comparable to the Mithraic bull, that is the bull of the beginning, the world bull, Abudabao (of Persian origin). You see the bull of the beginning is the blind unconscious creative force, representing in this case a great value, because the attitude of saintliness is a culmination, it is an end. For anything that is differentiated and has reached its completion is, of course, beautiful and respectable and good and noble — and sterile. It runs dry after a while. One can admit, "Yes, it is beautiful, it is marvellous." But it does not work any more. It is as if it had lost its efficiency, and in such a case the unconscious brings up the contrary, an undifferentiated blind impulse, a spring sign in astrology. Astrology is the projected psychology of the unconscious and there we see Taurus, the bull, as the sign of spring, the creative time, the creative part of the unconscious cycle.

[Shortly after this, the patient's first big vision occurred. – Ed.]

The Ram's Head

VISION: I beheld the head of a ram. Swiftly and with fearful strength the ram charged and was met full on the forehead by the spear of an Indian.

You see the new element is that it is no longer a static vision but is now in progress. It is a vision that has dynamis, it is moving by itself. Before, she had still retained her own activity, what you would call her own free will, she had not lent her own power to the contents of the mind; therefore they did not move, they had no power and no movement. This time her dynamis has wandered over into the unconscious objects, the contents of the mind, which are now moving by themselves, with that energy which was formerly her own and which is still her own if she is on another level; she is still capable of withdrawing from that vision and climbing up to the surface of consciousness where those things do not move, where there is no ram charging and everything is just as it always is. But at the moment, she sinks down through that, she gives up her own power, and, as you see, the unconscious contents are moving violently.

VISION (cont.): And in that moment (when the forehead of the ram was met by the spear of the Indian) the ram vanished. The Indian lay down beside his spear. Then suddenly he leaped onto his horse, which was black, and galloped over plains and hills until he came to a black pond surrounded by black mountains. Here the horse refused to go farther and lay down and *(illus. 1)* died. The Indian stayed on the shore and looked for the sun but it was no longer to be seen, for the sun had set, it was twilight. Suddenly the Indian turned into a Chinese man; he knelt down at the pond and bowed his forehead to the ground three times.

The Nature of these Visions

You see this vision is very much like a dream but not quite. If you did not know whether it was a dream or a vision, what would you say? What is the difference? What is the criterion? . . . Well . . . there is not one thing in this vision or in this series of pictures which the dreamer could have met with in ordinary life. If it were a dream . . . it would be what primitive peoples call a great dream, a visional dream, a dream of far-reaching importance. Now that is a criterion. If a series of pictures does not contain the ordinary stuff of life, say automobiles, relatives, aunts, and so on, then it is at all events very unusual, and therefore it is quite probable that it is a visional dream. But we have other criteria besides the absence of the stuff of everyday life. . . .

You see there is something very peculiar about this vision. In a dream you probably would find more emotional interference; it would be less clear in its sequence. The sequence here is peculiarly objective and it excludes the personal participation, while in a dream the person is not so much excluded. One is there, even if it is only as an onlooker. For instance, you very often have dreams where . . . there is no subject. You do not appear to be in the dream, but emotional contents of yours are there — you are in the dream. Whether our dreamer said that she felt very sorry when the horse died or that the Indian felt sorry would make no difference, it would be her own emotion, but here there is nothing at all; there is no emotion in the whole thing. So you get a peculiar impression as if it were a series of snapshots or a film; there is no participation of feeling. What is the reason for that?

Answer: Her conscious attitude.

Dr. Jung: That is true. Now this is a positive criterion for the fact that this must be a vision. Remember her dreams — they were full of feeling. She was afraid, excited, she played music. That last dream of the graveyard in France is full of it, there is an extraordinarily intense feeling atmosphere, but this series of images is completely devoid of feeling. That only can come from the fact that this vision has not been the exclusive work of the unconscious; if it were, there would be a mood in it. It is the conscious attitude that has excluded her feeling and, knowing that, you can see how these phantasies are produced. It is first of all her unconscious that operates; she does not know what is going to happen. If I asked her, "What are you going to see next? " she would not know, she would not have the faintest idea; the things that happen are sudden and unexpected, which proves the activity of the unconscious. But the unconscious, as we have seen from her dreams, is very emotional, it is full of feeling, yet here that does not appear. And the reason is that another factor is operating, namely, her consciousness. Her consciousness is extinguishing feeling, because her conscious attitude is intellectual and that blots out feeling. So the original picture that the unconscious is trying to bring up is peculiarly denaturalized by the searchlight of the intellectual consciousness, and what you see is a sort of compromise between the unconscious and the conscious functions. . . .

The swift strong movement here denotes that energy has entered the visions or images. . . . That means tremendous progress because then they have a life of their own and will continue to develop; but as long as they are static we can be almost sure that they will have no continuity, there is only a chance that the patient may catch a glimpse of life, a sort of snapshot from time to time. But as soon as there is movement, there may be a whole flow of images which will develop into a logical sequence, and that naturally leads to drama. It will not be merely an inconsistent flow of pictures; it will be drama. And as soon as it is drama it will catch the individual, the individual will be sucked in, as it were, and will enter the game. The patient herself will begin to play the assigned role in the drama, she will really be in the mystery play, she will be part of it, and she will be transformed. As long as

42

she is merely watching the continuity or the flow of images, she is detached, she is watching it as one watches the movies; she is perhaps interested or moved, but she is not playing an assigned role. As soon as you are one of the figures in the mystery play, then you serve the drama, you are part of it, and it catches hold of you and transforms you. You will know a higher power then, the power of the drama. That is the idea of the antique drama, namely, a sort of ritual which one could call a mystery or transformation. The antique drama seized upon the individual, or the individual assimilated it and became transformed; it was like the mystery of transubstantiation. . . .

Now, in interpreting what this movement means, we must start in very much as we always do in analyzing dreams. For instance, you remember that whenever we tackle a new dream we look back to the dreams before, or the last dream before, because we get there a sort of basis from which a judgment becomes possible. But this is not a dream, this is a product that has come about in the waking condition and therefore we deal with it somewhat differently than with dreams; we have to consider the admixture of consciousness, just mentioned, to see that such a thing is a sort of half-way product of unconsciousness and consciousness.

The last dream, as you will remember, was about the bull and the saint and that whole war atmosphere, and in this sequence of phantasies or images we see no connection with that dream. This is due to the fact that dreams really come from the unconscious sphere, and are not due to any conscious impression of will, though there is always naturally a certain amount of conscious atmosphere in any dream; otherwise we would not be conscious of them. Yet we are never quite certain whether the dream we see and remember is as it actually was in the unconscious. That a thing is in the unconscious we will never know. What we *can* know is something that is associated with consciousness; so if anybody should suggest the theory (and mind you, the theory has been suggested) that dreams are due to the interference of a remnant of consciousness, and would not be at all if there were not that remnant of consciousness, or that they are twisted by that interference of consciousness, I should say, "Sure enough, it may be so." Nevertheless, that admixture of consciousness is very small in comparison with the admixture of consciousness in these images; therefore we can assume that dreams really derive from contents that are much lower down than the contents of such a phantasy.

And so the dream of the bull and the saint is really referring to a problem that is far below or beyond the consciousness of the patient; that dream, if we go deeply into it, is really an anticipation of thoughts that will come back in this mystery play, but very much later. At this stage we are not at all sure

43

where that dream has come from, and if we want to find its starting point we have to go back to the ideas that are expressed in the visions; those of course derive from dreams originally, because the first thing that occurred was a development that took place in the unconscious — so right in the beginning dreams prepared the way for the first static vision.

Now you remember the first vision was the peacock, and then came the symbol of the rising sun, or the sun-man, the man with the halo or nimbus. . . . That sun-man derives from the peacock. The peacock is the unfolding of the sun, the sunrise, and therefore it is a symbol of the spring and of resurrection. This was all in a way an anticipation of the things that are now going to happen; so under this aspect we may understand the first movement that shows in the new series as a sort of spring or resurrection symbolism.

Astrological Symbolism

The ram is the symbol of spring. It is the astrological sign of Aries. Now astrology may be quite unknown to you consciously, yet to your unconscious it is very intimately known; because the fundamental ideas of astrology, for instance, the signs of the zodiac, are projections of our unconscious functioning to the skies. Of course the constellations have nothing to do with our earthly whims and sure enough there is no real bear, or lion, or any of the others. It is not as that famous amateur of astronomy believed, who was such a great admirer of science. "Why," he said, "besides knowing what the stars weigh and what they are made of, men have somehow even been clever enough to ask the stars what their names were!" There you see the fundamental mistake about astrology. We wonder how these constellations could influence us in such a wonderful way, but it is we who have unconsciously projected all those facts into them. It has nothing to do with those stars. Well, I don't want to go into that but, you see, the qualities of the different months of the year, in other words, of the signs of the zodiac, are really the projections of our unconscious knowledge of time and the qualities of time. It is as if there were profound knowledge in our unconscious, knowledge based upon unconscious experiences, that certain things originating at certain times of the year have such and such qualities, so that by that empirical knowledge stored up in our unconscious we are always more or less rightly adjusted to the time. . . .

So Aries, the ram, expresses certain qualities that characterize the spring time. Now Taurus, the bull, follows in the month after Aries, so we might say that Aries is more or less in line with the bull. The bull, we know, has always been looked upon as a symbol of fertility, the fulfilled form of

44

generative power, the whole of nature bursting forth with an irresistible rush. Aries is also a fertility symbol but smaller, only a beginning. . . . As a spring symbol it symbolizes the first shoots of green that come up again from the earth. The symbolism of the zodiac has originated somewhere in the south, most probably in Mesopotamia, so it would be the green shoots that come up there after the winter rains. There are no snow signs in the zodiac, because these signs originated in a country where there was no snow, only the early rains in February and March. You see, in February you have the sign of Aquarius, represented by a man with water jars. That is the rain God, and then follow the fishes. When Aquarius has poured out a flood then there are fishes to be found in that flood; the fishes are seed in the fertilized earth, like sperm; they are seed thoughts, unconscious contents. Fishes always mean unconscious contents.

So the earth is fertilized, and then come the first green shoots, symbolized by Aries; one could say, now the ram leaps up, the first green shoot leaps up. . . .

The Indian as Animus

But here a spear comes from the hand of a Red Indian and checks the movement of Aries — the first growth is checked by a spear. Now what would you assume about that symbolism? Who is the Red Indian? Remember, the patient is an American woman.

Answer: The animus.

Dr. Jung: The animus, naturally. It would be the representation of the unconscious mind, which means the relatively primitive mind. You know these unconscious figures like the anima and the animus are always a bit inferior in comparison with our consciousness — God knows what they are in themselves, we don't. So, you see, that Red Indian would represent her unconscious opinionating, which checks that movement, represses it. . . . (And the spear) is a typical weapon of the primitive man which is directed against that growth, that independent movement. The spear — like any sharp or well pointed cutting implement or weapon — symbolizes the trenchant quality of the intellect. You know the intellect is always dissecting and piercing, so the spear symbolizes piercing or dissecting opinion. It must be an opinion that has been aroused in her by that manifestation of blind impulse; instantly there is an animus reaction; it says, "Oh, it is nothing but this or that," and cuts the thing down if possible.

That is the way the animus works. And that is exactly the way the anima works, only the anima does not work in a masculine way with a weapon; she works with poison, she works in the feminine way which is an underhand way, it is not a square deal. What the anima does is absolutely not like a man's work, it is a woman's work, secret and venomous; so the feelings of the man poison the creative impulse by a sort of secret admixture of poisonous substance that kills that impulse from within, a sort of resentment. One could talk a long time about that, for that is a thing women do not understand, how Eros can have such, an effect, but it has.

Well, this reaction of the unconscious itself is the animus, and from it you can see a tremendously interesting thing in the structure of the unconscious, namely, the yea and the nay. There is the creative impulse, and then comes destruction stamping the thing down; also you can see the diversity of the figures of the collective unconscious. It is like a scene upon which many figures appear; there is the noble hero and the villain, the wonderfully virtuous person, the king, the beggar, and so on. Now the effect of this animus reaction is that the ram instantly vanishes, as it naturally would do. The reaction was so nasty — you could say, such a nasty opinion has been aroused — that the impulse was destroyed on the spot.

In the next image the Indian is lying down beside his spear. One could say, now his work is done, he takes his rest. One does not know exactly what this means, but it is obviously a passive situation. You see that very often — when the animus has reacted and everything has been trampled flat for about twenty kilometers in circumference — that the animus goes to rest; then people are utterly bewildered, they don't know what has happened, why everything is dead and quiet. And what can the animus do then, left all alone? He is bored to death and goes to sleep. But not for long, for when the animus succeeds in killing the creative impulse, there is no long rest for him because then the creative impulse goes into him. You know certain Red Indian tribes had the custom of eating the brain or the heart of the enemy they had killed in order to assimilate the strength or the wisdom or the cunning of the enemy.

Now this idea comes from the fact — again a fact of psychological observation or experience — that when you destroy a thing you simply inherit its spirit. . . . Therefore the next thing that the Indian does is to leap to his feet, jump on his horse, and gallop away; he takes over that power which he has suppressed in the ram. For it is quite possible that the blind impulse in the ram had to be killed. Things like that happen in nature. If the wolf eats the sheep, for example, is that right, or is it wrong? Naturally the owner of the sheep will say it is wrong, yet the wolf knows it is right — things happen like that. . . . So all that swift movement is now in the animus and his horse. And his horse is black. What would you say about this black horse?

46

Suggestion: Isn't it just the idea of elemental power which could be destructive? . . .

Dr. Jung: Yes, it is an elemental power. The color black always carries the connotation of evil. A black horse means a demoniac horse. You remember the horses in Plato, the black horse and the white horse with a man as charioteer, and the black horse was always unruly. . . . The blackness of the horse has the connotation of something evil, also chthonic; it is earthy and most certainly unchristian; therefore the devil rides a black horse, as do all sorts of evil spirits; the black horse is always somewhat uncanny. A good man never would appear with a black horse, he would appear with a white one, if with a horse at all. So a black horse in this vision means a chthonic, elemental power; it is simply a new form, but the direct derivation of the power of the ram.

In the case of our patient the black horse is the dynamis of her animus. . . . The animus, applying the energy he gained from the ram, has acquired the force which is now embodied in the swiftly moving black horse; and that horse, one could say, leads him to a very remote place, to a desert surrounded by black mountains where there is a black pond. There the impetus of the horse comes to an end. It dies, the impetus the animus has gained from killing the ram having now done its work — having carried him like a projectile to a certain place far away. Now when the horse dies, what would be the next effect? I told you that energy cannot disappear.

Answer: It changes form.

Dr. Jung: Yes, no other animal comes up instead of the horse, but this energy goes directly into the animus and the animus begins to act. So the only figure that is still performing here is the Indian; he stands on the shore of the lake and looks for the sun, but the sun has set, which means that consciousness has set, it becomes dark, and the animus is watching that pond. Then he suddenly undergoes a peculiar transformation, he turns into a Chinese and kneels down beside the black pond and bows his forehead to the ground three times. Here we see that the power of the horse which has gone into the Indian is a chthonic power, it is an elemental power that will most certainly seek the earth. The black mountains are, of course, black earth, the black pond is a deep hole in the earth, one might call it the womb of the earth, the black horse is the power that leads the Indian to the entrance of the underworld, to the pond, and turns him into a Chinese — the race that is probably closest to the earth, that is absolutely identical with that yellow earth, having the same yellow color, and whose philosophy, one could say, is the philosophy of the earth. And the Chinese puts his forehead

47

to the ground, that is, he lowers the seat of his consciousness, his mind, down to the ground, establishing thus a close connection with Mother Earth.

This is exceedingly meaningful because this woman's conscious type is intellectual, here tending more towards intuition, therefore the reality standpoint, sensation, is as it were below the horizon. You see the development of her intuition and sensation is about the equal — the emphasis on one or the other fluctuates, the scales are about evenly balanced; of course, feeling is always *the* inferior function. So though she herself is still functioning intuitively, her animus now migrates away, seeking the bottom, the function of the earth; he is obviously worshipping the earth principle.

Now this is an important lesson requiring no action on her part; it is a sort of performance in her behalf, a drama is enacted before her eyes, a series of pictures is shown to her, leaving it practically up to her to draw her own conclusions. . . . because it is an obviously logical sequence, leading up to a certain definite result. . . . It is as if some intelligence behind the screen were at work to put her onto an entirely new track of which she had not thought before.

White Birds

VISION: A white bird flew down and lit upon the top of the Indian's head; he tore it off and ground it underfoot with his heel. Then all became dark, it was night. The clouds parted and the face of God appeared and spoke, saying, "Now you will have to wander until you again find that white bird you have killed." Slowly the Chinese and the Indian walked round and round the black pond. Then suddenly from the black water rose up a swan and behind the swan a hand. For a long time the Indian and the swan gazed at each other, then the swan said, "Lo, I have come unto you." After that the Chinese pushed the Indian into the pond and the black water closed over him. The pond then grew long and narrow; at one end stood the Chinese, at the other end stood a crane. A long time later the Indian emerged where the crane stood. He was covered with black water. The crane said to him, "Wipe the tears from your face." The Indian then sat upon the bank with his head bowed low in his hands, for he was very worried. After a while a camel came up and the Indian mounted upon the camel and rode out into the desert. Soon they came to an Indian wigwam where the Indian went to sleep. When the dawn came he looked out and beheld three flaming crosses in the sky.

Let us add to this vision the one that followed.

VISION: I beheld a great white bird; the bird changed into a dark hawk which flew to earth and snatched an egg in its beak and then flew up again.

Again I beheld a bird with the wings outstretched, also white. The bird lit on my hand. I held one grain of wheat which the bird took in its beak and then flew up again into the sky.

Now I called your attention to the peculiar gesture that the Indian made in holding his head which is not quite explained by the contents of the first vision. The act of touching the ground with his forehead during his transformation into a Chinese might have to do with it, but I don't feel that that gesture is quite justified by those contents. But here we see why he holds his head. It is because the white bird has come down and lighted on his head and obviously the Indian takes this in rather a disagreeable way — he tears the bird off and grinds it under his foot, which is a brutal thing to do. From that act one would conclude that this bird must be very disagreeable to the Indian. Now what do you think about that: What is the white bird?

Answer: It is the ram once more, only in a different form.

Dr. Jung: Yes, the energy has passed out of the Indian again. One could say that the generative power was exhausted at the end of the vision. You should think of the visions in this series as something like spiritualistic seances. The patient herself called these conditions trances. Exactly the same word is applied in the East in the Tantric schools, *thyani*, which means trance. This is one of the techniques of the Tantric Yoga. You will also always notice in spiritualistic seances that there is a great deal of talk about a certain power, a power created by thought which manifests itself by moving physical bodies in space ... very interesting experiments have been made in order to find out what that power is, but it is most mysterious, most elusive; though we have very definite facts, we are still far from understanding what the thing is. Psychologically we would say it was libido, a form of psychological energy. Psychological energy, of course, does not exist, it is a concept, but in the physical — or phenonemal — equivalent of energy in these conditions you will find the same peculiarity, namely, that this creative power is after a while exhausted, and then everything sinks back into the condition that it was in before. . . .

So at the end of the previous vision, the bowing down to the ground might just as well be disappearance into the earth, which means into the body; that generative power is dissolved again into the physiological process, as if it never had existed. And then in the next *thyani* condition, in the next trance, it comes up again in its animal form, as it was in the form of the ram. Now the ram is chthonic, but this time it is a bird. What would that denote?

Answer: The Holy Ghost.

Dr. Jung: Yes, the Holy Ghost would be the interpretation. Now the

Holy Ghost alights upon the Indian. Any white bird alighting upon a person naturally means the Holy Ghost to anybody of Christian upbringing. But why does he give the bird such a bad welcome?

Answer: It would destroy his own way of functioning. The animus opinion could not withstand the Holy Spirit which wants to destroy it.

Dr. Jung: Well, one could say the Red Indian is a very unholy figure, a chthonic unholy animus, and the Holy Ghost perching upon him would not be welcome because the contrast is too great. Also when you interpret that white bird as being the Holy Ghost, as you are perfectly entitled to do, it is the Christian element; the Holy Ghost is a Christian idea, and the Indian is not supposed to be a Christian. Moreover he is riding a black horse and he seems to be in a black place, therefore we have reason to believe that the Holy Ghost would be something almost hostile to him. So the Indian destroys that form. The next thing that happens, then, is that when he has ground it under his heel, darkness falls, as if the white bird had signified a source of light; after he has killed the bird complete darkness ensues, which is exactly what one would expect, for in extinguishing the light of the Holy Ghost, he has eliminated the spiritual element altogether.

What follows is rather conventional, namely, the clouds part and the face of God appears, which means that the sin against the Holy Ghost has been committed and the Indian is cursed like Ahasuerus, who rejected his Lord, and has to wander until he finds the white bird again. This is rather conventional phraseology. The idea of having sinned against the Holy Ghost means, apparently, that she has surrendered to the powers of evil, to a sort of devil who is an eternal enemy of the spirit. The devil is a chthonic power, therefore he is represented as the darkness itself; he has not the ram's head, but he has the horns of the he-goat, he has also the goat's hoofs, he is half animal, a sort of satyr. In the Middle Ages he was also a phallic God, so the devil is an incarnation of all imaginable chthonic things, and it seems as if the Indian were some such thing, only much mitigated. He does not appear as the devil himself, he appears rather as a primitive, a man who is quite pagan, who clings to the earth, his goal is the earth, and therefore he resents any kind of intrusion from above, white birds and the like.

Now the two forms, the Red Indian and the Chinese, walk around the black pond. In the vision preceding this the Indian was turned into a Chinese, he suddenly lost his identity. Here he remains himself but the Chinese becomes an independent figure, so we may assume that these are two forms of animus, the primitive Indian and the civilized Chinese. This comes from the fact that the patient has read a good deal of Chinese stuff. She is particularly fond of Lao-tse and of the Chinese Taoist philosophy, and that of course produces a certain kind of animus, a certain kind of opinion. You see it is very funny, when we read such Eastern philosophy we are apt to be tremendously pleased; the sayings of Lao-tse are most impressive and we like to quote them and are not aware of the fact that we are putting on a garment which does not belong to us. How can we express ourselves through Lao-tse? It is absolutely impossible, perfectly preposterous, because we are not Chinese. . . . What happens is that she forms animus opinions which are not genuine, they have not risen out of her, they do not express a clear fact in her psychology. . . . That is the reason why the vision presents the primitive here, the Indian. He is the genuine article, you know, since she is an American woman. The oriental is a philosophical animus – an assumption. He plays his role – and that is not merely chicanery, of course – but what he represents is an opinion, a thing that can be changed, that can disappear. Opinions are just garments and if they happen to be exotic garments, well, that just means a bit of a mental carnival.

Now these two figures are concerned with that mysterious pond. Her primitive mind is concerned with the entrance to the underworld, the chances of going deeper into the black water, which means into the womb, into the place of rebirth. And the oriental is interested in her philosophical opinion, for being interested in Chinese philosophy through Lao-tse does mean something, it expresses something of her unconscious because Chinese philosophy can formulate certain concepts of the unconscious; but she has not formulated them, she has just borrowed them.

Now suddenly, through the effect of gazing upon the water, the water becomes animated by a certain thought, the swan. You see a lake or a pond is just like a mirror. Looking into it is crystal gazing, with transformations; and walking round it expresses concern – the two figures are concerned with that water, contemplating it, concentrating upon it. Similarly, in worshipping a shrine or sacred precinct, people walk around it. . . . That was the ceremony used by the Romans when they founded a new town. They plowed a furrow round it, the *circumambulatio*, the going round to the right in the sense of the sun, clockwise. Then in the center they made a hole in the ground called a *fundus*, where they sacrificed. . . . Now through this *circumambulatio* these two figures fertilize the center, through contemplation, they fill it with life. . . .

And then something happens in the center. The white bird again. The white bird has been ground underfoot, crushed into the earth, and it disappeared, it was dead. But with this magic rite it rises again, transformed and no longer a bird of the air but a water bird.

[In commenting earlier on her picture of the white bird, Dr. Jung pointed out that it had a peculiar shape with very much the appearance of a flying fish. – Ed.]

And behind the swan comes up a hand. Well, that is obscure. I would not venture into any interpretation of that hand. . . . (Although) later this symbolism of the hand occurs again, with either the idea of pulling something down or of creating something.

Now the Indian and the swan obviously do not recognize each other at once, therefore they gaze at each other as if they had known one another in a former life – until the swan begins to talk. Now this is also a very important thing – that often, when a vision has a tendency to remain static, if you concentrate upon it, then it begins to move. It might still remain quite silent – it might be mute – but if you concentrate still more, the picture begins to talk. The more you concentrate on that creative energy, on that image, the more you animate it with actual life. Of course, the more you fill the image with actual life, the more you lose your own consciousness, and that is why the *thyani* condition, the trance, has the effect of a contraction of the field of vision, namely, a sort of *abaissement du niveau mental,* or a *rétrécissement de la conscience.* It is a loss of yourself while you realize the life of the object all the more. . . . That is the reason the ancients were quite convinced that the figures of the Gods answered questions. . . . There are innumerable cases where a picture or an idol has nodded its head or talked to a worshipper.

Well, the swan now uses strange, rather Biblical phraseology. He says, "Lo, I have come to you." Now, of course, that is the Holy Ghost without any doubt, because you cannot kill the Holy Ghost; but here we see that spiritual element appearing from below, out of the blackness of the waters, out of Hades. What does that mean? It is of tremendous psychological importance in this case.

We must look at these things from the standpoint of consciousness. Her consciousness would assume spirit to be above, that there was no spirit in matter, in the earth. And here, for the first time, she becomes aware of the fact that spirit can come from the earth just as well and it is the same kind of Holy Ghost. The Holy Ghost is by no means only an air bird, He can be a bird of the water. A symbol of resurrection from below, the spirit of the earth this time, not of the air.

[Summary: Here follows a discussion of the pushing of the Indian into the black waters. Stress is laid on the idea that the animus is filling his most appropriate function when he relates a woman to the collective unconscious. The sometimes predatory character of the bird representing the Holy Ghost is also brought out and mention is made of the ruinous way that inflation by the spirit can disrupt an individual's normal psychological adaptation. – Ed.]

Something Lifts One out of Depression

At the conclusion of the vision this arrangement with the Chinese at one end of the pond and the crane at the other looks as if something was expected, and in fact something does happen. The Indian comes up from the black water covered with slime and he comes up on the side of the crane, which means that he moves in the direction of the representation of the Holy Ghost and away from the oriental, who is a system of Chinese philosophy. The crane is the living spirit – a sort of animal form – because the animal, being non-human, is the symbol for the super-human, the divine. It is as if the Indian had been pushed in at one end of the water, had passed through it, and come up at the other side by the Holy Ghost, the crane, who now speaks to him, saying, "Wipe the tears from your face." But nothing had been said about his weeping; it is as if the crane were interpreting the black water as tears. Now this black water is a mood, a deep darkness; it is a sort of short voyage under the sea which, looked at externally or observed through your own consciousness, seems like a deep depression – as when things are dark and the water is reaching over your head and you feel like hell; a terrible depression, melancholia, and it naturally means tears.

Then the Indian came out of the water. He "sat upon the bank with his head bowed low in his hands for he was very worried." That is simply the aftermath of his melancholia. And then after a while something new happens – a camel comes along and he mounts upon it and rides away. The camel is of course the animal that carries the burden. It is an instinct.

You see, when one has been in a deep depression and is still very depressed, after a while something comes up that lifts one out of that depression. I remember a patient who stayed in a relatively reasonable mood only as long as I remained on the premises; as soon as I took my vacation she fell into a hole, had suicidal moods, and everything. But I callously went away as usual because I knew that she would never get out of these holes except under her own power, and that even if I sacrificed myself completely she would not get out of them, but only deeper into them. So I went callously away and she fell into deep despair and decided to commit suicide. She was walking

down to the lake to jump in, and on the way down she passed a shoe shop
where she saw some very nice shoes that she had never seen before and she
thought they might perhaps fit her, so she stepped in and bought the shoes
and was all made over, perfectly reborn. She was completely cured, her
whole depression gone for not less than three weeks. She was perfectly
amazed when she told me and had already built up feelings of inferiority,
that a pair of new shoes could cure her of melancholia. If I had put a mountain under her feet it would not have cured her but that pair of shoes could
do it. It made her doubt her own internal values. I strongly advised her,
in case of another deep melancholia, to buy another pair, so the next time
she bought something else quite foolish.

Now such experiences are not to be invented, and from that she learned
that the whole melancholia was worth only about fifty francs. That is how
she learned to act objectively against those black water attacks. That was
a sort of camel that came along and carried her out of the situation. It was
a perfectly animal instinct, a most childish thing, but the point was that she
got into those black moods because she could not follow the indications of
nature. There were a number of camels around her but she never paid
attention to them, she kept to one conscious conviction and thus was
plunged into darkness because she did not want to follow the instincts. As
soon as she followed the instinctive indication — a pair of nice shoes is
instinctive — she was instantly cured. It was like sorcery to her, it was so
simple — she just followed a futile little intimation.

It is like the figures of helpful animals in fairy tales. When the hero is in
a tight place and does not know his way out, one or two animals appear
that prove to be very helpful; they show him the way, something very near
and very self-evident which he has not seen. That is the function of the
instinct, and it helps in situations where nothing else helps, where your mind
leaves you completely. There are certain difficult situations in life when
everything you have learned and built up crumbles away, nothing helps,
and then you have a most foolish little idea or hunch and you follow it.
And so people who can follow their instincts are better protected than they
would be with all the wisdom of the world — though of course if they had
nothing but instinct, well, they might be protected in the primeval forest
but they would not be protected in civilized situations where mind is needed.

Well now, the Indian, the animus, is represented here in connection with
simple impulse, he shows himself as a true natural mind, he is carried by
instinct. The great advantage of the natural mind is that it can live by instinctive impulse. That is, it is a great advantage on one side but on the other

it is, of course, a disadvantage, a sort of restriction because through continuous commerce with animals, a man assimilates too much of the truth of the natural mind and it alienates him from the cultural, spiritual mind. Sometimes it becomes quite difficult or awkward to deal with the natural mind because it is too far away from the opinion of the spiritual mind. So it is a great advantage if the animus follows natural impulses but, if left alone for too long a time with the animals, the animus could be carried away by them to deeper unconsciousness, and then connection with the conscious ego would be interrupted; the animus might begin to indulge too much in the animal world, which of course you never should misunderstand as, say, sex phantasies. You see, the earth has a spirit of her own, a beauty of her own, and there is enough to indulge in besides sexuality. The natural mind really has the world of earthly beauty to itself. You see, nothing is precluded. It is also not so terribly materialistic as one assumes, because the animal – we don't know – the animal might have a better knowledge of the deity than man, although, of course, an unconscious knowledge; and that is the danger, the unconsciousness. If the animus becomes too animal-like it becomes too unconscious and then the connection does not work any more; and moreover he animates the collective unconscious to such an extent that it is very difficult to deal with it; that is always the case where there is a lack of connection between the conscious and the animus.

Now they traveled out into the desert till they came to a wigwam, where the Indian was among his own tribe, and there he went to sleep. The Indian is of course in the right place in the wigwam, that is where he belongs, the animus has come to the position where he ought to be. He is the natural mind and should be in natural conditions. Instinct has taken him back into his natural condition which is above the water; he is not meant to live in the depths of the unconscious in the darkness, he is meant to live on the surface of the earth. He must be connected with consciousness, he should not disappear from consciousness, one should always know where the natural mind is. As soon as it becomes invisible then anything can happen. That he is in the right place is instantly shown in the vision, in the fact that "when the dawn came he looked out and beheld three flaming crosses in the sky."
Here the animus functions in the proper way. The animus must have vision, he must see what is going on in the unconscious; now he informs the conscious that he has seen three flaming crosses, which is something the conscious does not see.

The vision is represented as a sort of story because the conscious is still absolutely disconnected; the conscious ego is a mere onlooker and has as yet

55

no hand in the game. So far the animus and the animals are the active *dramatis personae*. But the drama shows the proper function of the animus, it reveals the laws of the unconscious to the spectator, and you will see what is going to happen after a while.

[Summary: What the patient failed to see consciously here is the inescapable importance to her of the sacrificial situation, also the enduring potence of the Christian teaching which still represents its most recent formulation. What is important is to have the Holy Ghost, the spirit of enthusiasm, in one's life, although "at times even the Holy Ghost," as in the vision of the white bird that became a hawk, "has to turn into a bird of prey in order to snatch the germ of life." And Dr. Jung repeats: *The content of life is not always above, sometimes it is below.* – Ed.]

Now the next thing is that the bird flies to a woman dressed in blue who is sitting like an ancient statue, and settles down on her hands. In her picture of this, the woman is holding a grain of wheat, the bird takes this grain in its beak and flies away with it into the sky. You see the bird is obviously bringing the egg to that figure and the figure is that of a mother. The blue is, of course, the celestial mantle of Mary, her typical garment, the color of the sky. This is the Universal Mother.... Then the mother holds a grain of wheat. This looks like the mysterious initiate or *epoptes* in the final stage of the Eleusinian mysteries, only there it was not a grain of wheat but an ear of wheat which the priest showed at the midnight ceremony. One could say that that ceremony represented the same thing as Christmas — the situation is the same. The son is born from the Great Mother, the Great Mother being the earth, and the son the ear of wheat. So this vision could be a sort of anticipation....

(By the way, when the patient had these visions I never explained them, I just listened, and we had enough work with dreams so that the visions as a rule remained absolutely untouched.)

The Indian as Redeemer

VISION: I beheld a horse which changed into a ram and then into a bull. (This is the typical series and you see how things begin at the bottom: the horse is the symbol for the animal, which means the unconscious libido associated with man, and that changes into a ram, and the ram into a bull. That is the spring symbolism, as we have seen.) I saw that the Indian was upon the back of the bull holding it by the horns. (This means that the animus is renewed by that renewed libido. Then:) The Indian was leading the bull, which followed very quietly. They slowly ascended a high hill until *(illus. 2)* at last they stood upon a pinnacle of rock. Below them many people surrounded the rock and raised their hands as if in supplication.

This is an interesting bit here. That resuscitated libido expressed by the form of the bull is a very primitive idea. The reason for the spring festivals is to shake off the past year and to renew the medicine power or the mana, the health for the coming year. Therefore such ceremonials are still celebrated in the spring to make us sound and strong for the coming year.

For instance, in my native town, at the end of January, when the first inklings of spring appear, they still perform a peculiar ceremony, a masked dance, which is highly primitive; with three figures in it — a very curious thing. First there is a strong primitive man, a wild man, carrying a young tree and wearing wreaths of ivy on his head and around his body — all quite green — meaning that he is a renewed demon of vegetation. He comes down the Rhine and is welcomed to the town by two animals, a lion and a griffin, who wait for him by the bank of the river and beg him to come to land; he comes to the bank, apparently with some reluctance, and then they dance together, a peculiar dance with drums. It is a very impressive thing and it is a really primitive ceremonial.

Now that is the renewed spirit of Aries, the ram or the bull spirit. The new vegetation power, the new mana for the whole town for the whole year, is what comes down the Rhine at the end of winter, or the very early spring. The carnival has the same meaning, and also, of course, the Dionysian festivals in Athens where they carried the phallic symbol. There is also evidence of such ceremonials in Italy in Etruscan times, symbolizing the renewed force of nature.

The renewed force has, of course, in this case a spiritual value, and it leads the animus, the Indian, up to a high place upon a pinnacle of rock where a remarkable scene ensues which is very much like a Bible scene, like Moses on the mountain, with the people down below worshipping the miracle that happened on Sinai, or something of the sort, because they all stretch their hands up to the Indian as if in supplication. From this scene we must assume that the animus and the bull as well have taken on a divine significance. Now this picture is based upon nothing in the patient's external experience. It is something that happens in her unconscious and she sees it simply as a sort of moving picture but you see the figures in that scene must express, or must be at least mirror reflections of, corresponding facts in her unconscious.

There is, for instance, in the unconscious a bull, the Indian, and all the people who watch the performance, a sort of audience in herself, and that audience is all the parts and particles and atoms of the collective unconscious. There is one leader, the animus, and there is one power which is the renewed libido, and for the unconscious those are the important facts. It is as if there

57

were a tremendous desire in the whole unconscious to be led — renewed
perhaps, too — for what they expect of the bull and the Indian is rebirth,
the spring miracle, and it is interesting to see how apparently the whole collective unconscious is just waiting for this miracle to happen.

You remember, perhaps, in the Epistles of St. Paul that interesting passage about the *apocatastasis*, a Greek word meaning the restitution, which
contains this same idea that the whole of nature is expecting the revelation
with us, that the animals and all creation are paralleling mankind. Just the
way we, as the children of God, are expecting a manifestation, a revelation
of the Holy Ghost, as St. Paul says, so everything, even the animals and
plants, are waiting for it too, because the spiritual miracle of the redemption
or the completion that is happening in man means the crowning of all nature
at the same time; so everything that has been fettered will be released with
the liberation of the children of God. You see it is the idea that man is the
representative of the whole of creation and that whatever happens to him
in a magic way happens to the whole world.

One finds the same idea among very primitive people. The members of
a totem clan, for instance, undergo certain ceremonials in order to change
themselves, and with that the nature of the totem will change too — the
totem animal is affected, too, in a way; if they get themselves into certain
psychical conditions then the propagation or the fertility of the totem animal is assured. In the center of Australia the growth of grass is exceedingly
important so they have a sort of grass seed as their totem; they perform
their rites and the grass seed totem is responsible for the crops. And there
is a water totem in places where water is very hard to get and they believe
that through their ceremonies the water totem will secure enough drinking
water. It is an exceedingly mystical idea. And as Paul thought, so the unconscious still thinks.

It is also a mystical idea among the common people. . . . (Sometimes)
they cherish the conviction of an absolute parallelism between man and
animal — the idea that when Christ appeared in the world, then a savior
appeared to each animal, a Doctor Fox, a Doctor Snake, a Doctor Hare, and
so on, and they all preached the same thing in order to bring up the whole
of creation along with man. It is the idea of *apocatastasis* again in a very
primitive form. And that still goes on. Of course, up above, in the thin air
of universities, nobody knows of such things, they come from far below.

And here we have the same thing. It is as if the unconscious were showing our patient how the hopes of the whole collective unconscious are aroused,
and as if the Indian upon the bull were really the savior for the collective
unconscious.

58

That brings us to a very paradoxical idea – you see, here on this plane of consciousness, we feel single and as if collectivity were a sort of opposite to us. Inside it is different, there is a multitude, and something similar is again the case but the situation is reversed; it is as if we were the multitude there, and as if the Indian upon his bull were confronting us. You could say it was a sort of private theater, if it were not so disagreeable; when you get into these things in the collective unconscious, you feel how terribly real they are and how utterly ungovernable, so you soon dismiss the idea of a private theater because you never saw anything as ungovernable in any kind of theater before; the theater idea makes it a bit too light. But it might be a sort of antique drama, a performance among primitive people where men are really killed, really tortured. It is something like that, or like a mystery play in which blood may even be shed. It is as if you were a whole small universe inside, while externally you are simply a unit . . . as if each individual were a little universe, a little microcosm in the macrocosm. But as if inside he were a macrocosm, too, and contained many microcosms. . . . You see, infinite greatness and infinite smallness are infinitely true, and it is quite possible that we contain whole peoples in our souls, worlds where we can be as infinitely great as we are infinitely small externally – so great that the history of the redemption of a whole nation or of a whole universe might take place within us.

Well now, here is a piece of such a mystery play. This woman is rather in the position of the people in this case because the Indian and his bull are still taking the lead, the Indian and his bull are the redeemers, or what amounts to the same thing, and this savior with his bull is, of course, the Mithras figure. But she has no idea that this Indian, being a warlike man, is Mithras. I am sure that if she had known of that possibility she would have adorned him with some symbols of Mithras, or would have directly called him that. But she did not, he remained an Indian and the bull a bull, despite that scene in which they appeared positively divine. Now the vision continues. She does not understand what is happening and therefore it simply moves on like a film.

VISION (cont.): The Indian and the bull crossed a high bridge over a swift mountain stream. (Such a crossing always means going over into a different condition, a new chapter begins. Then:) They turned to the left after crossing the bridge and descended into a wood. (So the situation now becomes quite different. To the left means to the side of the unconscious – the left is the sign of the unconscious as the right is the sign of the conscious. They are going deeper, descending into a dark wood, which is again a sign of the unconscious.) The Indian stopped to drink at a spring of water.

59

And then something very important happens, namely, the patient herself appears in the picture; she is now a figure on the stage. From now on the visions will be more like real experiences and not so much a series of moving pictures. She will be active in them, she is part of the mystery play, and this happens at the moment when the Indian comes down the hill and drinks. Now that is very close to earth: He leaves, as it were, the divine mystery spheres and comes down to the sources of the life libido which are deep in the body. You see he almost becomes physical and in that way he wakes her up, this is where he catches her and the means he uses is the drinking of the water.

You know the drinking of water has a transforming effect: it is an old symbol, the drinking from the magic well bestows all sorts of magic qualities upon one; by drinking from a certain well women become pregnant; and you know the symbolism of the well in the New Testament, the Samaritan woman, the living water and so on. In this case it is the going down into the body toward the earth, and down in the body he drinks the water; that means he establishes a moment of communication between the sources of life and himself, and so he brings her in. You see this again is something like bringing the egg to the mother. And it is also something like the grain that comes from the earth, because now she enters the mystery play, and she enters it in a peculiar kind of dress apparently — she is veiled.

VISION (cont.): And the Indian lifted the veil from my face and we gazed at each other. And he gave me water from the spring to drink. Then I followed the Indian, who was still leading the bull, and we came into a medieval town.

Now this drinking of the water has transformed the Indian in a way, it has brought him into connection with the earth, and the earth is the tangible reality. And her coming into the play veiled means that she does not see and she is not seen — she is unconscious. It is a sort of birth. You see, in the mysteries the veiling means the dying of the initiant, and the unveiling means resurrection; as, for instance, taking the veil for a nun means dying to the world, because she becomes veiled to the world; she is no longer seen nor has she any effect. . . . So lifting the veil would mean resurrection, going into action, having effect; and gazing at each other expresses that he has an effect upon her and she upon him. That means a close association from now on with that leading principle, which was first embodied in the Indian, and the obvious purpose of such a close union is that she should now acquire from the animus the function of leading. The animus should not lead any

60

more, it is not human enough for that office, it is only a partial figure, and she deserves to be led by something that is more her equal than the animus.

Backward in Time

The next move they make together is a move on the time machine, they go back in time to a medieval town. The unconscious can move in every possible direction, even in time it can go backward or forward because it knows no space, so they travel back to the Middle Ages and go to a medieval town.

VISION: There was a big square in the middle of the town and a cross was erected there; and we saw a woman who was holding up her baby to the cross. (Obviously, a Christian symbol.) The Indian walked silently on, and the woman then, in anger, threw the baby at the Indian, and instantly the baby was transformed into two little goats which followed along behind the bull.

Now this is a very involved thing. A movement back into the Middle Ages is a sort of regression but it is not of a personal character, it is a historical regression, it is a regression into the past of the collective unconscious. Such a regression takes place when . . . there is an obstacle ahead. . . . You regress and go to a medieval town, it is not a special town, but simply exemplifies the medieval atmosphere, that is, the medieval way of solving such a problem.

Well, the vision continues, they sacrifice a child, they offer a child to the cross. The woman offering the child is, of course, Mary; Mary brought forth a child to be sacrificed on the cross. That means that whatever is growing in the mind, reaching into the future, is to be sacrificed. Therefore no progress. . . . Our patient is shown to herself here as the medieval woman, she is shown what the medieval woman did, and naturally she has a *participation mystique* with that figure and she offers up the child to the cross. But the Indian passes on; that thing which is now alive in her, that guiding principle, cold-bloodedly goes on past the cross and says, "Nothing for you in that, it won't work." Then, as that woman, she gets angry and throws the child at the Indian, which means that she offers it to the peculiar thing he represents. It is as if she said, "I am this medieval woman and I offered my child to the cross, but since you go on like this, well, damn it, you can have it. Now take it with you."

You see she rebels against that new thing in her which is not respectful and disregards her medieval Christian intention. Then instantly, the future, the child, transforms and takes on an entirely new aspect. It is now two goats. . . . Now that would point to an unconscious beginning, a future that is still unconscious to her but in which her personal libido would take on the form of a goat. . . . In the frescoes of the Villa dei Mysteri near Pompei, where women were initiated into the Dionysian cult, the woman to be initiated appears with two little goats, meaning that she becomes aware of her absolute connection with nature. ·. . .

Then they moved on and climbed uphill again. . . . And now it is to her a most oppressive thought that she is following that shepherd, being herself two goats; that is rather disagreeable and she is full of doubts. Again she thinks, "As a Christian woman, who should I follow? Surely not the Indian, but Christ." Yet she is already so much the goat that she follows her shepherd, she *instinctively* follows the Indian and leaves the cross behind. There is no choice in the vision, she sees it, it simply happens like that; and mind you, she is not there yet, she has to go through many experiences before she gets there.

[In the remainder of this vision she throws a red rose to the Indian and the cortege is joined by an ostrich. – Ed.]

(illus. 3)

(The ostrich shows) that she puts her head into the sand in order not to see. Not to see what? Well, the whole situation, because she hands herself over to that Indian, body and soul, and it is better not to see it because she is afraid, which is quite understandable. You see things are moving, the cortege is wandering along, and the dream goes back in time, they come to Greek temples. . . .

The next vision is a very mysterious one.

The Vision of the Eyes

VISION: I behold a face with the eyes closed; I besought the face, open your eyes, look into my eyes that I may behold them. (She uses Biblical language, showing that these things have a hieratic character to her, it is not all phantasy stuff any more.) Then the face became very dark and slowly I beheld what no man is meant to see, eyes full of beauty and woe and light, and I could bear it no longer.

(illus. 4)

This is the first vision where she is positively stung; up to now she has been sightseeing, but here it gets under her skin. I will show you the picture she made. It is an animal — a dark hairy face with the melancholy eye of the animal. You see what really happened was that they traveled back, not only to ancient Greece but farther; the animals led her inevitably back to the animal age. That is, you remember, the purpose of the Dionysian mysteries, to bring people back to the animal; not to what we know as the animal, not that they should identify with it as we understand it, but to the animal within. This vision was really, as it were, the bottom. She looks directly into the eyes of the animal and they are full of woe and beauty. For they contain the truth of life, an equal sum of pain and pleasure, the capacity for joy and the capacity for suffering. Therefore the eye is exceedingly bewildering as the eye of the primitive is bewildering; the eye of the very primitive and unconscious man and the eye of the animal have the same peculiar expression of that mental state before consciousness which is neither pain nor pleasure. One doesn't know exactly what it is, it is both. That is what she sees and she does not understand what it is.

She looks here into the very soul of the animal and that is an experience she should have, otherwise she is disconnected from nature. That is the experience everyone should have in order to find again a connection with nature within, that is, with his own nature and with the God of the primitives. You could say just as well that these are the eyes of the beginning, of the Creator, who was unconscious because in the beginning all was unconsciousness; we don't know what it is in itself because sure enough if you are within the animal you don't feel unconscious but it is exactly the thing that from our standpoint we call unconsciousness. I cannot go into a philosophical argument about it but you see it is quite possible that what we call unconsciousness — that is, the sum of autonomous contents — that each of those contents has a consciousness in itself. Why not?

You see our conscious is only an autonomous complex and there are other complexes which might just as well each have an independent consciousness; and it is just as possible that the sum total of consciousness and unconsciousness has a center to which the autonomous complexes would be related, and that would mean consciousness, because that is the only definition of consciousness we can produce — namely, consciousness is the fact that things are associated with the ego center. So wherever there is such a center it is quite possible that there is consciousness. And so what we call the unconscious would be another form of consciousness, consciousness of something else in somebody else.

Now sure enough, when our patient has reached that level, or that bottom, one could say that she had undergone the essential experience of the Dionysian mysteries, which then forms a bridge between herself and the original man, the primordial man concealed beneath the historical layers of the past. And after that there is a chance that things can come right, be just as they should be, because the original pattern is unveiled, the original law is unfolded again. Then things take the course they must necessarily take because there is no possibility of loss of connection any more, the break between man and nature has been abolished, the bridge is there again, and so the possibility of creating dissociated systems in which she could go astray is abolished in principle. Of course, it is still possible to a certain extent, but the possibility of a corrector is always present and most probably she will no longer be as liable to wander off into arbitrary ideas or systems.

Here this woman touches the secret and the connection with the earth is established; she cannot go astray any more in conscious phantasies, inventions of the conscious mind, such things as have blindfolded her before, since now the bottom is touched. You see this is such a convincing experience, such an extraordinary and astonishing revelation, that one cannot get away from it. It becomes a truth. A truth, to be sure, which you cannot prove to anybody; you cannot say, "I have looked into the eyes of the animal." People would say you were just mad, but for the individual it is an uncanny and profound experience which contains absolute truth.

One feels something of that thing when one studies the remains of the Eleusinian cult; one finds there confessions of the tremendous impressions they received in those initiations. That also explains why the mysteries lived for more than a thousand years, perhaps fifteen hundred years — they lasted as late as 622 A.D., when they were abolished by a decree of the Byzantine prefect. It is not certain that they lasted as long as that in their original form but there was a decree at that time against them, and they were the most sacred thing in antiquity. If a man breathed a word about them he could be instantly killed, it was even a duty to kill him. That is the reason we have almost no knowledge of them, but the few fragments we possess indicate the reality of extraordinary experiences.

Now this vision has the value of such an experience, and the great emotion she felt in the moment when she saw that thing proves the reality of it, whatever it means. We are just trying to understand it in psychological terms but naturally we cannot suggest its profundity unless we ourselves have had it. But you can at least imagine that getting as deep as that down below all history into the regions of our blood must be rather an overwhelming experience, because one enters there a mental sphere or a psychological sphere that is still one with nature, which is, of course, an utterly different thing from our consciousness.

Now She Must Come Back

[Summary: The next vision is long. In it the Indian becomes involved in conflict. Then among a crowd of sun worshippers, he offers himself as a sacrifice, but receives no hurt. Later, he is wounded by an arrow and returns to his village. There all the animals greet him with joy. – Ed.]

The main thing to notice here is that the Dionysian cortege disappears, only the Indian is left. That Dionysian cortege was necessary to bring her back to the initial experience of the unconscious, the identity with the things below, and the experience of being at the origin of things, at the dawn of consciousness; the next move will be forward. You see going back in history like that means a sort of sacrilege, she has seen sacrilegious things in that regression, the dismissal of Christianity, also the passing of the Greek temples – all of that was left behind as if it were nothing.

Now she has to come back. Having touched upon the animal is naturally a thing that could hold her down, she could be imprisoned by the animal, so now she has to learn the meaning of all religion, all those cults, and she must move up from the beginning of consciousness to modern times. What she comes across first is a sun-worshipping people, and the animus is now being subjected to torture which would mean a sort of early Indian cult. . . .

She drew a picture explaining the situation. The Indian is in the center, the sun above, right and left are arrows, there is fire on the right side and water on the left. Obviously, this is a situation characterized by the pairs of opposites, hot and cold, fire and water, arrows from right and left. So it is a condition of conflict. . . . In this situation, then . . . the Indian shows how she can endure the battle with Indian stoicism, and with a sort of religious conviction, the relation to the sun being his guiding light. Finally he is relieved, he can go away to his people. And when he comes back to them relieved of that torture, then the *apocatastasis* takes place. It is an anticipation again. . . . (The animals rejoice) everything is reconciled, man with the animal and the animals with man, a sort of Paradise condition. . . .

The patient's conflict comes from the fact that she has touched the bottom, has looked into the eyes of the animal, and so the animal soul has gone into her; she has been united with the animal, with the deepest part of the collective unconscious, and that, of course, is an unforgettable experience which will cling to her and which will inevitably cause a tremendous conflict in her life. This you probably will say is a most deplorable effect, but you know if you don't suffer from such a conflict, it is surely that you are merely unconscious of it, because whether you have experienced it consciously or not, it is still there. In the one case you experience something which you don't understand, you don't know why you suffer, and you are absolutely dissatisfied with God's way of running the world and think it stupid of Him to torture you in this way; in the other case you know why you suffer — there is meaning in it. When you have such an experience as this patient did, then you know what you are up against, you know that you feel the animal in yourself just as much as you feel the cultured person, you know that the conflict comes from your wanting to be an animal just as much as a spiritual being, and then you have no one else to blame that you are in such a predicament. . . .

So this conflict in our patient is not too deplorable; she is very lucky to know what it is because then . . . she knows she is responsible, "Mea culpa, mea culpa, it is my guilt." And she will at least leave other people alone, whereas people who don't know their own conflict always want to improve others. They go around grumbling about education, or being habitual scolds, or acting as a public conscience. They are always interfering with other people and naturally they are always miserable because it is a neurosis not to be aware of one's own conflict. So she is pretty lucky despite the fact that it is difficult not to be a child any more.

VISION (cont.): The bull picked up an infant from the ground and carried it to an antique statue of a woman and laid the child at her feet. A naked young girl, her hair crowned with flowers, came riding on the back of a white bull; she seized the child, tossing her up in the air and catching her again. The white bull carried them to a Greek temple. Here the girl laid the child on the floor. Through a hole in the roof streamed a ray of sunlight. This ray of light struck the child on the forehead, imprinting a star there. She then changed into a youth, standing in a sacred grove. A satyr appeared and said, "Why are you here? "

Well, that infant is naturally herself, it is the newborn personality in her, because going down to the animal means a sort of night sea journey, which is the life between death and re-birth, the life in the womb. And when she comes out of it, she begins life again at the bottom of the long development of civilization, at first as a child. And now the bull, the full power of spring, is carrying that infant to an antique statue of a woman. Obviously the atmosphere is Greek — no longer exactly a primitive civilization; it is now a high civilization but of an antique nature. And then there is a naked young girl riding on a white bull. That is like the well-known picture of Europa riding on the back of the bull, the bull being the God. This is a very antique idea of course. She is an anticipation of what this little child might become if they continue on the antique level. That young girl, the anticipation of the future, now seizes the child, tosses it up in the air as if it were a ball, which means that the new personality is absolutely in the hands of that time, of the antique tendency. Well, that is a bit dangerous, this is the reason why people fear the collective unconscious because they are its absolute victims, they become as helpless as children, and then such visions can play with them, tossing them about as if they were balls, and there is no defense against it. Next the antique girl puts the child upon the floor, and in comes that ray of sunlight, which marks a certain point upon her forehead with the symbol of a star. Now this is a symbol which I am able to elucidate only by a parallel in Hindu philosophy. You see light always has the value of consciousness, it is the first ray of consciousness that strikes the child and therefore it strikes the forehead because that is the seat of the highest form of consciousness. . . .

She has become a child of the sun, a child of God in the antique form, a star herself, which means that she is now continuing her union or communion with nature on a much higher level, on an almost universal cosmic level. Now this is no poetry, mind you, it is history and it is psychology. You should not think the things I tell you are poetical metaphors. If you know the history of these mystery cults or comparative religions, then you know that these are the sacred metaphors in which man's psychology has expressed itself since time immemorial; they would not have come into existence if they did not correspond to very living and real psychological facts, and inasmuch as psychological facts are very real facts, these metaphors are equally real, provided that they are not used merely as words. . . . If they strike you as merely poetical words, as metaphors only, then it is your fault. Anybody who has the corresponding experiences will know that these words are the poor attempts of man to characterize very powerful psychological facts which can transform human beings completely. . . .

Now the vision goes on. The animus takes the lead again. The woman has stepped out of the mystery for a while, as it were, and left the active role to the animus, for she has changed into a youth and is standing in a sacred grove when a satyr appears and asks, "Why are you here? " Now that satyr is the reason why she suddenly stepped out of the play, because to meet a satyr is somewhat awkward, rather disagreeable, and you know she is enough of an educated woman so that when that satyr turns up, she naturally steps aside with a very innate decency; she leaves the place to a man, she sends her animus ahead and says, "Now you go in. I smell a rat, you go instead. There is a satyr inside. . . ."

Since the situation is awkward, you know something must happen. So she suddenly sees that young man irrationally standing upon the prow of a boat with his spear raised.

VISION: The boat approached a cliff, a sort of rock wall, and the youth threw his spear into the face of the cliff where it stayed, and a trickle of water came from the place where it struck. The boat then shivered and fell away and left the youth standing upon the rock. He looked into the water and saw the face of a woman. He leaped into the water and followed her and reached a cave where there were three witches; they said that they came from the land of the blessed. He tore the tooth from the mouth of one of the witches and ran from the cave. Then he was attacked by fierce and wild animals until he bled from many wounds. After that an old man appeared and drove all the wild beasts away. He wrapped the youth in a blanket and laid him upon a rock with his face to the sky, and that night there was a circle of fire which descended and burned in a flaming circle about the youth. Then the youth said, "I am the sacrifice," and the fire *(illus. 5)* consumed him. A white bird issued from his breast and flew up beyond the reach of the flames.

Now this thing that happens afterwards explains fully why we had such trouble before. You see, the satyr is an allusion to the goat God, or the goat man; he is emblematic, almost divine, and as she is afraid to meet that God, she sends the animus in, and he also is apparently in a rather perplexed condition. Then it is as if he were leaving on a new quest, for there is no going farther with that satyr. He travels away on a boat and then he strikes the rock with his spear, which means a sort of opening of the way, finding the way or the water, a sort of miracle, and you see what happens, he stands upon the rock and a woman appears, who is the patient herself in the depths of the unconscious. She made herself unconscious in order not to face that awkward situation, and he has followed her into a place where there are three witches, the three Fates you know, those three women who spin the threads of fate, adorning it with roses or cutting it with scissors. And he behaves rather roughly because according to the Greek myth they have only one tooth between them and he takes it away; obviously he is taking one disagreeable item away from them, robbing fate of one bad aspect. But that is, of course, an outrage against fate, it is what one cannot do, it is a presumption, and therefore the attack of wild beasts afterwards. You see this is the typical punishment for all those Greek heroes that show *hybris.*

What is *hybris*? . . . It is not exactly pride, it is more a proud arrogance. The German word is *Uebermut.* It is an increase of courage which amounts to insolence or freshness against the Gods, and the punishment for the assumption of divinity is dismemberment, getting lacerated, as for instance Dionysos

Zagreus was dismembered. He was torn to pieces by the Titans, the creative powers themselves. And so this youth who tried to rob fate of the poisonous tooth is dismembered or lacerated by the wild animals, for in resisting or outraging fate he puts himself into opposition to it, which he should not do, because in fate there is the divine will and one should not put oneself in opposition to it. But he is saved by the old man. This is again a typical fairy tale motive that always in the supreme moment something helpful appears; he would have been a helpless victim and the wild animals would have destroyed him were it not for the intervention of that old man. Now this is the wise old man, the medicine man, one who understands the speech of animals, who is lord of the animals and therefore can keep them at bay. And so the youth is saved, but he is saved for something better, for the divine sacrifice. He cannot escape the necessity of falling a victim to the Gods, but in a different form. So in the night that circle of flames descends from heaven and burns him up, the sacrifice upon the altar.

You see, that is the effect of the wise old man, that he makes him a willing sacrifice, not a sacrifice to blind passions but a conscious fulfillment of fate. He is consumed by the flames, but the white bird issues from his body and rises up to heaven, which is the escape of the immortal soul, represented since time immemorial by the soul-bird. Now I will show you the picture. Here you see the circle of flames descending from above and the idea is that the circle of flames descends upon him and consumes him, and there is the white bird flying up to the sky.

I leave out the next vision, which has to do with the union with the beautiful God. It is the union really with the animus, that youth who through fire became transformed — in the fire he acquires divine qualities; he is sacrificed and therefore attains to divinity. Then she is united with him which means that the role of the animus for the time being has come to an end. Having performed the ritual of self-sacrifice, having shown to her what would befall her, he has now given all his strength to her, he entered her and now she is *entheos*, meaning filled by the God. . . .

As she is now in this condition she naturally will have to face the thing from which she had recoiled . . . and so the vision goes on.

VISION: I beheld a satyr under a tree playing a reed. He stood up. Great stars fell down upon him and a very brilliant band of streaming light slowly moved across his face. I could only see his eyes which were green. I tried to part the band of light which hid his face from me but I could not. He stood with the palms of his hands upraised to me. He tore hair from his breast and threw it upwards. As he did so the hair turned into little flames. Then it became dark. He squatted down and blew upon a fire. I besought him to speak to me. He put a blue robe upon me and pearls around my neck. I knelt before him. Then he spoke to me saying: "I am the immortal one, I am the past, I am also the future, you shall know me." He made the sign of the cross upon my face and breast. Then he faded away and I saw him no more."

Now you see, this experience with the satyr takes an entirely different course than she had expected; for if I should say to any of you, "There is a satyr in there, now go in," you wouldn't do it probably, unless you were a policeman or an alienist. She was afraid, of course, she turned away and left the place to the man, to the animus. But now she confronts the satyr and the situation is entirely different from her expectations. What she had expected was something blurred, something sexual, and naturally it is a God. That is the prejudice we have when we speak of animals. So it is difficult to say to anybody, you should assimilate your animal, become acquainted with your animal, because people think of a sort of lunatic asylum, they think of the animal as jumping over walls and raising hell all over the town. Yet the animal is a well behaved citizen in nature, it is pious, it follows the path with great regularity, it is doing nothing extravagant. Only man is extravagant, the animal is never extravagant. So if you assimilate the nature of the animal you become a peculiarly law-abiding citizen, you go very slowly and you become reasonable in your ways in so far as you are able, for it is very difficult to be reasonable. You are something quite different from what you assume the animal to be, for only a man can behave outrageously. Have you ever seen an animal getting drunk on cocktails? That is man, only man can do that. We have an entirely wrong idea of the animal.

(illus. 6)   Now here is the picture of her confrontation with the satyr. You see the green eyes and the flames falling upon his breast; these are symbols of emotion, she is just tingling with emotion, a lot of little flames ready to burst into a big flame, the hopes that will arouse her to a big flame. But nothing happens. The woman is the patient herself with a blue mantle and a pearl necklace. And this satyr peculiarly enough is without any genitals, which is of course very uncommon for a satyr, for the usual fashion is to wear very conspicuous genitals as we know from antique pictures.

So you see the animal within is really meant and that God is the spirit of the animal. She expected something perfectly awful, but what that spirit of the animal is doing to her is to put a celestial mantle upon her, the blue mantle of Mary, and he gives her a necklace of pearls which, of course, means Mary's tears, the sadness with the divinity. He is crowning her in the mysteries. That is what the spirit of the animal does.

PART THREE

Initiation

The series of visions has now advanced to a very important point, namely, to the vision of the satyr who is the God Pan. You will remember, I compared this series of visions to the course of the mental phenomena that take place during an initiation. Now, of course, the process of initiation is a thing about which little is known. If you read about the initiation of primitives you think you are reading about something entirely new; or if you read about the antique mysteries, you feel that you have pretty well reached the end of human knowledge and understanding, because you come across the most amazing psychology. And these matters are not generally known, although, of course, they are known to the specialists. The corresponding psychological facts, with which we are dealing here, are also very little known — they have not been discovered yet — but I have found out quite a good deal concerning them. . . .

This whole series of phenomena takes place in a sort of fragment of the mind. It is not the whole psyche of the patient, but a part of her psyche that is having the vision. In primitive initiations the frame of mind of the man who is being initiated is different from his state of mind when he is fishing or hunting, he is not in his everyday state of consciousness. And the patient was not in her everyday state when she went through these experiences. You must realize that anybody undergoing such a process is in an exalted state, and naturally an experience in such a condition is quite different from an experience in one's ordinary condition. Now this last vision of the God is a very unusual one; it has all the characteristics of an ancient Dionysian image, just as the whole state of mind in which the vision took place had a Dionysian frame. . . . Can you tell me why it is important that she should realize this particular concept of God?

Suggestion: She is of puritanical origin and the Dionysian concept is very far away from her, so perhaps it is the next thing for her to see.

Dr. Jung: Yes. Because of her puritanical prejudices she naturally has in her unconscious mind a very peculiar conception of the supreme psychological factor — which is, of course, called God — and it is absolutely necessary that she should realize this entirely different form, as a compensation.

[From the lectures given between January 13 and March 25, 1931 (*Spring* 1962).]

71

For you see, the usual definition of God seems to be of something terribly abstruse and remote, and the definition is highly important psychologically because it expresses the supreme idea under which we work. Of course, we cannot assume that, if there is a God, He is exactly as we define Him. He prefers to be Himself, and what we say about Him amounts to no more than what ants might say about the Pope, or Mussolini. Just as we are untouched by the public opinion of the ant hill, so God is surely what He is, not what we define Him as being. But what the ant hill says about its own highest principle, its supreme factor, is exceedingly important because that shows its conception of itself, and we can be sure that even an ant hill is influenced by such a conception. For when a man formulates his highest principle, that is himself. Then he has formulated himself. But it is not necessarily true. When we say our God is love, we can be sure it is a compensation; we know it is not true. We say it to compensate the fact that we do not love enough, that we hate too much. Our ideal is love because we are too separated. People talk of community and relationship because they have none; they always talk of the things they do not possess. . . . The way people define their God is most characteristic.

But in a practical experience, like our vision, it is no longer a question of self-made formulations, or definitions made up for a certain purpose. Here, it is a fact. It happens. Such a vision just comes to a person. That is the point of the whole technique [of dream and vision observation]. The psyche is liberated from merely arbitrary management and is given over to itself, to a factor no longer identical with our conscious will or with our conscious intention. We train the patient to let things happen so that he can see what his psyche is; otherwise he labors under the impression that his psyche is exactly what he wants it to be, that he makes it. But if his relation to it is such that he is able to experience it as an objective fact, then he will know about the truth and the value of psychical events. Such a vision just occurs; it is not made up, it is not sought for, it is not elaborated. It just happens in a form like this and has the character of objectivity. But nevertheless it is a compensation. The original prejudice with which the patient starts is, of course, a conception of the divine that fits in with puritanical ideas, so naturally the kind of God that appears here is just the opposite. . . .

Now that vision of the God is a part of the initiation; it is the experience of the living presence and the absolute objectivity of the psyche. . . . If you can train yourself to the point of being able to experience psychical contents as objective, then you can feel a psychical presence, for then you know that the psychical contents are not things you have made. They occur, and so you are not alone in the psychical world. You can be in perfectly good company, most entertaining company, if you will train yourself to take such things as objective. . . . Naturally, all modern people feel alone in the world of the psyche because they assume that there is nothing there that they have not made up. This is the very best demonstration of our God-almighty-ness, which simply comes from the fact that we think we have invented everything psychical — that nothing would be done if we did not do it; for that is our basic idea and it is an extraordinary assumption. . . . Then one is all alone in one's psyche, exactly like the Creator before the creation. But through a certain training, a certain exercise — which is, of course, a yoga practice — something suddenly happens which one has not created, something objective, and then one is no longer alone. That is the object of these initiations, to train people to experience something which is not their intention, something strange, something objective with which they cannot identify. Then they can say, "Here is the object. Here is reality."

This experience of the objective fact is all-important, because it denotes the presence of something which is not I, yet is still psychical. Such an experience can reach a climax where it becomes an experience of God. Even the smallest thing of that kind has a mana quality, a divine quality. It is fascinating. A bit more and it is the whole deity, the giver of life. It is a decisive experience. . . .

The Regeneration of the Relation between Man and Woman

VISION: I beheld a scarab which opened. A man and woman emerged. They walked down some steps to a pond and gazed at their own images. Then the man went into the pond, dove into it, and emerged holding in his hand a ring. This ring he held to the forehead of the woman and the ring sank into the flesh of her forehead and remained there.

After the vision of the great God Pan comes a new revelation concerning the relation of man and woman. It is as if the relationship between man and woman had been regenerated [since the scarab in Egypt symbolized the regeneration of the sun], and the regenerated couple were now appearing. Have you any idea why the relationship of man and woman should have been affected by all this?

Answer: Is it that, just as the idea of God had to come in a new form, so the idea of love and relationship had to come in a new form, which would be an unacceptable pattern to her conventional ideas?

Dr. Jung: Yes, you see the conventional form is identical with the actual assumption of consciousness that it is all alone, that everything that happens

73

psychically is an arbitrary invention of our consciousness. If one thinks the same of love, there is only a love relation within the conventional forms, nothing else exists, nothing else occurs. The idea is practically the same. So if she has such an experience of psychical reality at all, namely, that something occurs which she has not made and is not responsible for, then naturally she has to admit also the possibility that something may happen in her feelings which she has not invented and which is outside of the frame of conventionality. This, of course, throws an entirely new light upon everything, and the relationship between man and woman is just one application of it. . . . Anything could happen and it could not be denied, don't you see? whereas the conventional consciousness always starts with the assumption that one can deny feeling the way one does because one doesn't want to feel like that. Convention handles such problems as if we should assume responsibility for the way we feel, but it is absolutely impossible because we have not invented that kind of feeling. It is as if I should say, "I apologize for the fact that the weather is bad today." But I am not responsible for the weather. . . . So coming out of the scarab is like the sun rising. . . . It is simply the coming of light. . . . She is in a way enlightened. Now she is in the picture — you know how important that is — and she sees her relationships in a new way. . . . She sees her feeling in a new light and this renewal is due to the vision of the Life Giver, of the God of Life, the great Pan. So, you see, the realization which takes place here is within the mystery experience, it is part of the mystery experience.

[With the mystery experience, however, there goes a certain exaltation.] This abnormal condition is by no means pathological. As long as humanity has existed, there has been that religious exaltation. It is an attempt at a sort of higher consciousness, which is legitimate. But one must be able to switch it off and get into one's so-called normal condition again. . . . In an exalted condition one is not necessarily in space and not necessarily in time, but one must know it, and that is exactly what insane people do not know. They become insane because they have no idea of what they are experiencing. The normal man knows that certain things belong to the level of the ordinary and other things to a more exalted level of consciousness. It is even possible that a thing may belong to both levels of experience, namely, that ordinary activity might have an *aspect* which has nothing to do with the physical level whatever, but belongs to a higher consciousness. But inasmuch as it belongs there, it has a divine or taboo character; therefore it is extremely unwise to let it appear in the sphere of ordinary life. It is necessary for us [as psychologists] to make these distinctions; otherwise we could

74

not enable people to live a complete life. People have to have experiences on an exalted level; it is absolutely impossible for them to bring all their experiences down to a physical level. This is the reason for religions — because formerly religions had something to do with exaltation. . . .

This last vision contains the realization of an aspect of the relationship between man and woman quite other than their relationship on the physical or conventional level. You notice that I say physical or conventional, and perhaps you are astonished that I speak of these things as practically identical. But convention is nothing else than the average truth. Just as the law or the penal code tell you what you can safely do, how far you can go, similarly the conventions are just poles that indicate how far you can risk yourself on the level of visible things, that is, in this conventional world. But there is another kind of relationship between man and woman which obviously belongs to a different order of things. It belongs to the exalted condition.

Now this is an extremely important recognition, and it is instantly followed by the image of a union which is of a very divine nature, namely the ring which the man brings up from the depths of the pond is inserted in the flesh of the woman's forehead. That means thought. You see, the ordinary ring that is worn on your finger can also be taken off; but when it is inserted into the flesh, grown into the flesh, then it is a different thing; even if you cut it out, it leaves a scar; it is far more securely anchored than when you wear it on your finger. And that is, of course, the idea. . . . This place on the forehead indicates the seat of thought, of supreme consciousness, and when anything happens there it shows that it has to do with the process of individuation, because supreme consciousness and individuation are identical.

So the relationship that the patient is realizing is closely connected with the problem of her own individuation, and at the same time it has the importance of an experience on the exalted level, which makes her twice-born, as they say in India. The statues of the Buddha, for instance, always have a certain sign on the forehead; it is the sign of the man with awakened consciousness, the man who is twice-born, who has undergone initiation. So that sign means that this woman has undergone initiation, but naturally at the time neither she nor I were aware of that. . . . [But] this vision really indicates the moment of complete initiation, or individuation; that is, she is definitely touched and marked, like a criminal who has been sentenced and who has a brand on his forehead — or the mark of the chosen one. . . . She has been just like somebody who believes that two times two may be five, or six, or perhaps four, but that there is no certainty about it. From now on she knows that two times two are four, and she can never forget it. Such an enlightenment or realization has that unforgettable character. That is why all these experiences have the character of the divine, of immortality. It is as if something of an eternal nature had happened.

Dionysian and Apollonian

(illus. 7)

VISION: I beheld a beautiful youth with golden cymbals, leaping high in the air with joy and abandon. He was followed by dogs who were also leaping. The hair of the youth was black and around his loins was a leopard skin. He came upon an old man in a turban, with a scythe, who stood with his arms outstretched. The youth stopped and his cymbals dropped. The old man gazed at the earth and flowers sprang up at his feet. The youth fell upon the ground and buried his face in the flowers. The old man lifted up his countenance. His face was dark but his eyes were white. He was blind.

Here we have again a case where the animus takes the lead. I explained in a former seminar that in a situation where the contents are too far from consciousness, so that consciousness is unable to realize them, then those contents are enacted or impersonated by the animus, as if it were the animus that was concerned with them. . . . (That is because it is a woman's case; in a man's case it would be the anima who performs.)

During the dance of the youth an old man appears who is described as a sort of Oriental — he wears a turban and stands with outstretched arms. This has a peculiar effect upon the youth. He stops and drops his cymbals, showing that the apparition of the old man has checked his enthusiasm. . . . This old man is the Apollonian side which has been called forth by what the Dionysian side is attempting. The whole thing is performed by the animus; when one aspect of the animus leaps forth in a Dionysian mood that instantly calls up the other side [the Apollonian]. . . .

[This] principle is expressed by an old man, obviously a sort of old wise man. It stops the Dionysian mood, which simply means that the patient's unconscious reasoning is undergoing a change [since both these aspects of the animus really represent unconscious opinions as to the way her future inner development should take]. . . . Now the old man shows *his* way which is quite unlike that of the youth; he stands still, as if rooted, and gazes down at the ground, and flowers spring up from the ground. The youth then falls down and buries his face in the flowers. You see, this is simply a demonstration of two contrasting movements: the first movement would be the Dionysian or extraverted way, leaping over things or into things, jumping over obstacles or slurring over difficult facts; and then the other principle, the introverted or Apollonian principle, would be doing nothing, not moving

on, not being enthusiastic, but being contemplative. So this old man gazes
at the ground, he uses contemplation, and that produces something, it produces flowers — to unfold and grow. And the youth, the Dionysian movement, comes to an end in those flowers. Now I don't know whether you
understand this symbolic speech of the unconscious. How would you interpret what the old man does? . . .

Suggestion: Reflection, such as that of the wise man, induces growth, it
is the inward principle of growth and the flowers unfold that way.

Dr. Jung: You are absolutely right. It is a matter of two ways here. One
would be the enthusiastic doing; the other is the reflective, contemplative
way, which also causes something to happen or to develop. The old man
wears a turban which points to the East — that is the way the unconscious
hints at things.

There is the further detail that the old man gazes at the earth. This means
that he is concentrating upon the earth, indicating that the earth is of particular importance in this case. It is as if he were saying, "Don't jump about,
don't get fussy. Contemplate the earth now, for it is from the earth that the
ultimate solution will come." Then the flowers grow up from the earth,
indicating that the solution will not come from any kind of excitement, or
great jumps, or anything of the sort, but through slow development, a slow
impersonal kind of growth.

Another detail is that the old man is blind. Only after the scene where
he brings up the flowers from the ground does this become obvious. His
eyes are quite white and he does not see. . . . Now that is a symbol. In our
Western mind when we see a thing we have almost an intellectual conception of it. Therefore we say, "Don't you see? Don't you understand? "
The seeing is a sort of intellectual understanding. But the vision states that
the old man does not see, he has no intellectual grasp, he gazes at the earth
without understanding. Of course, if you translate that into actual psychological consciousness it means that when the problem reaches the patient
she will sit down and contemplate it without understanding — with a sort
of blind contemplation, not knowing and not fore-seeing, and without any
intentions concerning the things which are to develop. And this is important
because if you understand — that is, if you opinionate that you know — if
you have a view about things, it is wrong; for then you kill them. It is just
as if you had the evil eye which poisons the thing it looks at. . . . The white
eye means an ecstatic condition in which the pupil is turned up and disappears under the lid; when you turn your eye inward, you hinder yourself
or your intellect by that means from seeing things too closely or too acutely,

and thus destroying them. One should never look at things if one wants them to grow. It is much better to be deaf in one ear and blind in one eye than to have an acute and conscious perception of a thing. It kills it. The seeing eye of our intellect has the quality of the eye of the basilisk. . . . That is the teaching of the unconscious to this particular patient, who has a very acute intellect and a very seeing eye.

Renewal of the Animus

VISION (cont.): (In the next part of the vision we see why the old man was looking at the earth because suddenly:) The youth drops upon the lap of an ancient mother.

One does not know where that ancient mother comes from. (But the most accurate way to understand these visions is to understand each sequence as if it were a picture projected against a wall, like a film.) In the scene before, the youth was lying upon the earth and burying his face in the flowers; then suddenly there is a dropping movement and he is on the lap of an ancient mother. The patient made a picture of the mother as a sort of enormous statue of far more than human size, rather of divine size. Now the lap of that ancient mother is, of course, the earth again, the lap of the earth mother. The hint we got before was that the old man looked at the earth because he felt it was the place where one grows. If the youth falls into the lap of the ancient mother, he can develop. He falls there, naturally, in order to be carried again, to be transformed into a sort of a plant in the womb of the earth. . . . One could say that this leaping youth is too elflike. There would be danger of his jumping into heaven or something like that; he has not solidity enough in the way of the earth, and therefore the earth is particularly emphasized.

(illus. 8)

But this is a general truth concerning modern people. One might come across cases where there is enough of the earth and not enough of the spirit, and in such cases naturally one would find continual insistence upon the air, upon the spirit. But here, there is emphasis upon the earth, and in our civilization and in the world of our consciousness the insistence [of the unconscious] upon the earth is generally more important. Therefore I say it is a *general* truth — not an individual case — it is a general truth that the earth is depreciated and misunderstood; so the unconscious regularly puts great emphasis on the fact of the chthonic. Nietzsche expresses this very beautifully: *"Ihr sollt wieder Freunde von den nächsten Dingen werden."* (You shall become friends of the immediate things.)

78

The immediate things are this earth, this life. For quite long enough our ancestors — and we ourselves — have been taught that this life is not the real thing, that it is provisional, and that we only live for heaven. It is because our whole morality has been based on that negation of the flesh that our unconscious so often works to convince us of the importance of living here and now. For, in the course of the centuries, man has repeatedly experienced that the life which is not lived here, the life which is lived as something provisional, is utterly unsatisfactory, that it leads to neurosis. . . . As long as it is a case of provisional life your unconscious will be in a state of continuous irritation. . . .

VISION (cont.): The youth now leaps from the knees of the mother and dives into the water below. [When he comes up his hair which was black has become golden.]

That shows that he is like a sun, a reborn sun; when he dived into the unconscious he released a sort of rebirth mechanism by which he was changed, and now he comes up with golden hair. This vision tells of a certain movement of the unconscious. The vision before was very spiritual; it was of the birth of the exalted man and woman from the scarab, and that followed the vision of the God, the spirit of nature, and such a vision, of course, causes exaltation. Beholding the image of the deity has the magic effect of deification. That is the reason why there are icons, for example, because gazing at the sacred image produces deification. . . . In this case, an unavoidable exaltation [has resulted]. The image of the God has had the effect of deifying this woman in the form of the divine satyr, of a sort of spiritual satyr. She herself has become in a way a divine being, which accounts for the particular kind of leap the animus takes. . . . That is the deified *part* of her. You see, she has not fully realized yet that she has been deified by the vision of the God, only her animus has realized it. Therefore he behaves like the divine goat man, leaping as if he were a nature being. . . .

A rebirth mechanism is always applied, in the unconscious as well as in real history, when something is in a condition that it should not be in. For instance, when something is sick or imperfect a magic rite is applied to renew it. Now if the semi-divine condition of the youth were satisfactory, he would not have to undergo renewal, but apparently it is not satisfactory because the Apollonian principle is against it, and therefore he is forced to undergo renewal. Now in this case jumping into the water has the connotation of a sort of ritual ablution, of a rebirth through water. . . . This means that since deification has taken place a *rite de sortie* must be celebrated to get him out of the condition of semi-divinity. . . . deification is an exceedingly dangerous thing; it is an exaltation which lifts people up to a sort of divine state in which they can do very bloody things, tearing deer or young goats with their teeth, for instance [as the maenads did]. . . . as if they themselves were beasts of prey. . . . After being in such a condition, one needs a *rite de sortie*. . . .

[So the Dionysian animus] has to go down to get purified, to get washed in the waters. Therefore also, his hair which was black — having the connotation of evil, nocturnal — becomes golden after he has been in the water. . . . [For] the hair is understood to be an emanation of the head, having to do with the mind and with very spiritual and magic forces. This hair being black gives the idea of darkness, black thought, or an obscured mind, and the golden hair means bright thought or consciousness. And, sure enough, in the state of exaltation one loses consciousness of oneself and one's mind becomes obscure. But in the state after the *rite de sortie* one is supposed to have bright hair again, light shining hair. . . .

When the animus dives into the corporeal sphere and into the deep layers of the unconscious he enters the patient herself, he is no longer in the air, he is now in the corporeal sphere where he blends with her, and so when he comes up with golden hair she joins the game. He has fulfilled his task as a sort of forerunner. . . .

The Role of the Animus

VISION (cont.): We ran together hand in hand until we came to a great chasm which we knew not how to cross. . . . Then setting foot on either side of the chasm the youth told me to walk over him to get to the other side. This I did. . . .

Here the animus is in the right place. He functions as a bridge [helping her to pass to a new area in the unconscious]. He is on the side of the patient where the collective unconscious is, not in front of her, that is, not on the side of the obvious, so-called material, world.

VISION (cont.): I took him by the hand but he could not come. He struggled to maintain his balance and then he fell into the water at the bottom of the chasm. . . .

There is always danger that the animus will fall off, as if backward, will disappear into the collective unconscious, and then for a while the connection with the unconscious will be cut off. The animus is like a drawbridge which has its moorings in the unconscious. When it is drawn up, it shuts

the gate to the collective unconscious. That is about the right image for the
animus because, if rightly placed, it really belongs more to the unconscious
than to the conscious. You see, the animus is not really created by the conscious; it is a creation of the unconscious. and therefore it is a personification
of the unconscious. It is the gate to the collective unconscious, and by a
certain attitude, one can provoke it to appear and function that way; but if
it returns to itself and pulls up the bridge, then it locks the gate to the unconscious.

I repeat, the anima and the animus have not just been invented by the
conscious, they have been *found* by the conscious. It is not that we have
done something in the conscious in order to build a bridge to the unconscious;
it is rather that the collective unconscious came to us in the form of an anima
or an animus and, of course, when we became aware of that apparition, we
reached out for it and thus established the relationship. All these insights
into the peculiarities of the collective unconscious were not originally produced by consciousness — because our consciousness is a curiously passive
and incapable thing. All that inside world really appears to us through its
own continual activity. When you study the activity of the human mind,
you will be impressed again and again by the fact that thoughts have not
been made by man but that they *appeared* to him. They manifested themselves in such a way that he often did not even see them as thoughts. For
instance, the primitives see ghosts or have revelations of mental things which
we might think consciously. It is the same with our dreams, in them we get
intimations of thoughts which we would not have thought consciously.

That is the reason why we analyze dreams; otherwise analysis of dreams
would be perfectly futile, perfectly sterile, because we would find nothing
that we did not know consciously. Therefore when we reach a conclusion
from analyzing a dream which is exactly what we have found in the conscious
already, we have not arrived anywhere near the truth, we have simply not
gotten to the bottom of the dream — because every dream is an intimation, a
creation, produced from the unconscious, not caused by consciousness at all.

You see that is the Freudian point of view: that you have a wish, and
you let it drop, and then it may produce a dream. But that is not so true.
As early as 1904, I remember, I wrote to Freud once and told him that what
he called repression was not exactly repression because there are cases where
you cannot find any traces of repression. I said that dream production was
an automatic function which had its roots in the unconscious and of which
the conscious is a perfectly detached spectator. And he said that was true,
that he had observed the same thing, but it never appeared in his theory, he

81

always kept his old point of view. That was, however, one of the first inklings of my own conviction that the unconscious has its own ideas and can
produce amazing changes in the conscious by extracting things from it or
putting things into it; and the conscious can do precious little about it. For
our consciousness in its origin was a mere passive awareness, and all that we
call concentration and active thinking, or any intentional conviction, came
very much later. It is, as a matter of fact, a very recent acquisition. It is
quite astonishing, for example, to see how little a primitive man can actively
think or do. He cannot concentrate, he has no attention. . . .

She Fulfills the Mystery Experience

VISION (cont.): And then I was afraid. I was alone in the dark woods.
(She realizes that her ghostly companion has vanished and she is left alone
to her own devices. And it is interesting to observe what happens when she
is left alone.) I lay down beside a stream and the animals came and licked
my face. (She is together with her instincts. . . . People who are more or
less on good terms with their own nature are friends with animals; the animals know it and go to them.) I stood up and walked to the edge of the
water. Then a woman rose from the water, wearing a high peaked cap. She
laughed as I stepped into a golden boat, pulled by a white sea horse. As I
went I saw rainbows arching everywhere over the sky.

The peculiarly high peaked cap which the woman wears is the *pileus.*
This derives from the cult of Mithras, who is a sun figure, a deity. The
woman is the patient herself; so this is a vision of herself in the exalted condition of being identical with the sun. It refers back to the initiation and
deification in the former vision, and it is the reason why she laughs that
divine laugh, which is beyond the uncertainties and doubts of an imperfect
mortal. She is the woman who rises as a vision from the unconscious. It is
also she who steps into the golden boat, which shows the sun identification,
and while sailing on the water, she sees rainbows arching over the sky. She
is causing the rainbows to appear – just as the sun causes rainbows – she is
now the sun.

You see, that makes the thing complete. Being together means being
together with her lower instincts, the earthly instincts, the instincts of her
body, with every thinkable animal fact, a complete awareness of her chthonic
being. This is, of course, a sort of utter humiliation; it is man degraded to
the animals, being among the animals as one of them. And that causes this
superior Self to appear; it is the only possible thing that can happen. Because
the Self in this divine form is the balance and the necessary counterpart to

the instinctual, the animal. So this figure of the Self, if you put it together, is divine above and animal below; like the vision of the satyr-God.

Now that is the end of this particular vision. . . . In the last part you saw that she succeeded in getting her animus into the right place and in making it function in the right way, as a bridge. Then she crossed the [animus] bridge to the other side, thus establishing a connection with the collective unconscious. The moment that happens, one could say, the goal has been reached, so the animus can plunge back into the collective unconscious. Then the drawbridge is pulled up and the gate is shut; she is left alone with the animals in the darkness, which is perfectly all right. Being with the instincts, being among the animals, means, of course, being consciously in the dark. . . . The more one reaches back into the ages, the more one has the animal feeling, the intuition of what the animal is. . . .

Then, on the other side, she has the vision of greatness, of the Self in its divine aspect, which is absolutely as it ought to be, because she can never hope to be more, or to have more, than the vision of the Self. She is glorified or deified. She is entering the golden abode of the sun and producing the rainbow, which is the halo you find round the heads of the saints. That halo symbol occurs several times in the course of her visions. So this is really a complete sanctification or deification in the sense of the antique mysteries. . . . It is all one could wish for, apparently. Now what would you expect? How can the visions continue? . . .

You remember what I told you about looking into the animal's eyes? There she had reached the bottom, she had gone down through all the civilizations. Now she is returning. You remember she was with the sun-worshippers, then she came to . . . the sphere of the Dionysian mysteries. Now she has reached about as far as the mystery cults of the second and third centuries A.D. . . . For she is the sun. The purpose of the antique mysteries was to make you the Helios. The whole upshot of the mystery ceremonies was that you should become the sun itself, like Apuleius in *The Golden Ass.* But that is surely an absolutely superhuman condition; to rise up from darkness to the tremendous height of the sun. And she is after all just an ordinary woman. This is merely her experience in an exalted condition. Now what is the relationship of such a condition to our life? That is still lacking, for the problem is now solved as it would have been two or three thousand years ago. Then it was sufficient for them to be almost unconscious, to be people who at certain times in life were exalted to unspeakable depths and unspeakable heights; that was the whole thing, and that experience sufficed at the time. We still have fragments of confessions of the initiants

83

at Eleusis, which tell something of what they experienced there, of what a wonderful experience it was. Apparently it was sufficient then, but it was not sufficient in the long run. Human consciousness developed, and new needs came up with new solutions. The next solution was Christianity.

Now something should happen in the visions which is akin to Christianity. We are already overlapping the beginnings of Christianity and something should happen in which she will discover the inner meaning and structure of early Christianity, just as she has discovered the inner meaning and structure of the pagan cults. For we must expect her to continue on her way through the ages in order to reach modern times. . . .

The Divine Punishment

VISION: (The next vision begins:) I beheld a sheep which had been sacrificed upon a stone altar.

You see, in these very words you discover the Christian idea, the sacrifice of the lamb; the sacrificial idea is already here. Up to the present we have had no sacrificial symbol, except the one with the sun-worshippers, and she had next to nothing to do with that. But now she obviously is coming to deal with the idea of sacrifice. Why do you think the question of sacrifice comes in here? If you can answer that, you will have answered what Christianity means as an introverted experience — not as the historians explain it. What do you think the connection is between the end of the last vision and the beginning of this one?

Answer: In order to get to the middle way she must sacrifice.

Dr. Jung: Exactly. While she is the sun, she is the supreme God, and down below in the depths she is an animal. She is reaching beyond herself in both directions, above as well as below; she is no longer human. She is almost torn apart into pairs of opposites, she is stretched to an amazing degree. Now that is exactly the situation described by an early Christian philosopher, the old bishop, Synesius of Edessa. He lived between the fifth and sixth centuries and wrote a very interesting book. In it he philosophizes about a certain *spiritus phantasticus* — this is simply the creative imagination of man — which causes dreams. We would call it phantasy, visual phantasy, or creative phantasy; but with him it is almost personified. The idea is that there is a *spiritus phantasticus* in man that does extraordinary things. The *spiritus phantasticus* can descend, for example, into unspeakable depths, or he can ascend to enormous heights. He can approach the figure of a God, and inasmuch as he goes beyond the reach of man he becomes divine — really divine, mind you.

84

So you see, if that woman's experiences had been more real — as it is, we can more or less think of them as painted on a wall — if she could really have felt them in her body she would have been divine, divine in the human category — I mean, of course, in so far as man can imagine anything divine. She would have experienced herself as a superhuman being. Now that is what Synesius held: that when the *spiritus phantasticus* in man, his creative phantasy, reaches beyond man in any respect, below or above, he really becomes divine. Then Synesius says an extraordinary thing: he says, "And being divine, he has, as such, to undergo the divine punishment." And the divine punishment is dismemberment: he will be torn in pieces, he will be sacrificed like a sacrificial animal that is cut asunder upon the altar. In these words Synesius gives away the whole secret of the transition from pagan religion to Christianity. He really formulates it.

You see the religious experience of antiquity was men's experience of themselves as divine; that was the enormous discovery they had made, and it was a living truth. They probably said to one another, "Have we not been divine? Have we not been Gods together?" It was a tremendous thing; they were exalted: they were no longer little citizens, they were lifted up to a higher condition. . . . But the tremendous disadvantage of it was that people got into a superhuman sphere, and this became impossible somehow, and therefore they fell. Then they felt that the only way in which they could cure the ailment they had gotten from this ascending and descending was to sacrifice. They must kill something. So it came about that they chose a symbol which really means the sacrifice of the animal, the lamb, but which is at the same time the God . . . the God-animal. . . .

That is why the Christian cult has a great spiritual advantage over the Mithraic cult, for it not only sacrificed the animal part but also the human-divine form of man, in the shape of the Crucifixus. This meant that not only the things below man should be sacrificed, but the things above man, too. This is a peculiar kind of interpretation, I am perfectly well aware, and if a theologian were here he would probably tear my head off. . . . Now, of course, we must find out what this means. . . . What did they really sacrifice?

Answer: A man sacrificing his divinity is no longer in *participation mystique* with God. After the sacrifice he risks putting himself in the place of God.

Dr. Jung: Exactly. You see through the antique religious experience the individual becomes entirely collective: he becomes a God. I become a Helios, you become a Helios, he becomes a Helios, and so we are all Helios. A man, who was very sad and terribly alone, once said to me that he could cure himself with the idea that other people were sad too. I am sad, you are sad, we are all sad; so nobody is alone. Thus the effect of *participation mystique* is strengthening. It is really a return to the primitive condition. The Dionysians were seeking that effect — namely, to be like everything else, to feel themselves in everything. The idea was that the blood of Dionysius circulated in every living being, that everything contained a piece of Dionysius. . . . This naturally strengthened the *participation mystique*; but, of course, it killed individuality, it offended against it.

It was the first appearance in man of the being that reaches beyond man, but the shot went too far. They identified with it and they were torn apart. They no longer existed. They were shattered to pieces, so that nothing remained but the remembrance of the divine moment. Then, since they themselves did not exist, it became necessary, for the sake of the individual, to sacrifice the *participation mystique*. That they did not really exist as human beings is shown by the fact that they had no real feelings as human beings. Think of all the horrible things they did in the circuses! That would not have been possible if they had had any live feeling for humanity. They had no individuality, therefore they had to worship one individual human being. That's why the Caesars were deified, and why after death they became stars, which the astrologers used to discover. Or in Egypt, the individual was the Pharaoh. This is because we are all individuals, and the individual cannot live if individuality is completely denied.

There was a general sadness in those days, which the poets pointed out, and a tremendous desire for a redeemer to come. So the next sacrifice was exactly the sacrifice of the experience which constituted the holy life, the real spiritual life of antiquity; that was completely abolished. (I put this very strongly, because we are in a time now when old things are beginning to crumble away. . . . There will have to be a tremendous abolition of old values. I mean if the time is such as it seems almost to be. . . .) We can surely believe that for the pagan individual, who was really religious, it was a horrible moral and spiritual conflict to sacrifice the experience which to him was most holy. For this experience of divinity is the real essence of religion, and these people had to sacrifice it. They had to accept the fact that we are all ugly, and miserable, and full of sins, before a humble poor God, hanging on a cross. That is the thing they could not understand and I can understand that they could not do so. . . .

Now I will give you the whole text of the series of visions referring to the sacrifice of the sheep. As usual, it consists of telegraphic sentences, just telegraphic impressions of changes taking place.

86

A Sheep is Sacrificed

VISION: I beheld a sheep which had been sacrificed upon a stone altar. Many Indians danced in a circle about it. (It is curious that this sacrifice is taking place in such surroundings. It is the *relatively* primitive man, the kind of primitive man that is immediately accessible to the dreamer, the North American Indian.) They threw the sheep into the air and smeared their faces with its blood. They tore the entrails out and hung them about their necks. The entrails changed into great red jewels. I appeared dressed in white.

First comes the objective part and then she herself enters the sacrificial scene. As usual the activity is first projected into the Indians. You know that her animus often appears in the form of a Red Indian, but here instead of one Indian it is a whole crowd — instead of one animus, there is quite a group of animi, a whole tribe. This is perfectly possible since the animus is always like a multitude; she might just as well have said, "One Indian is sacrificing the sheep." The Indians here are carrying out in an anticipatory way whatever is the real meaning of the whole ceremony.

[Dr. Jung explains here that many primitive ceremonies, similarly connected with sacrifice, were intended to help the sun to rise. This magic ceremony, he says, *means that blood is needed. . . that a sort of life renewal is planned.* Renewal is required because *through the fall of her animus into the depths and darkness of the collective unconscious, through that loss of connection,* communication has been cut off. In this, her condition resembles that of our modern consciousness as a whole, for we have lost the *symbolic bridge of dogma* that used to connect us with the collective unconscious. Just as she experiences *a sort of sun identification,* we are able to imagine ourselves supermen (like Nietzsche's superman who, having said God was dead, then thought of himself as God.) But this is an inflation, a *hybris* and must be paid for. At first, *it gives a wonderful feeling of elation and grandeur; but after a while one will be left high and dry because one is separated from the sources of life. That is the condition of the patient at the end of the last vision. Now communication ought to be reestablished because life is beginning to fade out. . . . Therefore this rite to make the sun rise.* Also, in what follows, the smearing of the face with blood has the value of a rebirth ritual. – Ed.]

Now they are tearing out the entrails and hanging them about their necks and the entrails change into red jewels. Do you know anything that could enlighten us about this peculiar symbolism?

Answer: They used the state of the entrails for augury in the classic times.

Dr. Jung: Yes. The entrails always played a great role in blood sacrifices. They needed the entrails for all sorts of prophetic purposes because they supposed that the entrails and particularly the liver contained the imprint of

destiny. Just as we have, for instance, little books about dream interpretation, or about the lines of the hands, or astrological books, so in antiquity
. . . . they prophesied from the particular condition of the liver, or the size
of the entrails. Naturally, the entrails can change; there are very individual
differences in their size and form, and these are enough apparently to give
an opportunity to read a meaning into them intuitively. In addition, the
liver was particularly important because it was supposed to be the original
seat of life, as the name indicates. The liver is the thing that lives. In German, it is *die Leber,* which means the same thing. . . .

Of course, it seems reasonable — I mean from the primitive point of
view — to assume that in order to get anywhere near to a knowledge of fate
one must go to the sources of life. That was the old idea and that is why
oracles were over wells or holes in the earth, like the springs at Delphi, and
there are many other examples of this in primitive myths and early literature. . . . That is why they questioned the liver, just as they questioned the
entrails which were supposed to be the seat of psychic life and of secret
knowledge. . . . You see, we more or less identify the brain and consciousness. We assume our consciousness is located in the brain; but the consciousness of very primitive people was not located in the brain; it was decidedly
below. . . . And in our day . . . it is still possible to bring to consciousness
that primitive form of mind which is located in the entrails. As I have told
you, there is hardly a case of neurosis where the entrails are not disturbed.
For instance, after a certain dream a diarrhoea happens, or there are spasms
in the abdomen. . . . I know of a number of cases of people who did not
know what they ought to do, people who got lazy when they should have
organized their lives on a somewhat larger scale, who omitted their duty
and tried to live like chickens, and they then got frightful spasms in the
abdomen. . . . So, when somebody whom I have formerly analyzed comes
back again with such symptoms, I say, "Now, what does that mean? What
is that symptom talking about? I expect you to have enough imagination
to tell me what that symptom is trying to point out to you — exactly as a
primitive man would do". . . .

Now this taking out of the entrails, using them as a sort of decoration,
a *guirlande*, really means bringing the hidden contents out into the open.
The sheep almost invariably symbolizes unconsciousness or unconscious
impulses — that is, sheep-like impulses to do gregariously exactly the same
thing that everybody else is doing. You know how, when one sheep runs
ahead, the whole flock follows it and they all go to hell together. That is
how men are when they are entirely collective; that is unconscious gregari-

ousness. A sheep sacrifice is always a matter of the sacrifice of a merely collective impulse, of imitation, of doing what everybody else is doing. The
sacrifice means, "Now cut that out. No more living blindly, like sheep in a
flock." One cannot just live in a herd. If one lives like a sheep one knows
only what a sheep knows, just a going along with the crowd. So sacrificing
the sheep means giving up the collective prejudice that one is one among
thousands. It is true that man is gregarious but, if he is nothing but gregarious, he is not human. Unconscious gregariousness is just animal, and with
it goes the famous kind of thinking that causes people to worry night and
day over what would be good for the eleven thousand virgins but never to
bother about themselves. . . .

Well, we have gotten as far as seeing that those entrails are closely associated with a very primitive form of psychical functioning. And we see that
bringing them out of the sheep into the open would be a sort of analytical
procedure. However, I have no evidence from antiquity which would confirm that there ever was such a rite and I rather doubt it. I think this is a
very modern attempt to symbolize a sort of dissecting or exposing of the
contents of the sheep, in other words, to symbolize the getting of the contents of the early primitive mind out of an unconscious form and wearing
them openly. And then a miracle happens. They become jewels, which
means that the unconscious itself says, "These contents, as long as they are
inside and unconscious, are just entrails of sheep and nothing else; but if
you turn them inside out, if you bring them up into consciousness, they
become precious stones, like rubies."

With this, we see that the thing has become very positive. Since the
patient enters the ceremony, it is now acceptable. Before, it was a primitive sort of blood ceremonial which was in a way horrible to her, but the
moment she sees that these things are precious she can accept it. You see,
the collective unconsciousness, which forces us blindly to join the herd and
be like everybody else (here it is symbolized by the contents of the sheep),
is a force that has great value when it is revealed to our consciousness. At
first, one finds contents that are rather disgusting and crude; then they reveal their inner value and one sees that they are really precious jewels. In
practical application, this would mean that the extraordinary force which
makes everyone resemble everyone else, which keeps every man as low as
possible — low in consciousness, low in quality, low in every other respect
— that force, if brought up to consciousness will reveal contents of priceless
quality. If you apply this to psychological life, it would mean that, up to
this moment, the patient has been too far away from her own reality. She

89

has been seeing things somewhat in the form of a detached vision – and even this might still be more or less of a detached vision – yet she is approaching the central problem as if in a spiral, seeing things nearer all the time. Now she is close enough to be able to see the great value in crudeness and primitivity, although at first she recoiled from it.

That disappearance of the animus into the unconscious, you see, shows the peculiar autonomous nature of the animus. It shows that the animus is capable of doing things without the control of consciousness, that consciousness cannot hold him. The collective unconscious can lock its gates and leave the human individual isolated, so that after a while the individual will find himself forced back into the herd, into unconsciousness, by the autonomous functioning of the collective unconscious. Therefore it is that functioning which has to be sacrificed; she has to kill the sheep in herself to *make* herself conscious. Then she will get the contents of that unconsciousness, the precious jewels.

The Great Red Jewel

VISION (cont.): Now dressed in white, I besought the Indians to give me a red jewel.

The white refers to the state of rebirth. It is the garment of the newly born – *quasi modo geniti.* Then she beseeches the Indians to give her a red jewel. Obviously, she is craving the value that it symbolizes. Now what is symbolized by this red jewel? What about this whole blood ceremonial?

Answer: It would be the life force, would it not?

Dr. Jung: Yes. Blood is always the life force, the symbol of the soul. In primitive beliefs blood is the real seat of life; therefore, drinking the blood of the enemy is supposed to give you his mana. Magic is also worked with blood. The blood is plain enough, but what about the jewels that appear out of the entrails? . . .

The patient is of a thinking-intuitive type so that, with her, feeling would have the position of an inferior function. The inferior function, when it is much repressed is located in the abdomen. In such a case, if the feeling function is aroused, there is trouble in the abdomen. For instance, you often notice in talking to people that at certain places in the conversation the abdomen suddenly begins to murmur, because emotions, which don't appear on the surface at all cause a peculiar kind of irritation in the entrails. . . .
Of course, we don't understand that language but, if we could succeed in getting the entrails out of the darkness, we would know what they meant

to say. When these things appear out of the natural mind, they are horrible, even insupportable, but one discovers, when one handles them for a while, that they are really exceedingly precious.

The inferior function is exceedingly precious on account of the life it contains. The superior function is like fine old material, a bit worn out though highly differentiated, while the inferior function is very crude, a sort of rough diamond, but full of promise. The person of the thinking type will very probably get a bit dry and sterile in his thinking. Yet, when it comes to feeling, he is still young and fresh; nothing has been used up; there is still a lot of life and that is a great treasure. This would explain the redness, for example; it refers to the blood, to the soul power. The inferior function contains the priceless treasure of life force and that is the reason it is so important. . . .

We have to bring up these inferior qualities in people because they contain the priceless jewel of life — things they would not miss for the world; for what is more precious than life to a living thing? If one only lives a half or a third of life, what is the use of living? What is its meaning? Life only has meaning when it is really lived. Otherwise, it is like a pear tree that blossoms every spring and never brings forth a pear. You know Christ himself symbolically cursed the fig tree that did not bring forth fruit. People who live and don't bring forth fruit are like the fig tree that had to be cursed, for such people do not fulfill the will of the Lord. If they want to live they must live with the whole of their being. Sometimes they cannot accept this because their entrails begin to murmur; they are too aesthetical or, as they call it, too moral. But then they don't live, they don't fulfill their meaning, they don't resolve the problem of their being.

That is the problem here. She is still too much of a sheep . . . and yet she is really a person who is not a sheep, most decidedly not. . . . Therefore, she ought to make the sacrifice, she ought to kill the sheep, in order to become individual and to be herself. Then, of course, she will be confronted with the necessity of taking up her inferior function which is no joke at all. But the vision tells her it is a jewel and the jewel is so beautiful that she wants it. It is interesting to see how the vision puts it: she wants it not in her ordinary form but in the form of the *quasi modo geniti,* that is, in the state of one dressed in white, in the state of newly gained innocence. This would denote that she does not want that jewel because she is greedy — there are people who want a jewel out of mere greediness, out of cupidity — she does not want it out of cupidity but out of innocence.

91

VISION (cont.): They fled from me and I was left alone. Then appeared an Indian who came toward me. "Why have they fled? " I asked him. He answered, "Because you have violated the blood." Then many animals appeared and stood behind the Indian. . ."

Now the subsequent symbolism does not explain what it means to have violated the blood, but what do you assume that it means? You see it cannot be anything personal, for these things with which the patient was concerned were way beyond the personal. . . .

Answer: It means that you have severed the *participation mystique* of primitive law by separating yourself off as an individual. . . .

Dr. Jung: The suggestion is worth discussing, but is there not perhaps some other possibility? It might be that "You have violated the blood" does not actually refer to the ceremonial. *She* has not killed the sheep, the Indians have killed it, so this may refer to something else; it may mean that she has violated the blood in another respect. . . . You see, to answer such a question one always ought to look back to the things that have happened before — although, of course, I admit that these things are bewildering and you might well lose your orientation. What happened before was deification, and naturally deification lifts a man out of the ordinary and inflates him, which is a violation of the human quality. And human quality means the law of the earth which is contained in the blood. It applies to anybody who imagines that he is more than he is, and we all try to be better than we are. The general idea is: "How can we be better than we are? " But we are just as good as we can be and not one inch better. Just as we cannot add an inch to our physical size, so we also have our moral size. We try to live above our level, like millionaires or princes, when we have not a cent for daily bread. It is just inflation. But, don't you see, that doesn't mean that we cannot improve. . . . Try to be what you are. . . .

Comment: But then I would not go to a psychoanalyst.

Dr. Jung: You go to the psychoanalyst just to find out what you are. . . . You see, we simply have forgotten what a human being really is. . . . Our inflations are prejudices about ourselves. They are our attempts to live above our level, or below our level. For there are people who live decidedly below their level. Our ignorance of the human being as he is really meant to be is a violation of the blood. This is particularly so when we try to live above our level, when we try to live with our feet in the air; that is the real violation of the blood. Because an attitude like that makes us so God-almighty-like — as, for example, when we say, "Where there is a will, there is a way," or "If you try seriously to get somewhere, you will get there."

92

As if you could get out of your skin! You see, all that is the same kind of foolishness, yet we are convinced of such things and they are taught everywhere.

Now, is that clear concerning the violation of the blood? She is not natural, she lives above herself, and assumes that she is better than she really is. She is divorced from her shadow, and because of that her animus has married the shadow and gone to hell. For that gives her animus power to behave just as he wants to behave. . . . If you want to control your anima or animus, you have to bring the shadow close to consciousness and so liberate it from anima or animus possession. If consciousness goes on without a connection with the shadow, then violation of the blood occurs; that is, people live beyond their means, they live in an unnatural imaginary way, above their own heads; and that is an offence against the earth. If one lives close to the earth, if one lives *with* the blood, then one simply cannot do or imagine certain things. . . .

At the moment when the Indian — being the chief of the ceremonies, the head animus, as it were — gives this explanation, that she has violated the blood, many animals appear and stand behind him. He is backed up by the animals, which means psychologically that the instincts are coming to back him up. Then he does something which initiates her to the blood.

The Reconciliation with the Blood

VISION (cont.): He spilt some blood upon my head and my robe became scarlet.

Now she is stained by the blood; it is a blood bath, the reconciliation to the blood, exactly as in the Mithraic *taurobolia*. . . . And this is very much the same thing. You see, people have to be initiated or baptized into that. which they are not, or that which they ought to possess but do not. Therefore, she has to be baptized or, in other words, reborn — since baptism is a symbol for rebirth. So blood is spilled on her head, as in a baptismal ceremony, and her robe, from having been the white of perfect innocence, now becomes scarlet. . . .

VISION (cont.): (With that peculiar revelation, she heard a strange rhythmic beating all about her. She says:) And a great swirl of blood encompassed me, vibrating with a strange and terrible throbbing.

This description sounds as if she were hearing the noise of the blood in her ears, or the throbbing of her heart. Evidently she is feeling the movement of the blood, the specific, rhythmic life of the blood. You may have noticed that here her language changes a bit, her style becomes less abstract. She is obviously describing some very physical sensation. When she talked to me about this particular part of the vision, she insisted upon the extraordinary reality of the experience; it was just as though she were in her own arteries, or her own heart. When a person has such a vivid sensory experience, it is as if the unconscious were emphasizing it by adding the quality of sensation in order to make the thing more real. That it should be very real is in accord with the natural tendency of the unconscious to insist upon the reality of the blood.

Then, you notice, she uses the words, "with a strange and terrible throbbing." The "terrible" means, of course, terror of the fact of being submerged in the blood, because then one is almost like a particle of it, like a red corpuscle, just being swayed and carried; one feels that one is no longer master of one's own fate. . . . If anybody is in the blood, then he is in the instincts, in primitive man, in the animals that lived before primitive man; he is in nature as it always was. Only by such an experience do we realize the extraordinary fear that we have escaped through civilization. . . . Civilization is a sort of thick wall against all limitless and boundless things, all the chaotic things that can happen to a man when he is in an uncivilized state. So, of course, anything that blasts the thick wall of civilization is a terrible danger; then things may happen which one cannot foresee, or rule, or do away with. One suddenly feels oneself just a helpless part of nature. In such a moment, it is as if one felt for the first time what it is like when things become real.

I am always reminding you of Tartarin de Tarascon, when he realized that the glaciers and chasms were real and not at all brought there and arranged by the Compagnie Anglo-Suisse, and that if you happened to fall down into a crevass you would be really dead. The attitude of such people is, "You don't mean to say that you really would be dead!" But it really means that you would be dead. . . . Many people live a whole lifetime, until they die, without noticing that things are real; it is as if they lived in a world where everything could be changed by shifting the scenery. I have seen people go mad, or badly neurotic, when they encountered a situation they could not shift; for example, when a child died — when even with the best doctors and nurses, and hospitals, a child really died. Then they were up against a reality of which they had never dreamed before. Or, when men starting out in the world, quite certain that they will get a position, find that that is not true; then the shock drives them crazy, or they become neurotic, simply from impact with reality. One could easily say that, for most civilized people, reality is a sort of a dream — far away. Whatever they touch, they touch conditionally. "Yes," they say, "You are real up to a certain point, as far as I allow you to be real. But if you turn out realer than I want you to be, then, curse you. Either I must kill you or I must kill myself." Then they go altogether crazy.

It is almost as if, for most people, the discovery of reality were a cause for panic. The interesting thing is that, if you tell such a thing to people who are living the provisional life, they nod their heads wisely and know all about it; then they go right on as they were, they continue their sleep.

VISION (cont.): (Now the patient has such an impression of absolute reality, a frightening impression of a situation superior to her own forces.) I lay back in the swirl which carried me upward in spirals.

Obviously, she surrendered to the movement of the blood, then discovered that the way did not go downward but that she was carried upward in spirals. What would you assume from that? When we are in a swift current of any kind of liquid, the natural assumption is that we will go down. That is what we fear, what causes our terror; but here she discovers that she is being carried up.

Comment: Blood is a peculiar kind of liquid; it is the source of life and therefore it would not bear you down like water.

Dr. Jung: What about the movement of blood? . . . It not only goes down but also flows upward. So one might quite possibly get into the upward and not into the downward movement.

Comment: Would not the association of blood with wine come in here? Wine carries you upward too.

Dr. Jung: The wine will play a role later, but it is blood for the time being. Sometimes one is allowed by the Gods to substitute wine for blood, but not yet. What I want to know now is the secret of the spiral.

Suggestion: It is a symbol for development.

Comment: The spiral expresses the functioning of opposites.

Dr. Jung: Yes. It is the very symbol of unfolding . . . in plants the buds or the beginnings of leaves are arranged in a spiral, a plant grows in a spiral. As you point out, it is the functioning of opposites, the reconciliation of opposites. The man who discovered the mathematical law of the spiral is buried in my native town, in Basel; on his tombstone is a spiral with this device, EADEM MUTATA RESURGO, literally translated, "In an identical way, changed, I lift myself up." That is the law of the spiral, a very

95

beautiful thing. . . . Sameness, non-sameness. . . . So the spiral is really a very apt symbol to express development. You see, this vision is saying, "If you surrender to the terror of the blood, you will discover that it leads to development." It does not lead downhill into hell, it leads upwards, but it is a really terrifying development.

Three Secondary Visions

VISION (cont.): (While in that swirl of blood, she has a rapid succession of visions.) I passed the white face of God. I saw the sun, and I saw a pool of gold. . . .

These are secondary visions, like thoughts visualized while she is in the movement of the blood. They are very difficult, but I ought to be able to explain them to you, to show how every word of these visions has meaning – exactly like dreams. Concerning "the white face of God," here she writes God with a capital, and she always does that when she writes of a modern Christian conception of God, as over against the old pagan Gods.

Question: Is the face white in contrast to the red blood?

Dr. Jung: Exactly. You see, her idea of God has been a very pale, ghost-like concept, the bloodless late-Christian concept, but she is carried past that, which is very significant. And now she sees the sun.

Comment: The sun is a deeper, more primitive God.

Dr. Jung: Yes. It is certainly more primitive, more real and concrete. But besides that, this is the way she has traveled: In the earlier visions, she left Christianity and landed deep down at the animal level; then she came up again through the antique cults – we have just been speaking of her realization of deification as the sun, Helios. Thus she has gone through the whole inner meaning of the antique Gods; that is the second phase [corresponding to the sun vision] and now comes a pool of gold. What about that? This is enigmatical.

Answer: She has found value.

Dr. Jung: Yes. Gold would mean value. But first try to visualize the face of God: in the ancient pictures God is often depicted with a very pale halo round his head – a very pale sun, apparently. Next she sees the real sun which is also a golden disk; and then a pool of gold, a disk of gold. The idea here is always the same but the quality changes considerably. . . . The pool of gold is the return to the earth. Gold is a very heavy metal and must naturally be at the lowest point. God is very far away, the sun is nearer . . . but the pool of gold is embedded in the earth – at her feet even – and very

96

concrete. People who unconsciously have this vision may get stuck there, they may, for instance, develop a great desire for money, for gold. You know, the whole philosophy of the alchemists was filled with the idea of making gold; it symbolized the precious substance made from valueless substance.

Suggestion: Sun and gold are identical in alchemy. So gold is the terrestrial sun perhaps.

Dr. Jung: Yes. It would be the terrestrial sun. In alchemy the sun is the astrological equivalent of gold. That is, of course, contained in this vision, too. But what do you think of this peculiar development? We can see that the sun could be a substitute for God; we know that from history, so we can easily understand such a transformation. . . . But how can the sun change into gold? What does this whole descent mean? How can you solve this riddle through the hypothesis of value? . . . The definition of God would be the Summum Bonum; the greatest value of all is certainly God. Then the greatest value to life is the sun, because it is the source of energy and it warms. But now this vision comes and says the greatest value is gold. That is terribly shocking, don't you think so?

Well, it would be, if this whole thing were to remain unconscious. As long as she is idealistic and actually up in the clouds, she is not following the law of the earth; therefore her highest values all flow out into gold. That is the reason why very pious people are usually very well to do. . . . In such cases, the spiritual evaluation has been undermined precisely because they proclaim too much that they believe in the spirit exclusively. . . . It is a depreciation of spiritual values by too frequent use; they get worn out, and all the value is in the gold.

Comment: It seems to me to be a very good thing for this particular woman. Gold is materialistic; so now she realizes the great value in materialism.

Dr. Jung: Yes. But it is good only if she is conscious of it. If it is unconscious, it amounts to an unconscious resistance against every conscious value. She believed that her God was a spirit in heaven, while in fact her God was secretly in a safe in the bank. He lived on earth, which was a horrible discovery. People are more afraid to lose their money than to lose God: He is not their highest value at all. . . . In fact the idea of God has become very abstract and unreal. It does not work as an actual determinant; yet there always is a highest value, a center of gravity, which ultimately decides. So, you see, this woman, as long as she is unconscious that her God is in a safe, is a materialist and is really hindering herself from living, because she more or less sacrifices her life ideals to her money. But here she discovers that her God is a pool of gold, and this is mighty good because now the thing becomes conscious. She knows where her fear of God is, her fear of God is all connected with that money. The moment such a thing becomes conscious she has to admit that it is shocking. It is entirely wrong, according to her ideas, that gold should really be her highest value . . . and naturally, it causes a terrific conflict with her idealism.

But she cannot get away from one thing, that gold *is* mana, whether one despises it or not. Just the fact that one despises it shows that it is mana, that it is value. . . . Gold is a superb thing: it is marvellous and most insinuating; it is like the sun — a wealth of light. It is desirable and one must admit that it is desirable. There is a mana that is peculiar to gold, as there is a mana peculiar to silver, and a mana peculiar to precious stones. They have an intrinsic value which people cannot deny. . . . So now she will realize the money value of the gold, and in doing so she will discover that gold is worth more than so many dollars, that it is a mistake to think gold can be valued in money. For there is always the mystical value. Just on account of the conflict, she will discover that in the mana of the gold there is a value beyond money. This pool of gold is a symbol. Do you know what it symbolizes? This is a very peculiar and unexpected turn of the story.

Answer: It is her Self. . . .

Dr. Jung: Yes. One can arrive at an interpretation quite easily, by the theory of highest value. The highest value is God, then it is the sun, and then it is the pool of gold. Now the question arises: "Is this pool of gold, perhaps, myself? Is it a value deep down below my feet — perhaps, the earth?" . . . Blood is the life of the earth and when you live in the earth you may discover the treasure that is embedded there, you may — very easily — discover that the highest value is in yourself. It is the next step.

Now these three visions which we have just dealt with are nothing but fleeting impressions, just glimpses, and naturally the patient herself is absolutely unaware of the meanings involved in them. It is very difficult, as probably you have seen, to assume that such things can even have a meaning. But when one meditates upon those fleeting impressions, one sees how they begin to sink in and enrich themselves with all sorts of associations. Then one discovers that they are really most important links in the whole procedure; they are like a marginal text that explains what is happening when the patient enters the stream of blood.

She Becomes a Tree

VISION (cont.): Then I was in a dark forest. The swirl of a flaming red surrounded the forest. I could perceive it through the trees.

The situation is completely changed. From the moment when she received the blood baptism she has been in a sort of trance, transplanted into the blood, swirled up by the blood into a new condition. This is now symbolized by a forest, which seems to be rather like a grove of trees, and round it is a swirl of flaming red. . . . It is as though a sort of blood fire were encircling her and she were in an enchanted wood. From the subsequent events we can see what that means.

VISION (cont.): My robe changed to green and my feet sank into the soft earth. I lifted up my hands and leaves grew from them. Then I knew that I had become a tree and lifted my face to the sun.

You see, what has happened is a real classical metamorphosis — man into tree. Arriving in the forest means that she is one of the trees; so she behaves like a tree, her feet become roots, her hands become branches; she is growing like a tree. She made a picture of it. In the background the color is *(illus. 9)* really blood red, therefore I hesitate to call it just fire. We have here a very peculiar symbolism. What is your opinion of it? . . .

Suggestion: The tree is a link between the earth and the sun. . . . Before, she was driven by the stream of blood and, therefore, could not influence her own fate and development. But now she becomes a tree and while it is true that, on the one hand, plant life is the lowest state of life; on the other hand, plants are the only form of life that can nourish themselves. They are autonomous in that sense, and that is what she must learn.

Dr. Jung: Yes, exactly, a quite apt symbolism. . . .

Comment: Would the tree not be a logical development of the spiral? Before there was the idea of the spiral, but now you have the plant actually growing — the spiral represented organically as a tree.

Dr. Jung: It is as if she had gotten into something here that was quite strange to the animal world. In the animal world the spiral is a practically unknown thing. But in the plant world it is all important to development and growth. While she is in the blood — that is, in the animal substance of her body — she suddenly discovers an entirely different principle. This is also a life principle, but not a life principle of the blood. We have already had several visions in which there has been a plunging down into something: there was the black pool in the beginning, beside which the Indian stood in thought, and the Chinese meditated upon it, too; then, recently, the Dionysian youth leapt down from one thing to another. Now here we find the secret of all that plunging, that attempt to get to the bottom: it was the anticipation of the final plunge into the blood, where she is going to discover the great treasure.

The great treasure in its first aspect — the gold was only a fleeting impression — in the feeling of the spiral, which we must take as a very immediate and real experience, almost a sensation. . . . That is the first discovery of an entirely different life principle, namely, the plant principle. As you know, life has developed mainly in two forms; one form is animal life, the other plant life, but, since both belong to the same life, plants and animal belong together. Moreover, animals live on plants, we are parasites, we are a kind of lice on the forests of the earth. The life of man and the life of plants is a sort of symbiosis, and it is unavoidable that whenever there is a symbiosis a partnership should result. Our whole system adapts to the system of the partner — in other words, the life of the plant is in us as well as our own — and in us it becomes the symbol for a non-biological quality, for what we call spiritual. The unfolding of the spirit is based upon an analogy with plant life. Thus the first discovery here of what may be called spiritual development is that sensation of the spiral. You can see from the vision that, according to the unconscious point of view, it is a thing of highest value; the development does not lead down, it leads upward to a higher story or layer, one might say, where there is a forest in which she takes root among other trees. . . . Plants get their nourishment immediately from the elements. . . . So the primary form of life is plant life. . . .

You see the animal always symbolizes the physiological and biological life in man because in those ways he is nothing but an animal. From that point of view we quite naturally deny the reality of the spirit. That's why it takes a very special kind of experience to make people believe in anything like a spiritual law. Exactly this experience is needed here to prove the existence of an entirely different type of living, though it is not in itself necessarily spiritual. One could say that this simply means the plant, the plant *per se*. But since we are not plants and cannot live like plants, it cannot mean a real plant; therefore, it must mean her *real plant life,* which is the *unconscious* way of the spirit. . . .

Because the life of the spirit is an absolute contrast to animal life, one sees that wherever spirit has manifested itself it has been hostile to many forms of our animal life, to many of our customs and conventions. Any new form of manifestation of the spirit has always meant a lot of trouble.

Think of the manifestations of the spirit of Islam, of Christianity — many tons of blood spilled, because plant life grows differently from animal life. You see, animal life is first a rising and then a descending growth. Also it is not regular: there are different seasons in animal life; the mating seasons, periods of heat, and changes having to do with seasonal migrations. And it is the same with man; he experiences *élévations et abaissements* because animal growth is always increasing and decreasing. Plant life shows some seasonal oscillation, too, but in the main the growth of a tree is steadily upward, without any real descent, until it dies abruptly in the end. Up to its last year it blossoms and brings forth fruit, just as it has done from the beginning. Also in this type of life the seasonal oscillations are far less violent. Naturally, they would be less violent in a thing that is rooted, for a tree cannot move, cannot pull its feet out of the ground. The animal can jump about, it can afford to get excited; so it takes advantage of the fact and indulges in its excitement, just as we do. Most people indulge in their excitement, they like to get excited and jump about. But people who have the idea of the tree feel that excitement is not good at all. Therefore, in the East, the very first principle of Chinese or Indian yoga is that one should forsake one's emotions, that one should withdraw; it is exactly as if one were to withdraw from that curve of animal growth with its foolish jerky motion. . . .

The Magic Circle

You remember, the patient is in the wood as one of the trees, and the circle of flaming red, of blood, is circulating round the wood. . . . In the picture, one sees it like a red ribbon oscillating round the trees.

Comment: I cannot see why the blood should surround the wood. . . .

Comment: It is like Brünnhilde surrounded by the ring of fire.

Dr. Jung: Or a fire round the earth. What would happen if it came onto the earth? The world would be consumed by fire. You see, as long as she was in the blood she could not develop spiritually; therefore, she withdraws from the blood and it is just as if the blood withdrew from her — as if it exuded from her. So now she is living as a tree, and the blood is all round her in a flaming red circle . . . as it is round Brünnhilde, while she sleeps; it is the great circle you find in mandalas as the circle of desire, the flaming circle of cupidity, or desirousness.

Question: Does it mean protection? . . .

Dr. Jung: It is a protection in so far as you do not identify with it. But if you become identical, I mean, if you put your foot into it, you will be consumed by the flame and dissolved. Just as wood is consumed by the touch of fire, so you too can be consumed. That is why this woman must realize that she can live without the fire, without the blood; otherwise, she would simply be the victim of illusions, the victim of desires, disease, and crime, and of the illusion of doing good and doing evil. . . .

When you try to visualize it, you arrive at something like this. I will draw a sort of chart (Figure 1). Here she would be, as a tree, in the center with the other trees standing around her, and the circle of red all around that. Then, you remember, the vision of the pool of gold which we spoke about before . . . that would be in the center . . . down below the tree [while the sun, of course, stands above].

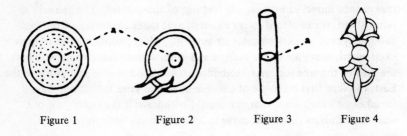

Figure 1   Figure 2   Figure 3   Figure 4

You see, the idea would be that the tree is really a sort of transformation symbol between these two equivalent symbols; what is the pool of gold below is the sun above, and the tree is obviously a function in between. The roots of the tree are equivalent to its branches and, as it sends out branches above to receive the sun — or the sun's rays — so its roots shelter the gold below, or take mana out of the gold to grow with. This is the kind of symbolic idea which sometimes occurs in fairy tales, when the treasure is buried under the roots of a tree, or else brownies live there and are associated with treasures in the earth, precious ore, precious stones, and so forth. The symbolism which this vision suggests is something like that. It points to the pool idea, which we shall come across again later. Also, in a later vision, we encounter the idea of descending into a cave, into darkness, which would, of course, be going down in the trunk of the tree to darkness below.

This picture is a mandala, a mystical circle expressing the totality of the individual. Now the totality of the individual is a very difficult concept. Psychologically, it would be the totality of the conscious ego and of what

102

one would call the unconscious Self; that is, of the subject (the ego) and the psychological object (the unconscious). The unconscious is of a very indistinct nature, so one can never delimit its borders properly where it touches oneself nor can one give a rational description of it as a psychological concept. We can only describe it as an almost arbitrarily circumscribed area of the collective unconscious. It is as if parts of the collective unconscious were selected by an unknown agency, which we would place at the center, a sort of living monad which takes its choice of elements that really belong to the collective unconscious and were not originally separated from its other contents by any magic circle. But through individuation it seems as if such a magic circle were actually produced. And sometimes a magic circle is really used. For instance, the alchemists, when gold was to be made or treasure gathered up, began by making a magic circle around themselves for protection, a wall to hold away strange influences, strange disruptive forces; because as soon as one starts the secret work of making gold or gathering treasure, one immediately calls up forces from the collective unconscious. Then ghosts begin appearing at the borderline and, if the circle is broken anywhere, they come in, and that means mortal danger. . . . Therefore the circle must be complete.

Naturally, this is a psychological projection; it is a visualization of the process of individuation. Gathering up the treasure is a sort of concretized symbol for centralization or the arrangement of one's psychological material around one's greatest value, around one's most important idea, the idea one has of the greatest strength, the idea one can designate as God. In antiquity this central idea was called the individual daimon. But such an important value is by no means identical with oneself because it is superior to oneself . . . yet it dwells in oneself; it is even supposed to die with oneself. Now if the idea of an individual Deity like this is put in the center, and if this element or factor then exerts a certain attraction on the collective contents, it will produce a more or less artificial wall between the collective contents in general and those that are attracted and thus picked out as being one's personal belongings. Yet if you analyze the contents of the Self inside the borderline, you will see that they differ in no way from any other collective contents: it is just the special choice of contents that produces the individual.

These matters are difficult to explain; it is quite difficult to understand the structure of the Self on account of the fact that its contents are of a collective nature, yet belong to the individual. From this comes the very ordinary mistake of believing that the collective unconscious is inside oneself. Everyone speaks of *my* unconscious, or even of my collective unconscious, which is perfect nonsense — one might as well say, "my stars, my planets, my continents." You would never assume you contain the world because you see it; you can see this room, but you do not assume, on that account, that it is there, inside your eye. Naturally, it is outside of you. But, psychologically, the center here is an eye, . . . the famous eye of Horus. It is this eye [which determines] what you see of the contents of the collective unconscious in your psychological field of vision. You can say that these things are yours in so far as you see them, but they are not yours to the extent that they form part of yourself.

Thus you always contain certain unconscious contents which are merely separated by a sort of magic circle from the surrounding collective contents, and that circle can be broken. That is why individuation is such a ticklish and delicate thing; because if the magic circle is broken at any time things begin to move out or else to move in, and you have what is called an eruption of the collective unconscious — that is, your Self is flooded by collective contents. From time immemorial mankind has insisted that the process of individuation and the production of a magic circle with this kind of center is man's greatest value, the most-to-be-desired good, and all the efforts of Eastern philosophy have as their purpose the production of this pool of gold, or this magic circle. It is considered the highest attainment, for example, in all of Tantric Yoga, and in Lamaistic and Chinese philosophy.

Mandala Pictures

Special pictures, such as those I have shown you, are used as instruments for the production of this kind of centralization. You will also find some reproduced in *The Secret of the Golden Flower*[1]. . . . Any mandala is a sort of two-dimensional map of the actual psychological condition. For there are conditions where one sees disturbed mandalas instead of normal ones. In them a proper magic circle will suddenly come to an end; a break will occur, disturbing the whole thing, and then it is just as if a flowing out or a flowing in of forces had occurred, or as if a quarter, or even a third, of what belongs there had been cut away and strange elements had been substituted. Such a drawing (Figure 2) reproduces a state of possession or obsession in which people harbor strange ghosts in their psychology. That is one of the reasons why primitives have their ghost theory; they explain every possible disturbance of body or mind as a possession by evil spirits, which simply describes the fact that autonomous contents of the collective unconscious have come in and taken possession of a part of the Self. These peculiar contents feel like strange thoughts.

For instance, sometimes you cannot get rid of a certain idea or a certain conviction. You know it is all wrong, but the thing has gotten hold of you and you cannot get away. Take a very simple case: a certain melody will stick in your head for days on end; it persecutes you; it is as if a little ghost went on and on whispering that tune. Of course, it seems absurd but if you analyze the tune you will always come across a content with a certain autonomy which explains why it has been able to take possession of you. Now the main purpose of constructing a mandala is to keep out these possessing forces, to keep out the strange so-called collective contents, and you can only achieve that when the magic circle is solid enough.

But one cannot build this circle by concentrating upon it; it can only be produced by concentration on the center. The more you concentrate on the center, the more the wall is strengthened. But if your attention wanders outside the center and you begin to concentrate on the surrounding wall, then it becomes a circle of fire — you fan the flames until the whole thing burns up. No sooner do you occupy yourself with that fire than it consumes you.

What we are seeing here is the reverse process. The patient was first in the blood and, through the blood, she discovered this particular little Garden of Eden, this circular place of trees, with the pool of gold and the Tree of Knowledge in the center. Thus she has escaped the flaming river, but it is possible that her eyes will turn outward again and be fascinated by the wall of fire; then instantly the flames will consume her once more. At the present moment, however, she is in the center and, in her vision, she describes what it feels like to be there. It is like being a tree, she is growing like a tree; her garment has become green, her arms have become branches and her feet roots. So we learn from this vision that being in the center is equivalent to being plant-like. Here we have the psychical life of the plant, which grows unconsciously, centered only on the Self. When one is centered like this there is a possibility that one may grow into something else, or give birth to something not otherwise attainable.

A Transverse Cut through Continuity

Now, if we return to the mandala represented in Figure 1 (page 102) we can see that it contains a little circle (a) at its center. This little circle (a) is shown again in Figure 3, where it appears as a transverse section of the trunk of the tree in the center of Figure 1. Looking downward from this cross-section, one would be looking toward the roots of the tree and into the pool of gold which would be, so to speak, beneath. But looking upward, one would behold the sun, which is what she describes. You can picture the branches and the disk of the sun above, as she lifts her face to the sun. This part of the mandala, therefore, is like a transverse cut through something that continues above and below. What one experiences here is the special unfolding tendency of the tree, the feeling of the branches opening out above her and the roots below. So [when seen in another dimension] the little circle at the center of Figure 1, in its simplest, most abstract, Lamaistic form, is actually the thunderbolt symbol (Figure 4). Pairs of opposites are united in the thunderbolt symbol; it is the sign of concentrated energy, because the function that unites pairs of opposites is energy; the clash of opposites produces energy.

[Now I will show you a Tibetan mandala with] the thunderbolt symbol right in the center and emanating from it are eight petals exactly like the petals of a flower, each containing the same symbol again, which means the unfolding of concentrated energy from the center.[2] (This is called the Diamond Wedge, because of its hardness, its extraordinary strength, and its great value. As the diamond emits rays of light, so this concentrated energy emanates the radiant energy which now forms the Golden Flower.) This is like a picture of libido; if you want to visualize the source of libido or energy in the unconscious, this would be the suitable image. . . .

And since this concentrated energy has not always been there, that means that it can be poured in, or that it has been poured in. So such a Lamaistic mandala always has gates, and in each of these gates is the same thunderbolt sign, meaning that this is the way or the gate. Much energy can, therefore, leave the magic circle through these gates and go out into the world – or into infinity. Energy can also be drawn in through them by concentration and contemplation, thus producing the treasure in the center, which is symbolized by the Diamond Wedge or the pool of gold – for gold, too, is concentrated energy. And wherever there is concentrated energy, there is the possibility of releasing it; then you have emanation again.

So you see, the Golden Flower symbol represents the drawing in of libido, and the possibility of emanating libido, and since the whole thing is the equivalent of a transverse cut through the trunk of the tree, that means that it can move up or down. If it goes down, the energy will be heavy, it will become earthlike, it will form the pool of gold; if it moves up, we shall have the disk of the sun, because the energy will become manifest in the form of radiation, light and warmth. Now is that plain? It is a very difficult sort of philosophy because it is utterly irrational. It is a typical Eastern philosophy, a modern Lamaistic form of Tantric Yoga.

Question: Did you apply the idea of a mandala to the tree, or is that also contained in the Eastern concept?

Dr. Jung: Well, in the Eastern idea the center of the mandala is not the cross-section of a tree. That is something I got from this patient's vision and from other phantasies of my patients. In the East you would see the symbol in the form of a lotus plant. The lotus flower itself corresponds to the transversal cut. That is the universal symbol of the cup. And out of the lotus cup appears the God. . . . The lotus has the peculiarity of rising above the water, the flower is not just upon the surface of the water, it rises out of it. . . . So it is like a thing that emerges out of the depths of the unconscious and unfolds, and in the middle is the golden center in which the God is supposed to appear — or where the sun rises. For this is sun magic. As the lotus rises from the dark depths in the slime below and comes to the surface of the water, so the sun rises. It is because the lotus is the image of the rising sun that it has become the most current symbol in the East for the birth-vessel of the God. You know the symbol, the figure of the God sitting in the flower. . . . And if you look down upon the lotus, you see the mandala. . . .

But the thing which is lacking in the East is the idea of continuation; this idea of a transverse cut through a continuity is not Eastern. The idea in the East is that the mandala represents a perfect condition, just the end of everything. . . . But our Western mandala — let us be quite modest and say, because we are not perfect, not finished, but because we feel utterly unfinished — is a transverse cut somewhere, and we don't know how far up. Probably, not very far. We do not assume that the mandala we perceive is the most perfect mandala, like the lotus in the center of the Eastern mandala, the lotus of absolute knowledge. So, in modesty, I assume that our mandala is somewhere lower down. And certainly at the stage of this vision, it would be quite out of the question for this lady to have perceived anything like a perfect mandala. My evidence for saying this is excellent, because later on she began to draw mandalas and produced several irregular ones and one that was obviously wrong — it was like an inflammation, a mandala half eaten by fire — which shows that her perception of a mandala was very troubled.

You see in the East we have to do with an absolutely finished kind of philosophy — as finished as it can be in that form — but here we are only beginning to divine the psychology of such things. . . .

The Gates

Question: You have just shown us an Eastern picture of a magic circle with gates through it. But, on the other hand, you say it is forbidden to break through the sheltering wall. What does that mean?

Dr. Jung: Well, the center is absolute. . . . The gates are identical with the four functions really, . . . the four gates through which libido may come in and go out. . . . (You find this in the *Bardo Thödol, The Tibetan Book of the Dead.*[3]) The idea is that one should not leave the center, yet one should function through the gates, like the governor of a city. He dwells in the innermost temple in the Forbidden City and his employees, his subordinates, go in and out through the gates; but not he. He remains in the center and is well protected. This is why there are gates and a wall; it shows that the aspiration of the East is not to be dead and buried in the mandala, but to function through the mandala. It is quite naive of the Westerner to attempt to form the mandala but not to function through it. As soon as he identifies with one function [intuition, for example] it is as if he became a balloon and were carried off by the winds; he becomes a gas bag himself because he loses touch with reality; or, if he identifies with another function [sensation, perhaps], he just gets buried in the earth and cannot walk because he is lopsided. The fact that we are more or less identified with our functions is, of course, one of the reasons for our disorientation. The Eastern idea is rather to make a harmony of the functions, but one should oneself be central, one should disidentify from them, one should feel apart from all that. "To be free from the opposites" is a phrase repeated again and again in the sacred texts. Therefore the mandala does not necessarily signify withdrawal from life, it may just as well mean a turning toward life.

There are certain mandalas, of course, where the gates are locked or where there are no gates, and these are intended to produce a standstill — for a standstill is sometimes quite necessary. For instance, there are certain civilizations that advance too rapidly — as we do — and if we cannot produce a standstill it will be enforced by circumstances. . . . So some mandalas really have the purpose of producing death, they are mandalas of complete withdrawal. And their symbolism is likely to be merely abstract. But others show Shiva and Shakti in embrace and it is marvellous to see how the embrace is repeated, how the reverberations of it radiate out into the world. Those figures are repeated in eights again and again, which means that all the embraces in the world are the reverberations of that one central embrace. Such a mandala is a mandala of life, not of death. . . .

[Summary: In order to complete the theme of growth as a tree in this section of the excerpts, we must now pass over several visions.

In the first of these she descends into a cave. This is what Dr. Jung spoke of as a going down into the trunk of the tree. Here she finally makes connection with the earth by swallowing a black snake. When she comes to the surface again this chthonic element leaps from her body and is burnt to ashes upon a golden disk, which means that it is transformed into a spiritual drive that forces her on toward consciousness. Next she comes to a black wall, the unknown future, on which she sees nothing but an eye and a star, symbolizing the emanation of light and its reception. This eye — that is, living consciousness — seems to be the place to get through the wall. Inside, she comes to a woman personifying the essence of all womanhood and sees a brutal scene of sacrificial prostitution. At a new depth, this woman shows her uncreated chaos and breathes life into the crystal figure of a man which takes shape there. The crystal man is "the 'diamond body,' the individual center and treasure of life. That she sees the treasure outside of herself in a man shows that she is still not ripe for it. ... She has to accept this fact and wait for her natural growth."[4] – Ed.]

The Tree Grows over the Wall

In the next vision she stands again before a black wall, she is still before the same obstacle, it is still the same wall with the star and the eye.

VISION (cont.): I stood before the black wall and I said to the eye, "How shall I surmount this wall? " The eye turned inward on itself. I also turned my eye inward, and within myself I saw a growing tree.

[The eye is like] a peculiar kind of gateway; it turns upon itself and looks. So she does the same, and then she has vision and sees a growing tree, which is, of course, a symbol of development.

VISION (cont.): Then I looked outward again at the wall and I beheld a tree growing near it. I walked over to the tree. It gathered me up in its branches and lifted me over the wall. . . .

She literally grows over the obstacle. She does it by assuming the position or the attitude of the tree, that is, she does not do it by will. She makes no violent attempt to force the wall, she leaves it to natural growth. This means simply that if she wants to get anywhere she will have to grow. There is no other way. She has to stand still and wait until she has grown enough to reach over the top. That is a very definite psychological situation.

You see, the unconscious always tends to create an impossible problem, and as long as a patient has not met such a problem — as long as he can promise himself a solution of his problem — he has surely not met the right one,

but merely something preparatory. For the unconscious always tries to produce an impossible situation in order to force the individual to bring out
his very best. Otherwise one stops short of one's best, one is not complete,
one does not realize oneself. What is needed is an impossible situation where
one has to renounce one's own will and one's own wit and do nothing but
wait and trust to the impersonal power of growth and development. The
vision says, "Here is this wall, the other side of which you can see only by
turning the eye inward. You can't get over it except by growing like a tree."
And that is, of course, an absolutely different mechanism from the animal
mechanism of running after things — or jumping for them, like a dog.

VISION (cont.): On the other side I beheld an old man. I looked in his
eyes and saw therein a great river full of many writhing bodies. A few men
stood upon the bank and called with a loud voice to the struggling masses
in the rushing water. The water cast a few souls upon the bank. Then the
men who stood there lifted them up and showed them a star and a sun.
Then I was myself in the eyes of the old man. He said: "You have perceived," and he sank back into the earth.

What is this intermezzo? She has come to the other side of the wall and
there she finds a wise old man. . . . In this case, the animus, but in the guise
of the old man. And she looks into his eyes. Here we have the eye again.
It means that she sees his view, she sees what he sees. This man is, of course,
of legendary age — I don't know how old. He is the personification of the
collective unconscious, which is of an immense age, and in that eye she sees
the view of the collective unconscious. . . .

It is the river of time, in other words, of life. The bodies are, of course,
individual fates, lives writhing, and twisting and turning themselves into a
sort of pattern that dissolves again and again. And a few men stand on the
bank. . . . Those are the people of detached consciousness, who are conscious
of themselves and of life. They are standing on the bank, calling to the
struggling masses in the rushing water. And the effect of calling to the
struggling bodies in that chaotic river is that a few souls are cast upon the
bank; they wake up, leave the great river, and come to land. Then the men
standing there lift them up and show them a star and a sun. What would
that mean?

Answer: Individual fate and consciousness.

Dr. Jung: Yes. The sun means the light of day and is, also, the symbol
of the deity. And the star is individual fate. Consciousness of the individual
life and of the deity, that is the idea. And the old man said, "You have perceived," and then disappeared. Now what has she perceived? . . .

110

Answer: To my mind, when he says, "You have perceived," without qualification, that means, perceived all.

Dr. Jung: Exactly. What she sees is really a point of view, a *Weltanschauung*, if you like to call it that. It is a very simple thought but, of course, has tremendous consequences. She sees the chaos of life, an interminable river .of life that rolls on to eternity, making no sense whatever because everything is merely chaotic. Only a few stand on the bank and are aware of it. Thus in our earthly world a few stand on the bank and really understand, really see with their eyes what is happening; all the others toil on just as blind as ever. So the unconscious here emphasizes the extraordinary importance of consciousness, of consciousness as a sort of redeemer from the eternal wheel of death and rebirth. That is what the wheel means in Buddhist philosophy, death and rebirth, the curse of eternal, illusory, meaningless existence. In this vision, as in Buddhism, we find the consciousness of what is happening as a redeeming principle. For the people who are standing upon the bank are conscious, they are aware of individual fate and the relation to the deity; or of the star and the sun. Those are the two important principles. Now, this consciousness is explaining something to the patient. What would it be? . . .

Answer: Things perish, of course, and this is a very pessimistic fact; but to realize this fact in one's consciousness is somehow to rise above it, to conquer it. To accept the fact that you perish in time is a sort of victory over time – perhaps that is the meaning of tragedy in the drama. This vision is a presentation of the meaning of knowledge – a conquest of fate by accepting fate. . . .

Dr. Jung: This vision is a sort of reconciliation of herself, or of her point of view, with the great nonsense of the world. It gives her a philosophical explanation. "You see," it says, "that whole river only makes sense if a few escape and become conscious." The purpose of existence is to become conscious. Consciousness redeems one from the curse of that eternal flowing on. This is an exceedingly important idea. It is another parallel to the central Buddhist teaching. Now, mind you, this woman has no particular education in these matters; this is really coming directly out of the kitchen of the unconscious. And she is being shown what the meaning of human existence is after all in a most impressive way. . . .

[For] according to this vision, the real meaning of life is that a few people should become conscious. Consciousness redeems from the curse of continually flowing onward in the river of unconsciousness. It looks almost as if, through consciousness, one secures a position outside of time. And this is exactly what the Lamaistic and Buddhistic philosophies teach, that consciousness forms the bridge over death. The dying man should never lose consciousness, he should retain continuity, so that rebirth will not overtake him unawares. . . .

Comment: I suppose to be conscious of time is to be out of time; it is to be timeless, and therefore immortal.

Dr. Jung: Exactly, as if consciousness were a means to attain to timelessness. Now this is a most interesting philosophical thought which is, of course, tremendously important for this woman from a practical point of view. And that is what I want to get at. Why from a practical point of view? What does it convey to her quite personally?

Answer: That it is worth working for.

Dr. Jung: Of course. It is highly worthwhile to work for consciousness and to accept life as it is; because it makes sense after all.

PART FOUR

In the Old Man's Eyes

VISION: On the other side of the wall I beheld an old man.[5] I looked into his eyes and saw therein a great river full of many writhing bodies. A few men stood upon the bank and called with a loud voice to the struggling masses in the rushing water. The water cast a few souls upon the bank. Then the men who stood there lifted them up and showed them a star and a sun. This I saw in the eyes of the old man. The old man said, "You have perceived," and sank into the earth. A few small animals and flowers growing in blood appeared where he had stood.

We have seen that this is the archetypal old wise man, symbolizing the acquired wisdom which is the common inheritance of man. At a certain depth of the unconscious mind, one cannot fail to meet this inherited treasure of wisdom. Here we have a piece of it: that what is within is also without — and it is stated as if it were a most vital truth. It is a truth which has little to do with our rationalistic values, yet it is most important for the life of our soul. For if you are able to have such a view, a way is opened up in yourself by which you can arrive at a peaceful mental condition where you are in harmony with things. Whereas if you adapt to the world as being only a jumbled causal chain, you never arrive at any settled attitude, you have no feeling of certainty or security.

What the actual condition of things seems to be is simply of no consequence because if your attitude is right, things are right; they are the things that belong. Whether, from another point of view, they are sound, or moral, or wrong simply does not matter; for this is your subjective experience at the time, and as you experience your life or the world, so it is. Naturally, from one point of view, you could say this was a most miserable life, or you could say it was the most beautiful imaginable. But such speculations are perfectly inane; the only question is how you live your life, how you experience it. If your attitude is right, then things are right. . . .

Here life is envisaged as a river in which human beings swim and are carried along — all completely unconscious — for they are submerged in the water, which means in the unconscious. A little group on the bank are conscious, and these call to the ones in the river so that some of them emerge

[From the lectures given between May 6 and June 24, 1931 (*Spring* 1963).]

113

and also become distinctive and conscious, but they are only a few. In the words of the New Testament: "Many are called but few are chosen." The central Buddhist belief is that we continue to circulate endlessly on the wheel of death and rebirth as long as we are not conscious, but if we become conscious through right meditation and right living — by following the Eightfold Path, as Buddhism expresses it — then we shall eventually reach emancipation. So a very central Christian belief and a very central Buddhist one come together here, and this is the wisdom of the old man. But our patient did not invent or think out the idea, she simply saw it as a picture. . . .

What she gets out of it is a very universal view of the goal of life. According to the statement of the unconscious many are carried away by the river but a few hear the voices calling and come out of the water; they become conscious, they are no longer carried away by the great unconscious movement. Thus becoming conscious is shown to her as the meaning of her life, and this reconciles her with the fact that she herself has been feeling completely at variance with her conditions. On account of her problems she has grown away from the atmosphere of her family and friends, from the convictions of her milieu, and naturally she feels isolated. Of course, she will be told that it is neurotic and wrong to be isolated, but the unconscious says that is exactly what she is meant to be. Such a vision may help to reconcile her to her own particular life task. For anyone who undertakes to live the individual life will be confronted with a situation like this, it eternally recurs. . . .

VISION: After the old man had spoken my robe became green, then turned to white. About my head played white flames. I walked through waving fields of wheat.

(illus. 10)   The picture that she painted to illustrate this state very obviously symbolizes enlightenment. This is typically Eastern symbolism. For in the Tantric Kundalini Yoga, when insight (or understanding of the unconscious contents) has reached the highest center (the seat of consciousness), then the light bursts forth — a white light. The fact that her robe first becomes green simply refers to the color of vegetation; it means that she becomes alive, that she is part of life. When it turns to white, that means that the life which has been unconscious before now becomes light; and light is, of course, understanding, consciousness. After this she should become conscious in an entirely different way. She should become conscious of life with complete distinctness — as well as of things. A white light is supposed to be the brightest light and the brightest light gives the greatest power of discrimination. . . .

114

And the fields of wheat are ripe — it is the time of fulfillment, of complete maturity. . . . What would this wheat mean?

Suggestion: Meister Eckhart says that wheat is the highest form of grain.

Dr. Jung: Yes. Wheat is very symbolical because it is bread, the fruit of the earth. Therefore Meister Eckhart says: "The innermost nature of all grain meaneth wheat, and of all metals, gold, and of all birth, man." So wheat would be almost like the essence of vegetative or plant life. And since plant life is a symbol for the spiritual qualities of human life, what would wheat symbolize?

Answer: Resurrection.

Dr. Jung: Yes, and it is also the symbol for the one who resurrects: for Jacchos, the divine son of the earth who is born in the winnowing fan; for Osiris, out of whose sarcophagus wheat grows; and for Christ, inasmuch as he is the Host, made of the flour of wheat. St. Augustine called Mary the virgin earth, not yet fertilized by the rain, and so Christ is the son of the earth, the wheat. Here again we find it to be a fact that as it is within so it is without. For in this vision our patient is enlightened, she has become fully conscious, and at the same time the earth has given birth to wheat. The mystery of Eleusis, the mystical birth of Brimos is accomplished, the earth has brought forth the God. This condition would be expressed in Chinese philosophy as a condition, for the moment, of complete Tao — namely, of highest illumination within and highest fertility without, the God born within and without, or resurrection.

[But this vision of illumination is immediately followed, as Dr. Jung explains, by a realization of the difficulties that await her. She sees a vision of "the face of suffering" on the ground (that is, in reality) which turns into a dead child. When she dips this child in a stream, it revives and puts around her neck a chain with a jeweled heart upon it that burns into her breast. Then the child grows to a man (a specific man) and leaves her alone to commune with a laughing face that appears in a flame shooting up from the water. — Ed.]

[Formerly a ring was burned into her forehead, which meant an intellectual conviction had come to her.] Now the symbol of the jeweled heart means that the realization has touched the heart. . . . The two rational functions have been reached; so we may assume that an important step forward will be taken. Usually in convincing a person one can wish for nothing better than to reach his heart as well as his head. But sometimes even that is not fully convincing; that is, it is not compelling. For though it may be compelling as far as the conscious personality is concerned, it is still possible that the unconscious may be against it, and in that case even a serious attempt of the conscious would be checked by unconscious interference. That often happens: people are convinced of a thing consciously yet cannot carry it through because of something that, in an obscure way, always interferes.

The difficulty is this: when one has achieved such a realization, then it looks as if the way were opening, as if one could progress; and one does progress but in doing so one always and invariably hurts oneself on the power of the past. The going is never smooth. Even if one's progress takes a most reasonable form, most welcome and useful in every respect, still one hurts oneself against the past. . . . Some serious obstacle intervenes and one cannot understand why. But if one looks back upon one's past and realizes the difference between the nature of one's present progress and the nature of events in the past, one can understand.

People rarely have such a historical feeling — a feeling for events as they formerly were. The world of our parents has vanished from our consciousness; we do not appreciate the enormous distance that exists between our world and the world of our fathers and grandfathers. We live so much in the moment that we can only reconstruct their taste or convictions with the greatest difficulty — to say nothing of those of our remoter ancestors. If we had more historical sense we would understand the meaning of progress better. In world history, too, any important progress has always meant bloodshed and warfare and revolution. We are, for example, all convinced that the spiritual attempts of early Christianity were a very good thing, that their general intention and purpose was wonderful. Yet Christianity produced a terrible upheaval in the world; it led to the destruction of thousands and thousands of lives. The reason for such conflict is the difference, the friction, between the actual moment and the past. All of which is an introduction to her next vision.

The Giant of the Past

VISION: I beheld a giant lying on the ground. Hideous, he appeared. His skin was white and flabby. He called out to me: "You will fear me, for I will rub your face in the dust and flay your body with whips." I spoke to him, saying: "O world, I am not afraid." Then all things became dark and seething with fearful forms and faces. I was in a river of boiling blood. The giant stood over me and cast such a great shadow that I could not see the stars or the sky. I was being sucked into the great boiling stream and I cried out in agony. The giant disappeared and I beheld a great egg blinding in its whiteness.

116

That giant occurs in another vision later on where she carries his great figure. I will show you the picture which she made then. It was painted at *(illus. 11)* a much later date, when there had again been a forward movement and when she had again hurt herself in conflict with the past. Not until then did she understand what should be done with the past — that it should be carried. This picture is the counterpart of the historical idea of the *transitus* — the carrying of the symbol — which formed part of several antique mysteries. In the cult of Attis, it was the carrying of the tree, the symbol of the mother. This was usually a pine tree and it was carried into a cave. Crossing a river or getting past an obstacle may also be the *transitus*. Mithras is often represented as carrying the dead bull upon his shoulders, and that too is the *transitus*; the bull is his own life and it is the world, it is the so-called world bull. There is an old legend that the world was made by God in the form of a bull, and that legend is still alive in Africa. . . . It was a bit of old Persian mysticism which was taken up by the Mohammedan mystics and, passed on by Sufism, then went down the east coast as far as Zanzibar. I mention this because in the vision the patient calls the giant the world; and the Mithraic bull is the world, it is the life of the earth, because the sacrifice of the bull made all sorts of edible things grow. The best-known form of the *transitus* is Christ carrying the cross, the cross being the tree again. It is the same symbol in Christianity as in the cult of Attis, and has the same value: it means carrying the mother — the world is the mother, Mother Earth.

So this strange picture — the tiny figure of the woman carrying the giant, that huge white body with hanging arms, that enormous mass of flesh — represents the past in the sense of the world as she finds it. And naturally, she would not now be finding the world if she had not lost it. She has lost her relationship to the world of her past because she has gone through a long series of inner changes; and all who have gone through such stretches of the inner desert — that inner wilderness, that jungle — have the same feeling of having thereby lost their former world.

It is a fact that most spiritual cults lead to an alienation of feeling from the world. In early Christianity thousands and thousands isolated themselves in the desert, whole cities were depopulated, and in Catholic countries a fair percentage of the population still goes into monasteries. Also there is now an enormous number of monks in monasteries in Tibet. Obviously, the spiritual life has a tendency to estrange man from his past and — with reservations, of course — this is its aim; it is a suitable and purposeful proceeding, for most people find it exceedingly difficult to maintain a spiritual development against the world. . . . Therefore every intense spiritual movement has been accompanied by such phenomena as nunneries and monasteries, places of retreat.

But the patient's forward movement now leads her naturally into the world. The world is the only place where she can create, for you cannot create when you withdraw entirely into thin air. You need the world because that is the raw material, the *materia*. You have to get your hands dirty in order to do a serious job; so you must touch the world, you must get entangled in the *materia*. A spiritual existence is really a suspended condition. You can be a hermit and live in the spirit and that is a life of a kind, but it is not visibly creative. On the other hand, although people say it is doing nothing, I am not convinced of that; I am sure that those hermits in the Syrian and Libyan deserts did an exceedingly good thing. Their lives were of tremendous importance because they demonstrated the power of the spirit to an absolutely materialistic world. . . . But when the times change, when the power of the spirit is amply demonstrated and mankind is convinced of its advantages, withdrawal from the world naturally loses its usefulness, becomes an obsolete reaction. For then there is need of the other side; a time comes when the power of the *materia* must be demonstrated.

Yang and Yin

Our terms for expressing this are very awkward. We really should use the terms of Chinese philosophy; it is much better to speak of a time when Yang prevails and another when Yin prevails. In our epoch there are many signs of the growing importance of Yin. (Perhaps I should explain that Yang is the masculine principle, bright, fiery, creative; it is the sky, the heavens, the south side of the mountain, and the dragon is its symbol; while Yin is the female, the maternal principle, humid, dark, receptive, the north side of the mountain, the night, the earth.) These two concepts, which the Western mind can hardly grasp, are exceedingly suitable to explain the basic principles of our psychology. At first we feel that they are vague, like clouds of dust; but to the Eastern mind they are quite definite, and when we become used to them, we see suddenly that they are absolutely intelligible and clear; that they characterize the two principles in an unsurpassable way. . . .

In this woman's case progress does not lead her into spiritual mysteries; she must go the downward way, the Yin way, and here Yin is something very impersonal. If I speak of following the downward path, no moral judgment is implied; it does not mean going to the dogs, degeneration, or complete moral or aesthetical self-destruction. Nothing of the sort. She is on the way to Yin, literally; she has just been initiated by the Great Mother. This is chthonic symbolism and not just the earth; Yin is not just the earth. Rather it contains the earth, the darkness of humanity — and perhaps the cave, perhaps the snake. That is all one can say, but it contrasts characteristically with Yang. You see the Eastern mind always thinks in these pairs of opposites, whereas we are always trying to establish the uniqueness of things. If we construct a complete picture of the surroundings of an object it is to differentiate that object as a unique fact, to detach it from its environment. But the Eastern mind cannot think of a definite Yin without having the concept of Yang in mind at the same time; so much so that in the *Tai-gi-tu* — that circular symbol containing the two fishlike forms, one black and the other white — the black fish which is Yin always has a white eye and the white fish which is Yang a black eye. In each fully developed form the germ of the opposite is already underway. That is the Chinese paradox, the sunrise begins at midnight. . . .

So the correct characterization for this woman's progress would be, not the downward way, but the Yin way. It does not lead into spiritual monasteries but into the earth. It leads to tangible things that are destructive when looked at from the Yang point of view, because the Yin is the negation of the Yang. But a Chinese philosopher would never think that only Yang was good, for Yin would then become something hellish to fight against; nor would he think — from the standpoint of Yin — that Yang should be overcome. He is aware of these opposites as a pair and he would never dream of having only Yin or of setting up a Yang party against a Yin party. But that is the way we think. . . . You see, that is our historical psychology, which is inclined to think that the thing which has alway been taboo is necessarily bad — once bad, always bad. It is a destructive point of view.

You find exactly the same idea in that early pagan book by Apuleius, *The Golden Ass* — which is practically the only Roman novel still in existence. The book recounts the life of a youthful philosopher, Apuleius himself, who lived the ordinary life of a Roman gentleman, a perfectly natural sensual life such as any young man lived — St. Augustine, for instance, lived it in his youth. The novel shows that, by his simple natural life, the philosopher slowly becomes more and more bestial, and finally he is bewitched and transformed into an ass. Then he is used in the theatre for the most abominable atrocities and obscenities. He is terribly unhappy in the form of the ass, till one day meeting the procession of the priests of Isis and seeing the High Priest carrying a wreath of roses, he snatches at the roses and eats them. Then he becomes spiritual, he becomes an initiant.

119

Mind you, that was written by a pagan, not a Christian. It shows the psychological necessity of the time; it shows that if one lives the natural life entirely one becomes an animal, and therefore needs a spiritual initiation. It was perfectly true that in those days anybody who lived in the ordinary style went to hell and the good way was the Yang way. But if the Yang way becomes so established that it leads into a complete sterilization and paralysis of life, then the Yin way is the living way; it is the way of grace, the way of salvation. Yet it appears to bring out all the devils in the world. To the Romans, for instance, Christians appeared to be the worst vermin a demon could have invented because they upset their families. A son was converted and then he became a perfect nuisance trying to convert the father. The main reason for the persecution of the Christians was that upsetting of the family life. Christ himself says that he comes not in peace but with a sword — separating families was part of the program. This was very unwelcome to the Roman citizens; so they did not tolerate that Oriental cult — even the Jews were tolerated but not the Christians. Naturally to the old Yin way the new Yang way was devilish and therefore they fought it. . . .

Today it is exactly the same but the reverse. We are the believers in the Yang way and we think the Yin way which is appearing now is all evil.

So this woman experiences all the fears and doubts of the new way. She feels that somehow it is all wrong; it appears under the aspect of a black snake, it is all sinful, destructive, impossible; yet all the time her unconscious is pressing her into the Yin form, and the more she can accept it, the more a great light bursts upon her from time to time, or she experiences a tremendous feeling realization and becomes increasingly convinced, against her will, that the Yin way is the way of salvation.

Now I think you understand the symbolism of the first part of the vision. . . . That tremendous giant lying on the ground symbolizes an enormous power associated with the earth. Giants are always chthonic powers, like the Titans for instance in Greek mythology, or the giants in Nordic mythology. The white skin of this giant is the whiteness of death and the flabbiness is that of a more or less decaying body. . . . He will press her into the earth, into the dust, and reduce her to nothing. That is, of course, the overwhelming power of her former world, in which she, as a frail spiritual entity, as a tiny spark of life, simply goes under.

The Relation of the Treasure to Yin and Yang

Here again we come upon very typical religious symbolism, it is the idea of the treasure. For instance, when Christ speaks of the treasure in the field, he means the Kingdom of Heaven that is within us. This small light, this germ of life, which is the beginning of a new consciousness is quite small and, like any germ, it can be easily destroyed. Even the strongest oak begins as a tender little plant which could be wiped out easily. And so this woman's new consciousness is fragile in comparison to the giants of her former world. In Buddhism the treasure is symbolized by the jewel one sees on the forehead of the Buddha and the Bodhisattvas. In Chinese art it is the pearl. In the classical Chinese dragon pictures one always finds a little moonlight pearl in front of the dragon, or a gold pearl when the whole thing is golden. It is never in the dragon's mouth; he always seems to be trying to get it. Of course, the dragon is for us an exceedingly unfavorable symbol but in the East the dragon is favorable; it represents the creative force, Yang. From the European point of view we think of the precious pearl, the sun or moon image, as the precious thing, the new light in danger of being swallowed by the dark forces, by Yin. But that idea would be a mistake, for here again the Eastern mind has a peculiar kind of objectivity. The Eastern mind is absolutely aware of the fact that Yang is just as dangerous as Yin — it is our prejudice that we think that Yang is all good and Yin is all evil. So perhaps the dragon might as well swallow the pearl; it is by no means sure, as the Eastern mind sees it, that the swallowing of the pearl would be particularly dangerous or undesirable. You see the pearl represents uniqueness, the small body, the great value, which is perfectly defenseless against the dragon; one does not quite understand why throughout eternity that dragon has not swallowed it. My idea is that the pearl symbolizes the uniqueness of the individual, the imperishable individual that is always there. It is the hero, really, who is swallowed by the dragon yet always reappears, having destroyed the dragon from within.

That tiny thing, that unique individual, that Self, is small like the point of a needle; yet because it is so utterly small it is also greater than great. There again is the Eastern formula and it is of tremendous importance....

But when the spark of light, which is a new consciousness, comes into the world, it naturally finds itself up against the great powers of banality. All finished things, all established things are big. A new thing is always small, ugly, unacceptable, while the things that are grown and fully developed are beautiful and powerful and choice. Think of the beauty and perfection of the Catholic Church for instance. It is an absolutely finished and perfect thing and naturally one loves beauty and perfection; and then there comes a tiny little spark that has a Luciferian tendency to deviate from that form

121

and, of course, the church swallows it or wipes it out, exactly as the church has done with all heretics: some were just cleverly swallowed like St. Francis, others were wiped out entirely. . . . For in the speculation of the Christian church individuality really is evil, an invention of the devil, because it means separation from God.

Enantiodromia

So we can understand that, when our patient defied the giant [who was the world of which she mistakenly claimed to be unafraid], then the world caught her. Then she fell into the abyss, seething with fearful forms and faces, and was taken back into the river of blood from which she had emerged. Here the giant is no longer lying on the ground like Goliath hit by the stone of David; he stands over her and causes such a great shadow that she cannot see the stars or the sky: all orientation is lost; there is complete darkness; or as the *I Ching* would say, she is "near the heart of darkness." And she is being pulled even further down, for she says, "I was being sucked into the great boiling stream and I cried out in agony." That is the death of the hero, it means the disappearance of the hero in the belly of the whale-dragon. Then in the overwhelming darkness even the giant disappears.

It could seem illogical to suppose that the power which has overcome one utterly disappears when one is wiped out. But that is true Chinese philosophy. If Yin succeeds in swallowing and abolishing Yang completely, then Yang penetrates all the darkness and sets it on fire, and out comes the light again. Therefore if Yin wants to overcome Yang, or Yang Yin, if a man wants to overcome a crowd or if a king wants to rule his people, he must be swallowed by the crowd, he must give himself over to them completely, because only thus can he appear in each one of them. That truth is symbolized in the Christian Communion. There Christ is supposed to be literally eaten; he penetrates the darkness of everybody and reappears in everybody. . . . Here the giant is swallowed up by his own darkness, as it were; but then the Yin at the height of its power overcomes itself and by the law of *enantiodromia* transforms itself into its own opposite. That is the famous concept which means the crossing over into the opposite. The concept was created by Heraclitus who said that all things move into their opposite. It is an exceedingly important psychological law which you find everywhere. You probably have noticed that in the sequence of these visions things are again and again developed through *enantiodromia*. Always when a certain thing comes to a head, to the top, then it falls off, then it changes into the opposite.

122

So here in the supreme moment when the darkness is absolute, even the giant disappears; and behold, an egg appears of blinding whiteness. . . . Completely defenseless, the patient succumbs to the powers of the world and out of that giant comes an egg — an egg which she can hold in her hand, which she can manage. Moreover the egg is a promise of life. This is, of course, not to be understood in a logical way, it is only to be understood as an intuitive image. As she has been that tiny figure, that little germ of light, before being swallowed up by the universal darkness, so the universal darkness suddenly becomes a germ of life which she holds in her hands as if *she* were a giant. Now this is a very difficult idea but as an image it is perfectly plain. . . . How would you explain such a tremendous change? This experience is by no means peculiar only to her. I have seen the same kind of change occur a number of times at moments as important and decisive as this. Now how could it be, that the thing which has been the world of the past, a corpse, is suddenly transformed into an egg?

Answer: The past is the womb of the future.

Dr. Jung: That is perfectly true. Is it also the germ of the future?

Answer: Yes, the past and the future are opposites, and yet the future issues out of the past.

Question: I want to ask if the same idea is expressed in putting a grain of wheat into the earth to produce the new germ?

Dr. Jung: Yes, the death of the grain of wheat in order to produce the new germ. Of course it does not die, it simply transforms, but that is used as a simile — as a corpse is put into the ground and is understood to resurrect at doomsday.

Well then, this idea, or this picture, is a symbolic representation of the idea that the past is the germ of the future. You see, here something very strange happens. We were speaking of her consciousness as a spark, a tiny light in the great universal night. She is, of course, overcome by the powers of the world and her light is put out; but then the world transforms — the world of heretofore transforms on account of the fact that she has been lost in it. . . . One could formulate it perhaps in this way: if we think of the individual as being an imperishable substance of magic or divine quality, and if the cosmic darkness overcomes that individual light, then the light disappears, it is no longer visible; yet it enters the heart of darkness, it is within the darkness, and since it is imperishable the darkness cannot destroy it. On the contrary, the effect of it is that the universal darkness becomes transformed, and Yang emerges from Yin again.

123

Comment: The Romans who conquered the Greeks were conquered by them spiritually. Is not that the same thing?

Dr. Jung: Yes, that is very much the same thing. A better example would be the conquering of Rome by Asia Minor and Egypt. The same thing is happening to us: we have conquered the East and the East is conquering us. Here in the heart of civilization we are talking Chinese philosophy and declaring ourselves to be unable to find anything better.

Rebirth of the Godhead into God through Man

What I am driving at here is an exceedingly strange thought and we must say, of course, that it is a hypothesis. I don't know whether I shall be able to make it clear. You see, it is obvious that an individual being, an individual light or consciousness, can go under in the world. We see that every day; it is just as obvious as the fact that we die. But this vision says, if your light is put out by the great darkness so that you don't see the stars and the sky, then something very great happens, then your light becomes universal; then it is just as if you had given birth to a God, since the universal thing is the God. Now that coincides with the mystical ideas of Meister Eckhart, for instance. He makes the difference between God and the Godhead, as if the Godhead were nothing – or something quite unconscious and not happy in itself. It is as if the Godhead must be reborn into God through man.

To the primitive, a God is something original, a beginning of things as they have been made or created hitherto, and it is just as if the whole thing had no head; and then the individual man comes with his individual consciousness, and it is as if that man were the head, as if he had given a head to the Godhead. That is the creation of light. It is as if he were making the whole Godhead contract into one egg which becomes a new light. He goes under, but what he produces is eternal.

We have the same idea in Christianity. Christ is that egg – the dogmatic legend does not quite fit in but the Gnostic legend does. I told you that Gnostic legend of the Demiurgos who created a very imperfect world but in his vanity thought that it was marvelous. Then far up above him he saw a light – something he had not created. So up he went and there he found a spiritual world that he had not known before, made by a strange God. It was this strange God who – looking down and seeing the misery of man whom the Demiurgos had made only semiconscious – took pity and sent his son to Paradise in the form of the serpent to tell man that he should eat from that forbidden tree. As it says in Genesis: "Ye shall be like gods, knowing of good and evil." This is good psychological advice: eat from the

124

tree, see all the evil, understand how much it needs improvement. But then all the people who ate from that tree and who were increasing the light in the world were persecuted. The strange God — mind you, this is not the God who was the Creator of the world — saw that mankind was struggling in vain against the evil intentions of the Demiurgos. So he sent his son again, this time as Christ, and Christ succeeded in opening people's eyes to the fact that this world is really quite rotten, very badly made, and that therefore they should liberate themselves from it. That is the reason why the Ophites — one of the Gnostic sects — worshipped the serpent as Christ, and why they had the serpent on the communion table with the bread and wine.

The Egg

We should say a bit more now about the egg. . . . for the egg is the eternal example of the perfect germ in a dormant potential condition. It is often represented on antique Gnostic gems encircled by the snake. That is important symbolism which occurs also in the Indian Tantric philosophy where the snake coils round the egg, the creative point called the Bindu. . . . The point is interpreted as the male God; it is called the Shiva point and has often been represented as a phallus, the symbol of the generative forces. The snake coiled round it would be the female principle that receives or surrounds the creative point; it is called Shakti, Shakti being the Goddess, the female. Through intercourse of the Shiva point with Shakti, the illusion of the world, or Maya, is created. Now when that system begins to act, it is symbolized in the Tantric philosophy by the springing up of the Kundalini serpent. The word *Kundalini* comes from *kundali* (coiled). And as that serpent springs forth, it emanates the system of appearances, which is called the world but which they say is essentially an illusion.

I mention these details because, as we progress in our interpretation of the visions, you will see that there is unmistakably a tendency in the patient's unconscious to approach such Eastern ideas, although she is totally unacquainted with them in consciousness. For reasons which we do not know, her unconscious is trying to express this particular aspect of truth. However these ideas are archetypal and distributed all over the world; we find the same kind of symbolism in the Orphic mysteries of Greece, where the egg, the world germ, is exactly parallel to the Shiva Bindu idea in Tantric philosophy.

Nothing is indicated in this vision concerning the serpent; we only know that instead of the giant an egg appears. Do you know why the giant disappears? That is very important. You remember that the giant symbolizes the overwhelming power of her past world. How is that dissolved?

Question: Is the giant not Maya?

Dr. Jung: Yes, but how would that be dissolved? . . . The answer is clearly stated here but one does not notice it; the dry telegraphic style of these visions blindfolds one. You see, the events that came just before were really the culmination of the power of the giant. . . . Now she is going under completely. . . . [She cries out in agony and] it is at this point that the giant disappears. . . . One might suppose that the giant would stand there throughout eternity and that she would be simply sucked under and disappear. But no, the giant disappears. How is that? . . .

Suggestion: She cries out in agony.

The Power of Suffering

Dr. Jung: Exactly, it is her piercing cry that kills the monster; it is her agony which overcomes it. That shows the creative value of suffering. So Meister Eckhart says: "Suffering is the fastest horse that carries you to perfection." It is the suffering that transforms; she allows herself to suffer agonies, and, expressed as it is in her telegraphic style, you can take it at its full value. It is a moment of absolute suffering and that makes the giant disappear. Now this is a very important point. Of course, for masculine psychology it sounds too soft and weak. We cannot understand how that could be, and therefore the man who is a hero takes a weapon and kills the monster actually from within. You remember my *Psychology of the Unconscious.*[6] But the woman kills it through suffering. Can you understand such a thing?

Question: Would the suffering of Christ on the cross be a similar thing? And he was a man.

Dr. Jung: Yes, exactly. And that is what we cannot understand. It is the same idea, the magic effect of suffering. . . . Acute suffering has the extraordinary effect that suddenly the whole past does not matter in comparison with the pain. . . . People who do not possess their center, who are somewhat outside of it, need a great deal of suffering before they can feel themselves — they almost inflict upon themselves situations in which they have to suffer. But nobody can prevent them because it is a need. Only through pain can they feel themselves, or become aware of certain things, and if they never become aware they never progress.

If mankind had not suffered from living in caves or in the branches of trees, houses never would have been invented. So even if suffering is not inflicted from outside, it is inflicted by people upon themselves with the unconscious purpose of feeling themselves. If you have a bad toothache the whole world does not matter; if you are really seasick it is a matter of indifference to you whether the boat sinks or not; you become demoralized. But the positive effect of it is that you feel yourself, you acquire awareness, and learn to assert yourself against the giant.

So through such an acute agony the patient becomes aware of herself and that is exactly what she needs. In that moment everything that has been overwhelming before becomes an egg; she says: "I beheld a great egg, blinding in its whiteness." She represents it in the picture that she painted as *(illus. 11)* being above her, and she holds up her arms to it as if it were a divine apparition. It looks like an invocation.

Question: You explain suffering as a means to achieve Self-consciousness. In Christianity the renunciation of the ego seems to be a part of the saintly ideal, as with Christ and the martyrs. What is the philosophy of suffering?

Dr. Jung: The idea of the Christian suffering, I mean intentional martyrdom, was to deny the egotistical interests of man, and his avoidance of pain. The martyrs asserted themselves as immortal units: it really was to emphasize the Self because to them the Self was identical with the Kingdom of Heaven. In the Logoi recently discovered at Oxyrynchus, it is written:

> The Kingdom of Heaven is within you; and whosoever shall know himself shall find it. Strive therefore to know yourselves, and ye shall be aware that ye are the sons of the Father; ye shall know that ye are the City of God.

So when the Self is asserted through pain it means that the Kingdom of Heaven is established, which was the purpose of martyrdom and the reason the Christians were taught to seek the arena.

Christian martyrdom meant the complete abnegation of the ego, which was absolutely necessary at that time. It is impossible to live as an ego forever because it is too childish. Of course, many people make the great mistake of taking the ego for the Self. The ego is nothing but the artificial Self. That is, of course, clear to us but in those days egotism was the self-evident fact. The Bible said: "Love your neighbor as yourself." It was obvious to them then that they loved themselves, everybody loved himself; and afterward it became our ideal that we should love our neighbor; nowadays we love our neighbor and not ourselves. Everybody hates to return to himself because he is most loathsome to himself. . . .

Now we will proceed to the opening of the egg. The egg contains something and the patient is quite curious to know what it is.

127

VISION: I said, "Open, that I may know what is within you." At length the egg opened and within I saw a black antique statue of a head. I took it out and wiped the dust of ages from it. As I did so tongues of fire leaped from the lips and the face said, "Kiss me, woman!" I said, "I cannot, I will be burned." The face again commanded me and I kissed it. Then I felt the fire going all through me. I stood up and the head fell upon the ground and broke into fragments."

. . . First of all we must go back and find the origin of this egg. It surely came from the past, it is instead of the past, or one could say it was inside of the past, an egg that had been hidden within the giant; that is, the world hitherto has been pregnant with an invisible egg, now this appears as that world disappears. It is a germ from back in the ages perhaps; for she says that head was covered with the dust of ages. In the remote past an egg was laid, or the germ of a new world originated, which remained hidden within the giant, but when the giant disappears the egg becomes evident and within it is that black head. The head must symbolize the thing which remained concealed in the past, and that gives us a clue as to its meaning. . . .

Suggestion: It is the Yin.

Dr. Jung: Yes, it is a germ of the Yin but it has been hidden in the ages. Black suggests evil, and the tongues of fire leaping from that head are not particularly friendly, it reminds one of hell-fire. . . .

You see, it is important to realize that, with us nowadays, the Yin or the earth has the character of evil very often. To what would that head refer? Have you the connection?

Suggestions: Is it the black animus again? It looks very American. Is it a Negro?

Question: Is it the black Messiah?

Dr. Jung: Well, you have heard the suggestion that it may be a Negro and you know about the instinctive side that has not been accepted. But really we must have a symbolic connection, we are interpreting without considering what has gone before. Do you remember the God without a head that we were speaking of before? The God without a head is the giant, and here when the giant disappears the head appears in the egg. The giant is white, the head is black. That is astonishing. What would it convey? . . . Of course, it was nowhere said that the giant had no head, but I say it, in speaking of the heavy load which has to be carried. We in the present are the head of the past; we are ahead of the past literally and we are the foreseeing eyes, the creative brains, that give the past a head. At least that is what we ought to do. If we do not assert ourselves, if we do not create a

128

new head, the past is then an overwhelmingly heavy body that crushes us. But if we put a head on the body, we give sense and meaning to the whole thing. That we do not know what head we should give is the complication; the past is a growing tree and we do not know what kind of fruit it should have, what kind of development it will need. Our patient does not know what the meaning is, but it is already in existence, it is in the egg. . . .

Suggestion: The black head is also Luciferian which is a principle of change.

Dr. Jung: Well, yes, I would say that every head given to the past is Luciferian because it brings light. But here it is quite obviously a Negro head; and this is confirmed by a later picture where the whole Negro appears. . . .   *(illus. 12)* We are concerned here with a living symbolism. . . . This woman is seeking an attitude that will help her to meet the problems of her life; she has not found the conviction or the attitude that would help her to accept her own individual fate. For that she needs a sort of religious attitude which she can find in no other way than through analysis. My reason for dealing with these visions is that they give us a really marvelous insight into the secret workings of the unconscious. They show us how the unconscious works out certain symbols through which she is helped to acquire an attitude that enables her to live, not conventionally as we understand it, but her own specific individual life.

Now the great trouble is this head without the body or the body without the head. I grant you it is exceedingly difficult both to understand and to explain this symbolism. . . . But let me show you this picture of the Christ without a head which comes from Autun Cathedral. You see he is not really without a head, a symbolic sun is the head; this does not mean just the disk of the sun, it means a spiritual sun. And the spiritual sun in Christianity is the specific truth of Christianity, it is the Logos, and it is symbolized as the circle with the cross which in the East is called a mandala. It is the symbol of individuation, of the completion of the human individual, or its *entelechia,* and at the same time it represents the new light of Logos, that is, the new light which shines in the darkness, as is said in the beginning of the Gospel of St. John.

In the early centuries around the time of Christ there was, of course, an entirely different kind of psychology. Then Christ meant the discovery of a new attitude, a new hypothesis about the meaning of life. Therefore he was called the new light, he was even compared with the sun. . . . That is the reason why Christ was not given a human head but a sun, meaning that the Logos, his mind or insight, was the sun, a new light. There is a Latin inscription which says: *Quisque resurget ita quem non trahit impia vita et lucebit ei sine fine lucerna diei.* This means that everyone whom the impious life does not ensnare will rise as the Lord rises — like the rising sun — and the light of day will shine upon him without end. The word pious really means obedient, so *impia vita* would mean the life that is not obedient or does not conform to the new light; but if anyone succeeds in fulfilling the new meaning, in living by the new Logos, then the light of day will shine upon him in eternity.

This is exactly the formula which we could apply to the symbol of the head. The head represents a certain idea, it represents the Logos, it gives insight, or consciousness of things, it explains; and if you understand it you will live in the light, inasmuch as the *impia vita*, or the life of the past, does not drag you off your path. This is always the great trouble, for the past world is the giant that may overwhelm you.

Now this woman has made the great giant disappear by her suffering. She became intensely conscious of herself and that caused the appearance of a new idea which now impresses itself upon her. Of course, she does not understand it yet, but it is quite obvious from the symbolism what is meant. The head that does not belong to the body is like the disk of the sun that does not belong to the body of Christ. You would naturally expect a human head upon Christ, but no, it is an abstract symbol, the spiritual sun. The body is the past, our earth, the world as it has been until now; but out of it rises a new light which is not identical with the body; out of the enormous white body of the giant comes an egg that contains this head. And mind you, here it has a new meaning, nothing abstract, it is very concrete, a Negro's head — black; but it gives life apparently. It is, of course, of great age, as primitive man is of great age. Indeed, instead of the word "Negro" we could say here "primitive," since the quality of primitiveness is what the black head in this vision expresses. . . .

The thing that creeps out of the egg then is a primitive mind really, the primitive Logos, and it speaks words of fire — those are tongues of fire which leap from its mouth. That is like the symbolism of the fiery sword which comes from the mouth of the strange figure, a kind of savior or mediator, in the beginning of Revelation. And that she should kiss the face simply means the union with it, an acceptance. In the Eleusinian mysteries, you remember, the initiant had to unite himself with the powers of the earth by kissing the serpent. There is no text which corroborates that ceremonial, but a sort of relief has been excavated where the initiant is depicted kissing the serpent that represented Demeter, the Goddess of earth; it is a repetition of what we

130

have already discussed concerning the symbolism of swallowing the black snake. This is simply another form, an original form of the primitive mind.

Of course, one could ask here why that should be so, but instead of speculating about it now I must say that it simply is so; the main thing is to understand or to accept it as a fact that primitive things are most suggestive and, to our unconscious, most acceptable, while everything else, all the beautiful things, are less stimulating. They are quite all right, to be sure, but they seem to be exhausted, while the primitive things have a peculiar suggestiveness, a sort of spell.

Our patient says she was permeated by the fire that escaped from the head; that is, the words of magic fire went through her. They are the tongues of fire of the miracle of Pentecost; it is the Holy Ghost, the Logos again, as it descended upon the disciples. Here, instead of descending on her, it permeates her; it is something like the black snake but it is not the black snake, it is the magic fire of grace; grace has always been represented as luminous. It does not come from heaven in this case, it comes from below; she holds the head and the fire rises from it.

Suggestion: In some Gnostic religion there is a savior, a God, who is sent down as the primitive man, Adam. The idea is the same, that the first man is nearer to the strength of life and that therefore he is the God.

Dr. Jung: But mind you, that is not the primitive quality as we understand it. That is the primordial man who was in the beginning, but he is an entirely spiritual force. . . . In the first century, they did not emphasize the primitive quality, they emphasized the primordial man who was really a God-man, the *Theos Anthropos* of the Gnostics of the East. Christ, the son of God, called himself the son of man. But the son of man is the God-man, . . . the spiritual being, while this thing here is to be taken under the aspect of the primitive, not the primordial man. It is her primitive man and only when accepted in this form will it reveal its intention — its brotherhood or identiy with the primordial man, the timeless, spaceless man, the *Theos Anthropos*. But we are not yet so far.

The patient's whole difficulty is that she is confronted with that blackness. She would be deceived if someone should say to her, "Oh, that is merely Adam." Some people, the theosophists, for instance, would teach you that it is Adam Cadmon when it is really Mr. Smith. But if anyone comes to a real situation, he cannot accept it if he is looking for Adam and it is actually Mr. Smith. If you tell a young man that a certain girl is his eternal soul, Mother Mary perhaps, or something like that, it is cheating; she is a very ordinary ape girl. So the important thing for our time is that

131

we should see things and accept them as they are. At other times, when the chthonic element is too obvious, it is important to teach people the spiritual aspect. In the days of Christ it was important to know that men were divine; therefore he said to his disciples, "Ye are gods." Of course, they did not understand it. We would immediately grasp the idea; we would be quite inclined to it because we want to get away from the ordinary Mr. Smith. But for this woman it is all important that she should accept the black aspect of things; if she can accept the earth she will discover the spiritual part of it too.

Now when she was permeated by the fire she stood up and the head fell upon the ground and broke into fragments. You see she has now accepted this peculiar manifestation of the primitive man; she is permeated by the fiery words, by the mana emanating from the Logos. Now that form can break because she has accepted it — at least in the vision.

Here we might say something about the general symbolism, and about the black Messiah who has been mentioned. You see this head, which we must put parallel with the mythical or legendary idea of the savior, has really the value of the savior. (This will be confirmed in the subsequent events where the Negro performs that role — giving his blood for mankind.) We are quite safe in assuming that she has discovered the savior in this, to her, objectionable form. And here again I must refer to the past. You see if we were old Romans and anybody told us that the divine savior of the world had been nailed to the cross — like a dirty slave — it would be most objectionable to us. With the strong aestheticism of antiquity we would reject that teaching because it would offend our taste — it would be too blasphemous. We would be as little able to accept it as good Christians would be able to accept anyone's saying blasphemous things about Christ. Yet there is eternal truth in the statement of Isaiah and other prophets, that the savior always comes from the place where we least expect him. Just where we don't expect life, there it will be; because the life that we know is almost exhausted, the new life always comes from an unexpected corner. Therefore the paradoxical idea of the black Messiah is surely a symbolic expression which fits in with our psychology.

That the head breaks into fragments means that this form can be abandoned by the woman because she has taken in the fire which emanated from the head, and that is a great thing. The fire that went through her is the essence of the vision; it is inspiration, dynamic force; it instigates action or enterprise — like the fire of Pentecost which inspired the disciples to go out into the street and to talk in different tongues. . . .

132

The Exorcism of the Fire

But fire, as has been said, is also Luciferian. Naturally you would not expect this black head to diffuse a particularly spiritual influence; it is a doubtful influence. She says:

VISION: I stumbled out onto a great plain where I saw a snake and begged of the snake to lead me away. The snake led me through some cool grass beside a river. In the river I saw the beautiful form of a man. I entered the water and followed him. He took me by the hand and we went up a bank and entered a temple. I said: "Expel the fire from me." He told me to kneel by the altar and he gave me water to drink, but I said: "The fire within me still burns." He took out his sword and struck the walls of the temple so that, with a noise of thunder, they crumbled to the ground. The man then put his hand upon my forehead and said: "Woman, you are forgiven. Arise and hold communion with the people." I beheld many people about us. I walked to them and they touched me with their hands. At last I said: "The fire is no longer within me, I am purified." I lifted up my arms to the sky while the rays of the sun descended upon me.

[The snake is here an indication that she must be wary, that she must look out, but it leads her to the river of life. The beautiful figure of the man she finds there] refers to the man who is the stumbling block in her personal story. This means that in the river of real life, in the course of events, that image will come up again and she will have to meet it. Here you see something concerning the piece of the primitive mind that she discovered in the egg; it says to her: "This is your touchstone. This is the thing that you must eventually face." And why, people often ask me, must it be brought down to such a test? Why must things get into reality? . . . Because if the thing remained a mere thought, then the egg would not contain life; it would be an empty shell practically. Then the game would not be worth the candle; it would not be worthwhile to open the egg or to bother about such phantasies at all. But we have to bother about them because they really contain the germs of life without which that particular life would remain mutilated or sterile. . . . Therefore when she opens the egg, when that head speaks to her, when the fire enters her, she will inevitably be confronted with reality. So you understand why the snake means that she must look out. Things are becoming real.

Now she enters the water; she trusts herself to the course of events and follows after the man. We have seen before that the animus usually precedes her in any situation where things are obscure and where she does not trust herself — anticipating her or performing the *rite d'entrée*. . . . Assuming again the role of the leader of souls, of the Hermes *psychopompos*, he takes her by the hand, and leaving the river, enters a temple which is on the bank. . . . This woman does not know what is ahead of her; she simply allows him to take the lead . . . and asks him to expel the fire from her. She is filled with the fire from that head but does not know how to apply her new acquisition. . . .

First, he tries the usual means; getting her out of the river into a secluded place where she is sheltered by the thick walls and the mana of the temple, he gives her water to drink with the reasonable idea of quenching fire by water. . . . But there are certain predicaments where reason does not help; she has to confess that the fire is still burning. . . . Now he understands that no holiness, no sacredness, can quench that fire. . . . He does not turn her out but he destroys the sacred precincts, the walled-in place of rest; after that all the surrounding country can come in, as it were. The sacred place is no longer sacred, it is now profane, and, of course, the effect of this is that she is put back into the river practically. That is very important. Then the man puts his hands on her forehead and says: "Woman, you are forgiven." Of what does that remind you?

Answer: They are the words of Christ to the prostitute.

Dr. Jung: Yes, the adulterous woman is analogous with this case — we had the scarlet garment, you remember. And here the Hermes *psychopompos* develops a bit further; he assumes the role of Christ and the assumption is, through the analogy with the story of the adulterous woman, that he will now quench the fire; that is, create a psychological situation which will deliver her from it by allowing the contrasting elements to blend. For you feel something burning you when it is incompatible with your previous system of adaptation; if you change that system, then the fiery thing can enter without destroying you, but if you leave it as it is, either the fire will be put out or your flesh will be burned — that would leave a terrible scar.

So the rite in the temple should serve the purpose of uniting two things which have hitherto been incompatible; there is an idea of adultery in this phantasy, which ought to be accepted into the whole of her system without burning it. She cannot simply destroy the whole idea — because that is life from the eternal fire; therefore she must change her system of adaptation. That is what Christ did for the adulterous woman, and, as he was the son of God, it worked; he changed her so that she could accept it into her system, so that she could stand herself, and no longer be morally destroyed by it.

You see, it is tremendously important that people should be able to accept themselves. Otherwise the will of God cannot be lived: they are somehow cramped or blighted; they don't really produce themselves so as to express the whole of the creative will which is in them; they assume a better judgment than God himself, assume that man ought to be so and so. In that way they exclude many of their real qualities. . . . What the Lord did for the adulterous woman was to change her system so that she could accept the fact and still feel redeemed. You are not redeemed by repentance, you remain the same old Adam, because by repentance you are not changed; you may get baptized or something of the sort but that is not a real change. It must be a change of the system, an acceptance of the things that were unacceptable before. When you accept the fact of your inferiority, it lives with you; you are it too, but not exclusively. You are not merely white; one part is black, but both make the whole man. It is not wiping out the white substance when you can accept the black — on the contrary; it is only when you cannot that things go wrong — when there is nothing but white and nothing but black. That is simply neurotic.

So the evangelical cure is a very wise one. Christ helped the woman to accept herself as she was, and that is what the animus is doing here when he assumes the gesture of Christ. Now we will see the effect of the cure. He says: "Arise and hold communion with the people." What is the meaning of this? . . .

Answer: When you accept yourself, then the world can accept you.

Dr. Jung: Yes, it is just that. You see people who have feelings of inferiority are not accepted because they do not accept themselves. If you want to be appreciated or loved, appreciate yourself, love yourself, do right for yourself, and everybody will do the right thing to you. To people who say, "Oh, I am very much interested in people, I love them, but I hate myself," I reply: "Nobody can stand you because you bring with you the stench of your stables; go first and clean your stables and then we will accept you as a clean human being; then we will like you if there is anything likable." That is what they always forget, which comes from our wrong kind of Christian education. . . .

To hold communion with the people means: to recognize that we are all the same, that we all suffer from the same problems; to be no longer isolated but rather to be human among human beings. That is, of course, a tremendous asset which removes this woman's feelings of inferiority; she is accepted, she is in mankind, she stands upon the soil that is common to all living things. She is just a tree among many which has succeeded in taking root; there is no feeling of inferiority. . . . It is only our minds that cause such feelings and make that tremendous and blasphemous assumption that we know better

135

than the will within us. . . .

From that we can draw the conclusion that we should learn not to interfere, in order that the thing may work. If only we could learn the art of not interfering! We hinder ourselves most by intellectual interference, always knowing better; that is the stumbling block. What we have to do in analysis is to remove those conscious opinions, to help nature along, so that nature can work in her quiet way through her symbols, without our most obnoxious intervention. You see this magic rite has now worked. The fire is quenched and she confesses in true antique style, "I am purified," as if confessing, "I am reborn." Through acceptance, not by cutting away the thing — that does not help — but by accepting it, she is purified and brought back into the lap of humanity. And then she says, "I lifted up my arms to the sky while the rays of the sun descended upon me." She is now upon the earth and the light can descend upon her. When she is human, when she holds communion with mankind, she can receive the blessing of the sun which is, of course, a religious experience.

Only those people who really can touch bottom can be human. Therefore Meister Eckhart says one should not repent too much of one's sins because it might keep one away from grace. One is only confronted with the spiritual experience when one is absolutely human. . . . A great deal of old religious truth is put here into very unusual form; for this reason the patient does not recognize it, and that is very helpful — for so she cannot destroy it. . . . This is a beautiful example of an eternal truth stealing into her system when she is not aware of it, and so it can work. . . .

The Whole Negro Appears

VISION: I beheld a Negro lying beneath a tree. In his hands were fruits. He was singing with a full throaty voice.

(illus. 13)

Now I will show you the very beautiful picture she made of this. Whenever patients produce an especially beautiful picture, one can be sure that the thing they are trying to express represents a particular value to them, so that all their abilities are brought out and come into action. Usually my patients have no knowledge of painting or drawing, but when a picture suggests itself that expresses a particularly comprehensive idea, then all the faculties of the individual are called forth, and it is as if the body itself were supporting them in their endeavor. They often begin by making sort of ideographic pictures, using their minds only, with nothing natural about them, but the moment an especially comprehensive image is constellated in the

136

unconscious, their body suddenly helps them to produce a real picture. . . .
Now what does this picture suggest to you?

Answer: He looks like a man in a Dionysian rapture.

Answer: It suggests the God Attis to me.

Dr. Jung: Attis is a God of vegetation. Perhaps you know other parallels?
They are the dying and resurrecting Gods, and Christ belongs to that category too.

Answers: Mithras. Osiris. Adonis. Odin, pierced by the spear. Jacchos
who is really Dionysos again, the specific form born in the winnowing fan.

Dr. Jung: The lamented Gods belong in this group too. In Greece there
was Linos, the famous God who dies young, and in Babylonia Tammuz, who
was lamented by the women every year. The dying and resurrecting Gods
represent one special idea which is, of course, of tremendous age — like the
idea of Osiris in Egypt. All the different forms of it were, so to speak, combined and rescued for a later phase of civilization in the form of Christ. For
he is also the grain of wheat that is resurrected. These Gods are called the
vegetation Gods and their rites were usually performed in the spring — you
know the sudden appearance of spring in the southern countries after the
winter rains and the way it vanishes quickly before the burning rays of the
sun. The miracle of spring is particularly impressive in Mesopotamia where
these figures probably have their origin. . . .

Yet although these so-called vegetation Gods are expressed externally by
the coming and the vanishing of spring, they are of psychological origin.
One does not see a God when the flowers spring up, but that is what one's
psyche makes of it; it is a kind of reverberation in one's psyche, a psychological phenomenon which originally coincided with the processes of nature;
that is, it coincided as long as man was like the animals in complete *participation mystique* with nature. In the paradisiacal state he was so identical
with his surroundings that he experienced all the different phases of nature
as they came. . . .

Through development, however, he became aware that it was not the
spring outside, the spring or the vanishing of spring in himself which concerned him; so the process became detached from external events. . . .

Now in this vision the Negro has taken the place of that archetypal figure
of the vegetation God, the God that dies early. His relationship to vegetation is perfectly obvious through the fruits. In America you have Mondamin,
the God of the grain, who is a close parallel to Jacchos or any of the others,
for they are all Gods of the harvest. Therefore this Negro holds fruit in his
hands. Then he is under a tree, which shows that the tree is in a way his

attribute. (In that respect these pictures are like the ancient representations of the Gods who were always shown with their particular attributes.) . . . Also the blood pouring forth would be a manifestation of the fertility of the earth: plant life pours out a river of riches over the earth, the rich fields are like a stream of golden wheat — these are well-known poetical figures.

In connection with his being a vegetation God what else would the blood symbolize? We must see that aspect too.

Answer: Wine.

Dr. Jung: Yes, wine and wheat always typify the fertility of the earth, and they are also symbols in the Christian Communion; so the blood might just as well be a stream of wine. Therefore this absolutely Dionysian gesture of the Negro. All these attributes and the whole mythological context confirm an idea that we had about this Negro. What was that?

Answer: The black Messiah.

Dr. Jung: Yes, he is a mediator. All those Gods were mediators because they shared the lot of man. Gods usually do not die but those Gods did die. Therefore, in later periods of Egyptian history, Osiris was simply a designation or a technical word for the soul itself, the immortal part of man. The Osiris of the king or the Pharaoh was spoken of as an immortal substance, as the thing he had in common with the God who died like man and could overcome death by resurrection. This Negro as a mediator is really performing some such archetypal role; he represents the reconciliation between man and the thing that is against him or from which he has become detached. In this case he is a sort of psychological mediator. . . . One could say that he mediates between her modern point of view with its exclusiveness and one-sidedness, and the instinctive and natural point of view which is compensatory to it. . . . You know we have already found the animus going ahead, making a bridge to the next point, and here he performs in the same way for our patient again, he shows her the reconciling symbol. What attitude can she learn from that particular gesture?

Suggestion: *"Stirb und werde."* Die and become.

Dr. Jung: Yes, but that is exactly what people do not understand. . . .

Suggestion: A sacrifice?

Dr. Jung: Yes, but very involuntary. It is natural, a sacrifice within nature's purpose. Again I use a phrase of Goethe's, *"Die Natur verlangt einen Tod,"* meaning nature demands a death. It is natural, nobody has inflicted it. Like a pod bursting open, or fruit falling from the tree, so the wine or the blood pours forth. It is a natural flow, a natural manifestation, not an inflicted death, nor a self-inflicted sacrifice. And the attitude is one

of . . . joy, or the love of one's own fate — *amor fati*. A sort of enthusiasm
. . . for following the way of nature, for following the law that is in ourselves.
The Negro shows a complete abandon to the laws which are operating in him,
and that leads to fertility. . . .

But really a long commentary is needed to interpret such a picture. To
say, "Follow the way of nature," is not unmistakably clear because we have
preconceived ideas about nature. If I were to say that to a society of philosophers or theosophists, they would reply, "Exactly, naturalism, Rousseau,
that is what we would expect." But you see they entirely forget that nature
demands a death. That is what Christ says in the recently discovered Logoi
which the early Church Fathers were very careful not to admit into the New
Testament, despite the fact that they are older than the Gospels and equally
authentic. The disciples asked Christ who would lift them up, because the
Kingdom of Heaven was so far above in the sky (the old Egyptians used to
put a little ladder in the tomb for the dead to climb into heaven), and he
said, "The fowls of the air and all beasts that are upon the earth or under
the earth, and the fishes in the sea, these are they that will draw you into
the Kingdom." That means the instincts — the blind instincts almost; the
way of nature will bring you quite naturally wherever you have to be. That
is the idea of Tertullian: *anima naturaliter christiana*, meaning the soul is
naturally Christian; in other words, a natural process leads one to the Christian formulation. . . .

According to many of our preconceived ideas man is all wrong and sinful, but those ideas are absolutely false. For who but man has created the
religions of the world? Who has produced Christ? Who has produced
Buddha? All that is the natural growth of man. If left to himself, he can
bring about his own salvation quite naturally. Man always has produced
symbols that redeemed him; so if we follow the laws that are in our own
nature, they will lead us to the right end.

You see how things develop here; this woman does not go astray, not a
bit. One might expect, if a person were delivered over to his own phantasies,
that it would result, as Freud says, only in wish fulfillment, that everything
would go to hell completely. The theologian thinks man is of the devil,
that all evil comes out of man himself; so he thinks you cannot trust your
own law. But if you don't trust your law you must content yourself with
a neurosis. You have to trust yourself with your own experience because,
according to the natural law, it will lead to a state of completeness; I do not
speak of a state of perfection — that is prejudice — but of completeness,
which seems to be a kind of growth and which contains all the spiritual

values one can wish for. You see this vision is not leading to anything destructive; it leads to a natural fertility.

Question: Would you say that self-judgment and self-criticism are parts of human nature also?

Dr. Jung: Of course they are, and we know it.

Question: Not only accepting your nature but judging it, modifying it, that is also part of you?

Dr. Jung: Yes, and we do it with more or less success. The question is, are our criteria good? . . .

Must I Know You?

VISION: I said to the Negro: "Must I know you? " He answered: "Whether you know me or not, I am." I asked him: "Oh, Negro, what do you sing? " He answered me: "Little white child, I sing to darkness, to flaming fields, to the children within your womb." While he sang blood poured from his heart in slow and rhythmic beats. It flowed along in a stream covering my feet. I followed the stream of blood. . . .

Whether we know it or not the thing happens, whether we call it the law of nature or just that particular thought; it always exists — the question is only: Do we contact it or not? Can we become conscious of it? This figure of the Negro is, in a way, completely detached, not particularly interested in her. He exists for himself, like nature; nature is not especially interested in man, not in such a way that we feel it; yet since nature is also in man we must admit that she is interested in his existence. . . .

That the Negro does, in fact, take a certain interest in her is shown by his answer in which he explains that he is singing the darkness, singing the flaming fields and singing the children of her womb. She says singing *to* but the proper technical term would be without the preposition — as the Scottish fishermen, when they set out to sea for the oyster fishing, sing the oysters; or as the Australian bushmen sing the water, or they sing the grass seed, or the kangaroo. It is a sort of incantation to produce plenty, a magic procedure by which fertility is secured. . . . So the Negro is obviously performing a magic incantation, giving additional power, a productive or fertilizing value, to her consciousness.

One should be aware of such symbols for otherwise their effect remains either invisible or almost nil. It is as if somewhere in a pocket one had a banknote, but if one does not know it, it has no value, it is as if it did not exist. And so it is in nature. Of course, even without one's knowing it, it will produce certain effects, but they will be queer, they will interfere with one; for not knowing about the unconscious means that one has deviated, that one is not in harmony with it, and so it works against one. It is quite possible that if this woman were not conscious of that figure, it would simply form a complex which would work against her. As a matter of fact it always has worked against her, and she only can be aware of the positive power of such figures by becoming conscious of them. The value of these visions is that they help her to become aware of the unconscious contents, for they cannot work properly unless admitted to consciousness. But if one can perceive unconscious contents, that in itself is already an asset because it is close to nature, and then the next step is to admit them. Otherwise the conscious is not supported, it has no roots, nature assumes a contrasting attitude and even becomes an opponent. Then the unconscious is not interested in man, it simply rolls on in its own cycles, and man is left somewhere high and dry, stranded.

For instance, I told you about that case of the insane person who dreamed the most gorgeous myths of death and resurrection, but nothing happened to her conscious; it was unaffected. Had she been able to understand them, the unconscious would have been attracted, it would have welled up and increased her consciousness. People often point out that the Freudian school regards the unconscious as something alien, wild, barbarous, opposing, and criminal. But even assuming that the unconscious has such an attitude must result from the fact that consciousness has been hostile to the unconscious; it must be because consciousness has gone a very different way and therefore has brought out the negative aspect of the unconscious. But if one approaches the unconscious in a friendly way, it loses its dangerous aspect, and what has been entirely negative becomes positive. One sees that from dreams. One often has dreams that one thinks are destructive and evil, which present the thing one cannot accept, but it is merely due to the fact that one's conscious attitude is wrong. If one says, "It seems quite wrong and black but perhaps I have to accept it," instantly the thing changes color, it becomes compatible with consciousness.

So this Negro's interest in our patient's welfare or her fertility is due to her willingness to contact the unconscious or to accept it; so while he sings and while she engages in conversation with him, she notices that he pours forth the stream of blood. You remember that we encountered that stream of blood in a former vision; she swam in it, and by following it, she came to the central place, or the center of her own Self. Here is the same thing again — she has to follow the stream of blood.

VISION: It led down and down. At last I found myself in a rocky cavern beneath the earth. It was very dark. I saw a glowing fire. Above the fire I saw a phoenix bird which continually flew up and beat its head against the top of the cavern. The fire created small snakes which disappeared. It also created men and women. I asked the bird: "Where do they go? " The bird answered: "Away, away." The bird said: "Stand in the fire, woman." I said: "I cannot, it will burn me." Again the bird commanded me. I did so and the flames leapt up, burning my robe. At last I stood naked."

What is this cavern to which the blood stream leads her? . . .

Answer: The abdomen.

Dr. Jung: Yes, she is led down . . . into the abdominal cave, which here is a psychical localization. . . . [It means that] she reaches down with her intuition, as it were, into the region below consciousness; and there she finds a fire already glowing. . . . Now what is this fire? I did not know about it for a long time myself.

Answer: The Kundalini Yoga.

The Kundalini Yoga

Dr. Jung: Yes, the serpent fire. There are peculiar ideas in the Hindu Tantric system which were discovered through the practice of yoga, and we find practically all the same symbolism in these visions [as was suggested before in connection with the egg]. By descending into the cave of the unconscious the Tantric yogins discovered [a series of bodily centers, beginning down in the abdomen, through which they said the Kundalini — that is, the serpent power — mounts when once it has been awakened]. The lowest of these regions is *mūladhāra,* in the perineum at the base of the small basin. That is the root center where the whole system starts [and where the Kundalini lies coiled about the Shiva Bindu]. The next region above *mūladhāra* is the water region, the region of the bladder at the entrance of the basin. [There is no evidence of any values other than physiological being attached to either of these regions] but the third abdominal region, corresponding to the solar plexus, and called the fire region, seems to be clearly a psychical center. There are still African tribesmen who assure you that their thoughts are in the stomach. And one can actually feel certain emotions there. Therefore one says that it is difficult to digest an idea, or that one's stomach is upset when one cannot digest certain emotions or anxieties. . . . The next center above is about the region of the diaphragm. The word for diaphragm comes from the Greek *phren,* meaning mind. This center is identical with the heart which is of course a sort of feeling center; it is also an emotional

142

center but of a different nature, for above the diaphragm consciousness, the possibility of reflection, seems to begin. . . . A sort of moral continuity starts here. Then above the heart comes another center in the larynx region, and still another in the head. Six in all.

You understand, of course, that these centers are merely metaphorical. People sometimes assume that there really are such centers, but the Hindu himself says only that it is "just as if" there were such centers; it is not to be taken literally. But the interesting thing is that the symptoms which occur when, as it is said, the Kundalini mounts through these localized centers almost point to physiological facts; it is really "just as if" there were centers like these which influence certain organs. People in whom the Kundalini serpent has reached the heart region will probably suffer from neurotic symptoms in the heart; and as long as the Kundalini is unconscious they suffer from abdominal difficulties. As I told you, there is hardly any case of hysteria that is not accompanied by abdominal trouble; also by peculiar sex excitements. When the Kundalini starts there is sex trouble, and the next thing would be bladder trouble, like forced urination. Then comes the stomach, then the heart, and then the higher psychological regions. . . .

Here we have come to the fire center, in the center of the abdomen, and the fire is living but dormant. In the most primitive myths this is the fire which the hero makes in the whale-dragon's belly. . . . But in us the fire is already kindled, we do not need to do that any more; for the time of the primitive myth is over. So this woman finds a fire there already and she sees a phoenix continually flying up, beating its head against the cavern roof.

The phoenix is a symbol of rebirth — like the eagle or whatever it is in mysticism or alchemy that rises from the fire. That means that out of this glowing center of passions, of emotions, from down in the solar plexus, something can rise into the kingdom of the air, into consciousness; it is a germ of higher consciousness which is contained originally in the fire below but which can become airlike and mount to the head, or perhaps to a great height beyond the head. This is really the idea that gave rise both to the Tantric system and to our alchemistic system of philosophy in the Middle Ages. But here the bird is shut in; he is beating his wings against the roof of the cave and cannot get out; he is caught. This obviously means that the germ, that form of higher consciousness, cannot break through and develop; it is kept below the diaphragm — for the diaphragm is the roof of the cave. . . . Now what would that bird be? I called it a germ of higher consciousness, something that is really meant to rise to a great height.

Answer: Spirit.

Dr. Jung: But what does the phoenix myth really mean? Well, in psychological language, this fire center is the center of passion and enthusiasm, and that is exactly the center of emotion of the primitive; and it is down in the belly, it is pre-psychological. Anything that could be called spirit or soul takes its origin in a sort of fire on that pre-psychological level. Consciousness takes its origin in passion. . . .

But now the product of that fire, or the product of the passion in this case, cannot escape into consciousness; it is caught in the unconscious. Why can't it get up into the air, into visibility? Obviously consciousness is not ready to accept it, but why not? A phoenix would seem to be rather nice.

Answer: Because it comes from the abdominal region.

Dr. Jung: Exactly; it comes from the primitive black head, it comes from the abdomen; so it seems to her to be somehow inadmissible. There is still a remnant in the consciousness of our patient which does not allow that particular kind of mind or spirit to appear. . . .

Comment: But it is the unconscious itself, which prevents the bird from flying out.

Dr. Jung: That is perfectly true, the unconscious has no chance to come into the conscious unless the conscious makes a hole for it to come through. . . . But here her vision is centered upon the fire and she says: "I saw the fire create small snakes which disappeared." Now that is why the Hindus call that coiled-up snake Kundalini, the serpent fire; it is because they have observed visions like these. This woman, not knowing of the Tantric visions at all, reproduces exactly the mythology of the Tantric philosophy. . . .

That the bird cannot come up to consciousness is perhaps due to the fact that her conscious assumes that only snakes are down there, for snakes are supposed to be dangerous and venomous. But you see the fire produced both; the snakes would be a counterbalance to the harmless bird. Then she says that the fire also created men and women. It is an extraordinarily creative fire; it seems to be the creator of the world. And that agrees exactly with the idea in Tantric philosophy that fire *is* the creator. . . . Finally the bird said, "Stand in the fire, woman!" She replied: "I cannot, it will burn me." Again the bird commanded her. She did so and the flames burned her robe, so that at last she stood naked.

The Fire of Purification

This explains why she stays below with that living fire; it is the fire of purification. . . . Apparently she is now the phoenix itself and she goes into the fire in order to burn up. But what happens? Only her robes burn and she stands naked — evidence again that she is becoming herself. This passage simply means that through the fire of passion, in the pre-psychological condition when you cannot and do not reason, when you surrender completely and allow your pain or emotion to have full sway, you become purified, you become yourself. This is the test of the gold: true gold will show its quality in fire. This is also an alchemistic idea — she becomes the true substance. Then the fire dies and the bird disappears, because she is now the bird herself. That higher consciousness is the consciousness of the Self. And she has been made aware of the fire by talking with the black Negro. . . .

Why is it so important that our patient should be forced like this to absolute nakedness? Why cannot she indulge, at least to a small degree, in a mild persona indulgence?

Answer: Because she would only take half measures; she would not face the whole situation.

Dr. Jung: That is perfectly true, but there is another point. Of course, she must see herself as she really is; she has already faced a great deal, but now she is called to a still more intense consciousness of herself. Let us assume for a moment that she has really convinced herself of her problem. What more could there be? . . .

Answer: To know what she has got to help her to go on.

Dr. Jung: Exactly. To be conscious of herself as she is helps her to face her own problem because then she is convinced that it is her own individual problem. Most people do not believe this. They assume that it is just a mistake that they are confronted with certain problems in life. For instance, a person tells me that in the year so-and-so he made a fatal mistake. But there is no such thing — that is fate, there are no mistakes in fate. Fate is greater than we are. What happened to him then was just what had to happen; it was no mistake looked at from his inner structure. When he knows himself, he will know that the mistake is himself and that therefore he has to face it.

But that is only half of the value of the knowledge of one's own individuality. If a person does face his problem, if he lives it, if he really manages his own life with a full knowledge of what he is doing, even then he still may carry it through with the sort of limitless lack of consideration which is a peculiarity of the conscious. . . . The danger of our conscious way of living is that we constantly lose sight of the real goal and go after imaginary goals. This hinders us from advancing at all; it always induces a sort of limitlessness. Your conscious processes as well as your unconscious — that is, the power from the back, from your instincts — are always pushing you out with a centrifugal momentum against which you must have some protection, and the only protection is the knowledge or consciousness of your individual limitations, of what you are without a veil. You must know what you can do. . . . If you have a conscious image of what you are, you know what kind of life coincides with your individual pattern. But you may be quite certain that you will go wrong if you imitate somebody else, or follow a conviction or a principle that does not fit in with your individual pattern.

So in this moment, when things become hotter and hotter, our patient is again emphatically called back to the knowledge of herself; her picture is put before her eyes, so that when the visions move on she will never again lose sight of herself; she will always know who she is. For the figures of the collective unconscious which appear in these visions could easily insinuate that she is quite other than what she is, and then she would lose conviction about herself and lose her path. It is a tremendous temptation because on that path people make astonishing discoveries, they discover things of which they have not even dreamed. . . .

At all events, here she is in that abdominal cave, in the region where the fire starts and where there are absolutely no preconceptions. It is just as if life were starting again, as if nothing had happened yet.

In the beginning of life, in early childhood, one sees what an individual really is; children who are already introspective at an early age have an intuition about themselves which perhaps never leaves them. They know just what they are. Later on they lose this knowledge; it is partially squeezed out of them and partially they succumb to certain illusions; and it is only much later that they discover themselves again. That is the reason why the Freudian theory makes so much of the reminiscences of early childhood: if you can remember those facts, you know what you have been, because whatever happened to you then was yourself.

Of course, in a way nothing ever happens to you which you are not. The life you live is your life. All your experiences are yourself — that is exactly what you are. So when somebody complains that he has been a victim of a sexual attack, say, in early youth, and explains his whole life by that occurrence, one must say that it is lamentable, yet it was himself, he experienced it. You see, if such a thing had happened to him but it had not been his own experience, it would have made no impression; it would have passed him by. Usually neurotic patients think that one thing or another has had such and such an effect, but other people go through numbers of potentially devastating experiences that leave no impression because they are not theirs. Yet sometimes experiences are traumatic, and one has to be a mental acrobat to explain why — because a dog waggled his tail at one or something like that.

Danger of Calling Forth the Serpent

Now this woman's fear of becoming demented because she is caught in the cavern is not out of the way, for there is a particular risk in that close association with the lower centers, and any yogin studying the Kundalini Yoga is conscious of the fact that he is treading on a dangerous path; he is quite aware of the peculiar dangers of calling forth the serpent. For it will certainly complete its path if possible — that is, if the yogin is able to stand it. The further the snake progresses, the greater is the danger, and the most dangerous point is when the snake reaches the head. Therefore it is probable that few yogins reach the stage when the snake enters the sixth, or *ajña*, center of consciousness.

Now this Kundalini experience should not be mixed up with our ordinary consciousness; that has nothing to do with it. One can be quite conscious without having the kind of consciousness that is brought about by the serpent. This whole yoga process is something additional to normal mental development. I always try to make clear that this development of consciousness is not a normal process; it may be said to be abnormal, an additional consciousness. One cannot possibly tell what the result of such a thing might be; somehow it will be different from anything we know. You see the experience of the awakening of the serpent is not merely a sex experience; there are millions of sex experiences and there is not one real yoga experience among them. This is something apart, it is a particular kind of sex experience. So the yoga process is really something that happens on a different plane, as it were, and there are dangers and risks which do not attend the usual development of consciousness. . . . Should one, for instance, reach the lowest place, *mūladhāra*, one might be caught in the roots. Such experiences are so real that people who have not the faintest knowledge of Eastern philosophy have painted pictures of a human figure caught in the roots of a tree; there is one in *The Secret of the Golden Flower*,[7] a recumbent female figure dormant in the roots — in *mūladhāra*.

It is associated with the danger of insanity because insanity really is that attachment to the roots of consciousness. It is just as if in this Kundalini process one were giving up all the attainments of civilization and living the whole experience of the world over again, and naturally there is the danger that when one returns to the state of the animal one may get caught in the animal; the animal psychology may sway one's consciousness and dement or dissociate it. Therefore a typical case of insanity might be called a yoga experience that had gone wrong; something was touched in the roots of such people so that the serpent leaped up and they were caught; a piece of

147

psychology came up which they were unable to swallow. When one studies
a case of schizophrenia or dementia praecox, one nearly always finds some
such experience in the beginning of the disease. . . .

Question: And what is the difference between such cases and the case
of this woman?

Dr. Jung: Oh, she can cope with it.

Comment: But what she does is more than normal psychology?

Dr. Jung: Yes, it is supernormal psychology. You see, Providence really
meant the neurotic psychology to be supernormal, but it often remains
infranormal.

Comment: So the neurotic ought to use his neurosis, to make something
out of it?

Dr. Jung: "Many are called but few are chosen"; that is an esoteric truth.
It is true that the neurotic can only be really cured by supernormal psychology, additional psychology; and if that cannot be accomplished they are
just maimed. They are either crippled, or they are supernormal. . . .

This connection with the roots is a new and very peculiar experience. As
I said, it is as if the whole process of becoming conscious were repeated; so
it is expressed as a second birth, and the one who has undergone it is called
twice-born and is supposed to enter into a condition which is mana, or taboo,
or redeemed — whatever the religious term may be. At all events, it is an
experience that creates a new kind of consciousness, which could be characterized psychologically as a detached consciousness, a consciousness which
is no longer in *participation mystique*. I do not want to go further into all
that now, but I mention it in order to explain to you the experience our
patient is undergoing, her fear of insanity. . . .

Now this woman has to remain for awhile down in the dark, in that very
understandable fear, until she can stand it. Usually such states of panic or
great emotion last or repeat themselves as long as one cannot stand them.
When one can stand them, they are overcome; if one can tolerate such a condition and remain quiet, then it vanishes, it is overcome. It is as if one had
taken the energy out of the emotional form and transformed it into a sort
of consciousness. That is the Kundalini process.

The Negro Opens the Way

VISION: At length I heard the Negro descending. (That Negro who was
lying on the ground with his hands filled with fruit, that God of vegetation
who had been above while she was below.) He sang: "I sing to you of darkness and of flaming fields." He opened the door of the cavern.

You see, he is the one who opens the way for her. What is the meaning of his being above while she is down in the unconscious, of his being outside while she is inside? . . . It is because he is that power which is in the serpent fire, the part which she could not stand and which was therefore projected. He lives, he holds the fruits of the earth, and he is pouring out his blood. Now that is a Christian idea, the hero idea. We are not capable of living it; therefore if we have a burden we cast it upon the hero as quickly as possible and get rid of it. We think the hero can carry it, and moreover he promises to redeem us — which is exactly the reason why nobody is redeemed. That is quite impossible: it is a mere projection, a sort of historical illusion which was a truth once and worked for a certain period of history, but for us it will not work any longer. We know very well that if we cast all our sins on the Lord it won't work; nothing happens and we only get neurotic. So the Negro simply anticipated what she was intended to do — to come up to the surface, to receive the fruits, and to pour out the blood. Now he is the opener of the way, the *psychopompos.* Then she says:

VISION (cont.): He laughed when he saw me. He said: "Now you are wedded to me." We ascended the steps into the daylight. He said again: "Now you are wedded to me."

That means that they are in absolute unbreakable union. As the Christians would say: Christ became my brother and my brother is myself, so I am Christ. Now that is, of course, a most blasphemous assumption; anyone who said that would be considered insane. But no, Christ was simply a modern individual. He just lived his own mind. He had an interesting kind of conviction and he made an experiment: he identified with his own way against all traditions, against all the respectable people of Palestine. That is what he meant to do and he paid for it. And that is what this woman is meant to do, nothing else, just that. It is like an early Christian going into the arena, or like Christ himself who was doubtful how the whole thing would turn out so that he had his bad hours in the garden before he was crucified.

You see, these things are as serious as in the early days of Christianity. Tertullian taught his disciples to seek the arena, and that is the idea here — to become oneself and risk even going to the dogs, or being blasted to bits. That is what is waiting for this woman and therefore she needs superpersonal consciousness.

PART FIVE

Looking for Roots

Starting from the modern point of view, this woman's visions have led
her back very rapidly through the ages, from medieval Christian times, down
past the temples of the Romans and Greeks, to the borders of the animal
kingdom, where she had a vision of the eyes of the animal, really the soul of
the animal. And then she began to ascend again, coming back first to sun-
worship — a cult the meaning of which she now understands completely
through vital experience. But, of course, besides experiencing these things
herself, she also sees what their present-day meaning would be. Her point
of view is not that of an antique person, but of a modern person having the
experiences that men used to have in the remote past. . . . She has now
ascended to the time of early Christianity when the transition from the
Dionysian cult to Christian ideals took place. . . .

In the last vision that we discussed [the Negro vegetation God with blood
flowing from his side] there was a peculiar transformation of the symbolism
of the Communion; for in the Christian Communion the wine means the
blood, but here the blood gushing from the side of the Negro means the wine.
. . . The religious ideas of the patient seem to be returning in a very interesting fashion to the pre-Christian point of view. . . . It is as if in our late Christian era she reached a point which contained no more life, so that now she
has to look for the springs of life, or for roots from which new shoots of
life may rise. . . . At the time of the transition to Christianity there were two
figures, Dionysos and Christ, representing two different principles. The Dionysian principle was decidedly archaic and Christ was its new opponent. . . .
But this woman is not coming forward from Dionysos to Christianity . . . she
is trying to develop something new from the Dionysian ideas. . . . It is as if
she were giving up Christian abstraction for Dionysyian concreteness, the
blood changing into wine, the wine becoming sacred. . . . Also here we have
fruit instead of bread [an immediate expression of nature instead of a product
refined by man].

At the end of the vision the Negro says, "Now you are wedded to me,"
and he repeats the phrase. Obviously this means that she is now united to

[From the lectures given between November 11 and December 16, 1931 (*Spring* 1964)]

the new savior, that strange Dionysian spirit. And if she is really united with him, that spirit will act as a sort of instigator within her; it will continue to work, it will lead her through life on a special path. For without that Dionysian spirit she would envisage the problems of her life from the late Christian point of view, that sapless, almost sad, dusty point of view which made her neurotic before. But now she has this other form of life which is far from being sapless; it has an *abandon*, a spirit of abundance, which will influence her strangely. So she will be confronted with the most amazing problems on her way and in the next visions we may expect to come across serious obstacles to her continuing on the road with the black Dionysos.

The Black Stallion

VISION: I beheld a black stallion. With his hoofs he struck fire from the rocks. I was in the sea and I called out to him, asking how I could mount him. The stallion came down to the water's edge and I mounted upon his back.

Now what about this black stallion? In medieval psychology the devil rides on such a stallion. But why should it be the devil's animal?

Answer: Because it is black.

Dr. Jung: It is black, like hell, and black stallions are said to be particularly ill-tempered or nervous. You remember the famous simile of Plato: he says man is like a charioteer who has to guide two horses: one is white, a docile pious horse, and the other is black, disobedient, always obstinate and rebellious. This is obviously the evil horse, because for ages past black stallions have been understood to be bad, not only on account of color, but because they really are quite often dangerous and evil-tempered. And what does it mean here?

Answer: It is the force of nature in her.

Dr. Jung: Yes, but why a male and not a female?

Suggestion: It is an animal animus, I suppose.

Dr. Jung: Yes, it is an animus force . . . it means that the animus is in possession of her libido. He is identical with it, he is the black stallion. . . . So her vision is acquainting her with the fact that the thing which is now going to carry her is by no means herself, but her animus. Do you think that is right? Or is it dangerous or wrong? How would you take it if such a thing happened to you? That's what makes all the difference. If, for example, such a stallion should come to me, who am a male, it would go with all the rest and I would say, "Of course, I accept it." But if a black mare should come along, I wouldn't be so certain that it belonged to me.

151

Question: But if it is already in you?

Dr. Jung: I hope not! I'm not at all sure I could accept it. You must put yourself in the place of that woman. Suppose you were confronted in reality with a black stallion. You would not be in the least sure that it was yourself. You see the general assumption is that this is her personal psychology, but it is not. It is quite possible that it is something strange coming to her, a non-ego manifestation. That black stallion does not belong to her, and it makes all the difference in the world whether she assumes it to be her personal psychology or not.

Remark: But only by recognizing it can she really become acquainted with it and gain the power of exorcising it. . . . It is there and she has to recognize it.

Dr. Jung: Surely, it is there. But the question is, what shall her attitude be? Shall she identify with it and say, "This is myself"?

Answer: She must do what she did.

Dr. Jung: Suppose the devil offered you a black horse. Would you ride it?

Answer: One could try for a bit.

Dr. Jung: Well, it is really quite a problem. How can she trust herself to it? Might she not refuse?

Question: Couldn't she control it?

Dr. Jung: Why should she control it? Would you feel the need to control all the wild elephants in Africa if you encountered them?

Remark: But she was in the sea, and it would be desirable for her to get out.

Dr. Jung: There you are. . . . This horse comes as a sort of rescuer; it is the only means by which she can get away. In such a case one would ride away on a tortoise or on the devil, if he presented himself. . . . But what does it mean that she is in the sea? In the last vision she ascended from the underground cave to the light, to the surface of the earth, and now she is in the sea. Naturally that refers to the unconscious, so we might just as well ask, "Why is she suddenly in the unconscious? What could have happened after she made the acquaintance of the Negro savior? " . . . I want you to remember the end of that vision particularly, where the Negro said, "Now I am wedded to you." He emphasized it strongly, he repeated the remark. What might the consequence of such a fact be?

Answer: That she is possessed by him and would follow him.

Dr. Jung: And what would happen then?

Answer: She would lose herself.

Dr. Jung: Yes, she would become unconscious like that primitive figure, who was in a state of ecstasy, of *abandon*. That is what has happened between this vision and the one before, and therefore she is in the sea; she has wound up in an unconscious condition. This is exactly what we usually observe in such a psychological situation. If a person follows the Dionysian spirit of *abandon*, he will get drunk, for instance, beyond all reasonable proportions, until he is unconscious, until he is in the sea; then something seems to come and pull him out. Moreover, being in the sea means being below the level of the land, that is, being in too low a condition; he should be lifted up to a higher condition, and for that nothing is better than instinctive force. For very often when we are in an unconscious state our will fails us; we cannot employ will power and then something must give us the necessary kick to get us out of the unconscious. Here the instinct is represented by the stallion; this woman's only way out of that condition is by getting on the back of the horse.

You see the close connection between the black horse and the Negro; it is the same idea practically. So the thing which has brought her down into the unconscious is also the thing which lifts her out of it. That is a very paradoxical statement but it is a piece of the most ancient wisdom of the East. Therefore the saying that the man who falls upon the earth will — in getting up — be supported by the earth. . . . So the Negro brings her down into the unconscious and the black stallion lifts her up once more.

The Giant Again

VISION: We galloped for a long way. At last we came to a great giant who stood across our path. The stallion melted into the ground and I was left alone facing the giant. "Who are you, O giant? " I asked. He answered, "I am the voice of the world." His teeth were long and from his mouth issued fire. I tried to pass him but could not.

We have encountered this giant before. Do you remember the picture where she was carrying the great corpse? This is the same giant; it is the voice of the world, of public opinion, in other words of the gigantic human being that represents society.

Comment: I thought you said it meant the past, that she tried to carry the whole past.

Dr. Jung: I did say that. Our human society, all our functions, the whole *opinion publique*, is the result of the past; therefore it is gigantic. Everything old is big. The new things are exceedingly small and weak and tender. So you see she is up against a great power. The giant represents the *opinion*

153

publique of her whole world, the convictions of our present society. And there the stallion melts away. Now why should that libido disappear just when she needs it? It seems most regrettable that she should be left high and dry by the instinctive power that has been carrying her. Why should such a tremendously strong and vital animal suddenly collapse completely?

Question: Is it that she drops back into her old attitude?

Dr. Jung: You think this is really a regression? Then we must explain why she draws back.

Suggestion: Fear.

Dr. Jung: Yes, but what happens to this black stallion, to this battle animal, that he should suddenly be overcome and fade away? A stallion is very courageous.

Question: Is it that the stallion is an animus opinion?

Dr. Jung: Of course. The great obstacle in her way is the public opinion which functions in her own psychology as an animus opinion, and the stallion vanishes before the giant public opinion because he himself is the energy of that opinion. You see an animus horse is libido in a certain opinionated animus form, and at the same time it is public opinion. Animus opinion is always public opinion, universal opinion. That is why I asked if you would have mounted that horse right away. It would have been a bit dangerous, but here it was necessary. The point is that she had gotten into the unconscious by following the black savior. That was not too bad, it had to be; but then she had to get out again, and that thing that helped her out was public opinion. For public opinion holds that what you do in the sea, in the unconscious, is all wrong. It says, "Now be a man, don't degenerate, be morally responsible" — a very general slogan — and on the back of that slogan she comes to land. . . . [For] public opinion, conventional morality, conventional ideas, are naturally helpful; they would not be in existence if they were not good for something; such ideas are exceedingly useful for everybody who is down below, down in the sea. But if you go with them too long, in the end you will find yourself completely deserted because your unconscious libido vanishes.

You cannot force yourself beyond a certain point. You have to live within the boundary of the conventional point of view if you follow that collective libido; if you try the individual path, it will leave you. You can trust yourself to the conventional standard only as long as you remain below the standard of the fictional normal man. If you try to go beyond that, you come up against the giant and the horse vanishes, it simply leaves you; you are deserted by what one could call the collective instinct.

The White City Beyond

Then an entirely new problem arises: what can help you when your instincts leave you? When you are carried by instinct things are comparatively smooth, life is easy, you sail along; you make many mistakes but they matter very little because you are with your instinct and you remain more or less unconscious. But what will help you when you come up against the giant, public opinion? When your instinct collapses and is transformed into fear, what will carry you further? There is no "thou shalt," no admonition, and nobody will give you support, because it is not a collective matter. If you go further it is an entirely individual enterprise. What will help you then? I will let the phantasy answer.

VISION (cont.): I tried to pass the giant but could not. Beyond him I saw a white city. I said to him again, "I must pass you," but he only laughed.

Now what is that white city which she sees beyond the giant? What does such a glimpse ahead mean psychologically? It is an encouragement, hope, as if she were seeing beyond the obstacle something that will follow when the obstacle is overcome. It is a promise and therefore it is a white city. Do you recognize it?

Answer: The New Jerusalem.

Dr. Jung: Yes, the heavenly Jerusalem is a white city. And there is another example. You know Christianity does not cover the whole world; there are religions that are greater than Christianity in numbers and perhaps also in ideas; Brahmanism, for instance. The city of Brahman is the highest city in the world; it is a huge city upon the Himalayas. I think it is made of diamonds — something gleaming white — and it is on a mountain whose sides are supported by four other mountains. . . . This idea of the city of Brahman — which means Brahma himself, of course — is very much older than Christianity. . . . Now what is this city?

Answer: It is a symbol of individuation.

Dr. Jung: Yes . . . the white celestial city conveys the idea of the final, definite, and complete condition, the idea of the goal.

Comment: Again it is a collective symbol, not an individual or isolated thing. One might suppose the refuge would be for oneself alone, but it is there for everyone.

Dr. Jung: Exactly, but we must look at it first from the standpoint of its belonging to her exclusively, because she does not know yet that the thing that seems to be hers alone is the most collective thing of all. That idea comes very much later; the first realization is of the innermost thing, the absolutely unique thing that belongs only to oneself. That this thing should also be collective is a terrible paradox. . . . We cannot get around that, but we can say, in order to mitigate the paradox, that in speaking of it we make it collective inasmuch as it is a word; inasmuch as it is a fact we can never make it collective. But this is a bit difficult; so we had better stay for the present with the symbolic or metaphorical formula of the thing that she sees beyond, with the idea of the heavenly Jerusalem. Is there any one of you who knows the outlines of that celestial city?

Question: Is it not a mandala?

Dr. Jung: Can you prove it? We must read the Bible or we shall not understand psychology. Our psychology, our whole lives, our language and imagery are built upon the Bible. Again and again one comes across it in the unconscious of people who know practically nothing of it; yet these metaphors are in their dreams because they are in our blood. Now I will read you some news.

> And I John saw the holy city, new Jerusalem coming down from God out of heaven, prepared as a bride adorned for her husband. (Rev. XXI:2)

You know the mandala is a *yoni*, a female symbol; it is a bride.

> And there came unto me one of the seven angels which had the seven vials full of the seven last plagues, and talked with me, saying, Come hither, I will show thee the bride, the Lamb's wife.

> And he carried me away in the spirit to a great and high mountain, and shewed me that great city, the holy Jerusalem, descending out of heaven from God. (Rev. XXI: 9-10)

[Here Dr. Jung read the entire description of the celestial city. – Ed.]

That is a most beautiful mandala symbol, the foursquare symbol, the four corners; it is a square like the cloister in the center of the Buddhist mandala. The mandala is the symbol of individuation, so the white city is the city of individuation; it is the perfect abode, the eternal dwelling place that knows no sun and no moon. The same is said in the *Bridhadāranyaka Upanishad*. There, in a conversation which I will shorten a bit, the king asks the sage Yanjavalkya:

> "By what light does a man go out and do his work and return?" And the sage replies, "By the light of the sun." "But if the light of the sun is put out?" the king asks. "By the light of the moon." "And if the

light of the moon is put out? " the king asks. "By the light of the fire." "And if the fire is put out? " the king persists. "Then," the sage replies, "the man will go out and do his work and return home by the light of the self."

No sun or moon is needed because the city itself is made of pure light.

This is surely the light of consciousness but it is a symbol of the consciousness which is not ego-consciousness. That collective aspect of the city comes from the fact that a city is never one ego alone, but a multitude. So we come up against the tremendous paradox. The Self means the inmost uniqueness and oneness of this particular being, yet that is symbolized by a city. This is an early Christian idea also. One finds it in the famous fragments of papyrus that date from the first century A.D. and that were excavated at Oxyrhynchus in the beginning of the twentieth century. In a talk between Christ and the disciples, they ask him first how they shall get to the Kingdom of Heaven and he explains in that wonderful passage about the animals leading them there. Then he says, "Strive therefore to know yourselves, and ye shall be aware that ye are the sons of the Father; ye shall know that ye are in the City of God, and ye are the City."

Question: Is this not an exact parallel to the Indian conception of Atman-Brahman as the spark of life eternal within man, to find which in oneself is the most individual experience and at the same time the most collective one, since Brahman is life in all creation and beyond creation?

Dr. Jung: It is exactly the same thing. It is also absolutely in accordance with the evangelical teaching that the Kingdom of Heaven is within ourselves. It is our innermost nature and not in the least what certain theologians want to make of it, something between ourselves and other people. To say that the Kingdom of Heaven is between people — like cement — is degenerate theology. No, it is the entire man, the completeness, the wholeness of the individual, and that is not identical with the ego; the ego is never the Self, it does not include the whole man at all. . . . That is why we have neuroses: the ego-consciousness is too narrow. Whatever the strange non-ego consists of, it is quite certain that our ego-consciousness is not sufficient to cover all of it. So the symbol for the Self conveys an idea of a totality that is not identical with the ego. It is a consciousness that is not exactly our consciousness, a light that is not exactly our light.

That agrees with what I said formerly: that these visions are psychological processes having nothing to do with the conscious ego life; they are manifestations of the psychological non-ego. It is, one might say, a widening out of the ego-consciousness into the vision of *absolute* consciousness, or non-indi-

157

vidual consciousness, the consciousness that is beyond man. This sounds terribly abstract or metaphysical, but it is by no means metaphysical. It simply means the development of a wider and more abstract consciousness which is related to the other narrower, more concrete consciousness in the same way that algebra is to arithmetic, for instance, or abstract thinking to ordinary everyday thinking. So our patient's vision of the city beyond the giant is the intuition of a consciousness beyond ordinary ego-consciousness, a more complete, a more perfect, a more detached consciousness. For in the white city, one is surely in a state that is fortified against the surrounding destruction; the city has always conveyed the idea of a fortified place, surrounded by walls and towers and moats, inside which one is protected. I do not want to say any more at this point about the symbol of the Self as a collective symbol; our text here does not justify us in going so far.

Dwarfs Are Mythological

VISION (cont.): I said to the giant again, "I must pass you," but he only laughed. (Evidently this vision of the white city is not enough to help her.) While he laughed many dwarfs sprang up from the earth and tore my clothes from me and I was left naked.

Where do the dwarfs suddenly come from and what do they mean?
Answer: From the earth. They are instinctive factors.
Dr. Jung: Dwarfs are peculiar. They are more than just instincts.
Suggestion: Chthonic forces?
Dr. Jung: Yes, but also the dwarf is mythological. The dwarf against the giant, David and Goliath, the thumbling against the great man. In antiquity dwarfs were thumblings and they were also called *dactyli*, which means fingers. You see they are more than just instincts; animals of all kinds would symbolize instincts, but dwarfs are mythological, which is something else. The instincts come up from the earth, very often in the form of snakes or other animals, but mythological beings also come up from the earth. Now the dwarfs tear off her clothes until she stands naked. . . . To elucidate such a thing one needs knowledge, one must study the literature about dwarfs. What do they do in mythology?
Answers: Dwarfs are clever. They are creative. They are imps. And also they are the helpful *cabiri*.
Dr. Jung: Orginally the dwarfs were teachers. They taught people the preparation of ore and all sorts of arts and crafts. They were supposed to have a particular wisdom, and therefore they often have an educational

significance. The youth Horus was educated by the dwarf Bes, for instance.
And Siegfried was brought up by Mimir. They really represent the wisdom
that is buried in the earth, the extraordinary cunning and craft of nature.
They are always keepers of the secret treasures in the earth. They hide the
treasures; they know where the precious stones are. There you get the connection with the Self. But why do they tear the clothes off this woman?

Answer: Because she has hesitated to be true to herself against public
opinion.

Dr. Jung: Yes, she has kept up appearances, worn certain clothes, adopted certain external attitudes – she has kept up all that to ingratiate herself
with public opinion. But naked, she is nature. Things will change, public
opinion will collapse when she has the forces of nature on her side, the innate
spirit of things.

Question: Why do you say they are the innate spirit of things?

Dr. Jung: Well, in one connection they are the so-called *Kanopoi*. These
are the spirits of vessels, of amphoras and pots and so on. There was an idea
that the ancestral spirits lived in the household vessels. This probably came
from the fact that in old civilizations the dead were buried in great wine jars
or in the kind of amphoras that were used to hold grain. In Peru, as well as
in the Near East, such vessels were used for burial, or, if the bodies were
burned, the ashes were put into amphoras.

Perhaps that is the rational origin of this idea, but we have another much
better psychological explanation of why the dwarfs may be thought of as
the spirit in things in the peculiar fact that, according to legend, they were
always doing the housework. For instance, when a woman was kind and put
something aside for them – a drop of milk perhaps – and when she wasn't
curious, particularly about their feet, then in the night they would clean the
house with brush and water. When she got up in the morning it would all
be done, all cleaned by the brownies, the dwarfs – the German word for
them is *Heinzelmänner*. There is a beautiful drama called *Der tote Tag*,
written by a German artist named Barlach – he is not a writer, he is a sculp-
tor or painter – about the spirits of things; he gives them names, he calls
the ones who go about cleaning the house in the night by a German name
that means broom-legs.

The real origin of this peculiar animation of objects is psychological; it
comes from the fact that our psychology in the beginning is by no means
our psychology, everything is psychical through *participation mystique*.
That means by projection, you might say, but it is never done by projection.
Nothing has ever been projected; that is a wrong conception really; the term

projection is wrong. Such a psychological content always has been outside, it never was inside. A so-called projection is simply a thing which is discovered to be outside and then integrated by the discoverer with himself. Our psychology was all found outside, it never was in our pockets to begin with. And that's how it is with the primitive; his whole psychological functioning is exteriorized; it is identical with things and the things are his mind . . . his thoughts are spread like a network over the whole country.

Any country with old traditions has that network of the unconscious over it; we still have places in Switzerland with legends attached to them. If you say to a peasant that you will give him twenty francs if he will tell you all the local legends, he doesn't know what you are talking about. But in the evening, over a glass of beer and a pipe, he is likely to say, "That is a bad place over there. A man has built a stable there but he should not have done so. He will have trouble." If you ask why, he will repeat that the place is not good, there is something bad about it. That is folklore, local legend. They have agreed upon projecting a part of their psychology, a certain psychological effect, upon a certain place, and if you happen to buy that land and build a stable there, you associate with it and it becomes a psychical fact. It is a part of the general unconscious of the people which is still alive.

So to the primitive, not only his land, his rivers, woods, and hills are alive, but also his personal belongings, his spears, swords, canoes, whatever belongs to him, and that goes so far that it is even expressed in the language. In all primitive languages there are prefixes and suffixes to express whether an object is living or dead. Instead of simply speaking of "an ashtray," you must always say whether the ashtray is male or female or neuter, living or dead. Even in German or French you have to say *der Aschenbecher*, showing that it is a masculine ashtray, and in a primitive language you would have to say *der Aschenbecher lebendig*, the masculine ashtray living. If it belongs to me it is living, if it belongs to you it is dead. In certain languages you have to go even further and say whether it is upright or lying down, whether it is inside or outside; if you speak about it at all you must say: ashtray, male, alive, upright, inside the house.

All this shows the origin of dwarfs; they are the spirit of objects. . . . The dwarfs are the last representatives of that original mental condition, where objects were *my* life, or where *my* life was the objects. And those psychological parts, the dwarfs, become personified because each is part of the psyche. . . . Lunatics hear voices coming from objects, from the smallest things, perhaps even from matches, as if they were small human beings. Therefore it is extremely difficult to convince such people that the voices are not real, which makes them almost incurable. If they can get past that stage, if the personality becomes synthesized again, they can realize that the voices were something outside; but as long as the voices go on speaking they cling to the conviction that they are real. . . . One sees the same thing in mediums or in very sensitive people. They have one door still open, one part of their mind is not theirs, it is outside in an object and it knows what the object knows. Such a person can produce one's own thoughts, as if he were in possession of one's goods, so to speak. From the experience of people like that one can draw conclusions about conditions in early times when the human mind was still in objects. Then man had only to perceive and apply what was suggested to him by the things themselves. One hears remarks of this kind from artists, even now, if they are a bit primitive: that certain materials suggest such and such forms and so on.

Now out of these facts the ideas concerning dwarfs have come. On a higher level — in modern times — the dwarfs have been obliterated as domestic spirits, but psychologically they are still there; that is, they are not yet part of the ego-consciousness. It is questionable whether they can ever become part of it. But they are no longer found in objects; they are now in our unconscious where they are the equivalent of objects, and there they function psychologically in the same way as objects functioned before, namely, as spontaneous suggestions, which may be either helpful or injurious. Of course you can say that nothing was suggested to you, that it just happened to come into your mind; since you cannot trace the origin of the suggestion, you are inclined to deny that it has been suggested; you think that seems almost pathological and that you will be accused of hearing voices or of depending on things you cannot admit. But they *are* voices, no matter how you understand them. Here we have such a case: these helpful powers are suggesting that this woman should appear naked. And we said that being naked means being as she really is with no particular adornment, no particular fuss and conventional make-up, to deceive others or herself. She should just be as she is with no veil. Now why should that be necessary? Remember she wants to pass the giant who stands in her way to the white city.

Answer: The giant is made of essentially the same stuff as her clothes; if she takes off her clothes it will take away his power.

Dr. Jung: That is it. Her clothes are also a persona, and throwing that veil or deception away would be what is called sympathetic magic — a charm by analogy. To produce rain by magic, one sprinkles water or milk or blood on the ground; or one imitates the sound of wind or rain in order to create the mood of rain. . . . So by throwing away the thing in her that is like the obstacle, she would be throwing away or overcoming the obstacle.

Bluff

VISION (cont.): I threw stones at the giant, blinding him in one eye. Still he stood. I stabbed him in the breast many times. Still he stood. I looked up into the sky and beheld a star which sent down rays to my forehead and the crescent moon descended upon my head. "Behold," I said to the giant. But still he stood.

... It all makes no impression on the giant; he is not put off apparently. ... Even when, very naively, she points to a crescent on her head, it does not work. Now what would it indicate that she has a crescent on her head?

Answer: That she is the Goddess of the moon.

Dr. Jung: Nothing less! But it makes no impression upon the giant and the reason is that it is just bunk, it is not real. She could never be a moon-Goddess, that is mere inflation; she is trying to bluff him. You know certain people when they are up against their own fear or public opinion quickly identify with one divinity or another hoping for help; but it is no help because it is just bunk. So the identification with the moon-Goddess proves to be useless. ...

It is something like a fascination that comes over her; she is caught in her own concepts, in her own words; she has a feeling of divinity through an inflation from the unconscious. Her continuous preoccupation with these unconscious contents has given her a sense of power and importance, which is quite apart from the usual little effects, the little vanity of being able to produce something of interest to the analyst. The other thing, the inflation one gets from occupying oneself with the collective unconscious, is much stronger. After a while one gets the feeling that it is all rather simple and very beautiful; that one must be very gifted to see such marvelous things, that it must be a divine influx filling one with such pictures. Also the idea that it is all coming up from one's own creative depths indicates that one is perhaps the originator; so slowly an identification with the deity filters into one's psychology whether one likes it or not. With due modesty one says, "Of course I am not a God, but it is wonderful after all what one can do, what beautiful things one sees." ... Then when a difficulty comes, one falls back on being Napoleon, or something like that. It is a sort of unconscious readiness to bluff.

This is quite legitimate up to a certain point, but here it will not help, because that giant is not human and cannot be killed with ordinary bluff. For the bluff is made of the same stuff as the giant. He knows all about it. Once more she is wearing a garment, a divine veil; this time a divine nakedness. ... Quantities of people would do the same at such a moment.

Even when there is no particular difficulty to face, people are apt to remind themselves of their own greatness and importance. We had a very nice
case here in Zürich — I really should tell the story in Swiss — which shows
the bluff and the self-importance on a very small scale. Once a very popular
man here met some boys in the street playing ball and he played with them
very foolishly. Then after a while he could contain himself no longer, he
found it too marvelous that he, such a man, should have bowed down to
play with these little creatures in the street; they ought at least to be able to
tell about it at home. So he said to one of the boys, "Do you know with
whom you are playing? Do you know who I am? " The boy replied, "Oh,
yes, you are a — " — well, the equivalent of a jackass; we have a marvelous
word for it in Swiss: *Löli.* You see the child saw through the veil.

The White Bird Helps Her

VISION (cont.): Then I saw a faun who beckoned me into the woods and
gave me a goblet to drink. When I had drunk a great strength entered into
me and I returned to the giant. A white bird flew at the giant's throat, sucking the blood therefrom until he sank to the ground. Then I stepped over
the body and walked into the white city. The light was blinding, the white
stones hurt my feet.

The faun suggests an antique reminiscence; it is a regression into the
woods. She goes back into the Dionysian mentality: therefore the goblet
which belongs to the cult of Dionysos, the blood or the wine. And that
touch of the earth is sufficient to give her the necessary strength to overcome
the giant. Not that it is she who does it; it is the white bird that flies at him.
What about this white bird?

Answer: It is the spirit that was once killed by the Indian.

Dr. Jung: And later it flew down to the Great Mother figure. Here we
have that bird again after the Dionysian intermezzo. . . . It appears, not as
her possession, but as the typical helpful animal, apparently because she followed the beckoning faun. Drinking the blood meant a re-identification
with nature . . . and after this nature proved helpful, sending the white bird.
In modern Christian psychology a white bird always has an association with
the Holy Ghost, but it is difficult to understand how the Holy Ghost can
enter the scene here at all . . . when a Dionysian mystery has been celebrated.

Question: Can you look upon it as the result of the union between her
and the Dionysian?

Dr. Jung: We must; it *is* the result. The animals become helpful because
she has been reconciled to nature, but how is it possible that the Holy Ghost
should enter the scene after that faun episode? That is hard to explain.

Answer: The spirit is also a part of nature.

Dr. Jung: Are you conscious of what you say? The spirit as a part of nature! I hope we have no theologians here! But I am quite of your opinion; I am certain that there would be no spirit if it were not a part of nature.

Comment: So it would undergo the same laws as nature generally.

Dr. Jung: By what principle would you explain that or make it plausible? Well, we must not forget that *les extremes se touchent*, which means that when we reach one extreme, in the very next minute we encounter the other. It is the law of *enantiodromia*, the law of Heraclitus, that when things have reached their culmination they transform into their opposite. That is the teaching of the *I Ching*. So this woman goes to one extreme with that faun, back into a pre-Christian cult, and in that moment the turn comes. . . .

In an instant the situation is quite transformed, the bird is really the nature spirit, and that is the Holy Ghost. The Holy Ghost is always expressed by a natural thing, either by fire or by a bird. Jesus said it was the animals that led you to the Kingdom. I will read you again that passage from the Oxyrhynchus papyrus:

> Jesus sayeth, ye ask who are those that draw us to the kingdom if the kingdom is in Heaven? The fowls of the air and all beasts that are under the earth or upon the earth, and the fishes of the sea, these are they that will draw you into the Kingdom. The Kingdom of Heaven is within you; and whoever shall know himself shall find it.

Without realizing the animal that is within you, how could you ever understand yourself? Yet you avoid the knowledge of yourself. And if you ask why, the answer is: on account of the giant. You can only know yourself if you really get into yourself, and you can only do that if you accept the lead of the animal. . . . So one could say that through that regression to the Dionysian point of view, through contact with the earth, the miracle of Antaeus has occurred. The giant Antaeus, as the son of the earth, was so strong when in contact with it that he could not be overcome, but when Hercules lifted him up he became powerless and Hercules overcame him easily. Getting down to earth means strength; then one touches facts that cannot be denied. And instantly when the earth is touched the other phenomenon belonging to nature comes up; the compensating phenomenon is the spirit. Therefore one finds them together in the Dionysian cult. . . .

There is nothing without spirit, for spirit seems to be the inside of things. Dionysos is concerned with the outside of things, with tangible forms, with everything that is made of earth, but inside is the spirit, which is the soul of objects. Whether that is our own psyche or the psyche of the universe we don't know, but if one touches the earth one cannot avoid the spirit. And if one touches it in the friendly way of Dionysos, the spirit of nature will be helpful; if in an unfriendly way, the spirit of nature will oppose one. Therefore the countless legends of people who have offended the spirits of things.

That the white bird sucks the blood of the giant means that the power of public opinion is completely hollowed out by the spirit. The spirit is that which makes us free; this woman is instantly freed from the weight of convention when she is helped by the natural spirit. Without it she is quite powerless. Now what is the spirit? That is the question. Well, the spirit is really a certain attitude – one speaks, for example, of doing something in a certain spirit, or of being moved by a certain spirit, meaning a sort of general idea or archetype. But it is not made by man; no idea made by man can move one. The best this woman could do was the moon-Goddess idea; that was her own invention and it proved to be completely ineffective. But if the bird is on her side the giant collapses; that is, when a natural spiritual attitude is present, it works immediately; it is as if the giant had never existed and as if there had never been any conventions.

Now it is necessary to have conventions; nothing would be more foolish than to destroy them. They would never have come to be if they were not really needed. And it is right to collapse before convention; we are meant to. Otherwise we could not overcome the giant, or if we did, it would do no good, it would always be too early in life. It is much better that we collapse, for thus we remain at least in an orderly condition. To fight convention by futile arguments and attacks upon society only leads us into a new convention worse than the one before. We really cannot circumvent it. The only thing that may break conventions is the spirit; it is worthwhile to break conventions for a new spirit. To oppose convention for a whim or a fad is nothing but foolish destruction if we succeed at all. But for the spirit it is something else. Spirit is constructive; out of spirit something can come, because it is a living thing and a fertilizing thing. So, naturally, it has a great advantage over mere conventions. Convention is never creative but spirit is always creative. You can find this psychology in the Epistles of St. Paul; everything that I am saying here he has already said.

The Light of the Heavenly City is Blinding

When the giant collapses she steps over his body and walks into the white city, that is, she arrives at the Self, and one could expect here something very impressive. But the light is blinding and the white stones hurt her feet. So her arrival in the white city, which should have been a sort of triumphal entrance, is not so wonderful.

Suggestion: She cannot stand it yet. She is not ready for it.

Dr. Jung: But why not? Probably she has had an illusion. When she saw the white city from the distance, she naturally thought, as anybody would, "There is the place of rest, the place of completion, the real goal." But the vision says, "By no means." Well, that is often the case. It is the Christian prejudice to connect the idea of a perfect, almost paradisiacal condition with the idea of redemption. . . . But in reality it is not so simple as that. The Self can be, and very often is, the most difficult task; it is almost insupportable. That is why people avoid it; they do their level best not to become acquainted with themselves, because everything else seems to be easier.

It is as if people had a very clear notion of the Self and therefore avoided it most carefully, for if they became acquainted with it they would probably run into trouble. That is also anticipated in the Christian legend — we learned it there — because, for us, Jesus was the first man to show what happens when one becomes oneself. And we are not ready to go so far as that. He got into terrible trouble and his real followers got into trouble too; they died in the arena [and in other disagreeable ways]. . . . Our arenas are of a much subtler nature. Things are getting very psychical in our time, far less visible — in and out of backyards and around corners — the torture is much more refined. But life has not become easier in any way.

The fact that the stones hurt her feet and the light dazzles her simply shows that she is not at all ready to meet the light or to accept it; she is not capable of standing that dazzling consciousness. One would have thought — and she certainly must have expected — that having overcome the giant, who appeared to be the greatest obstacle, her entrance into the white city would be like the entrance of a Christian into the heavenly Jerusalem. . . . But heaven is by no means suitable for everybody. . . . Some particular achievement or accomplishment is demanded to make the heavenly conditions satisfactory. At all events, she found the new situation unsympathetic. But then she suddenly saw something and what she saw probably explains her condition: why she was not up to that whiteness and did not feel particularly redeemed.

(illus. 14) VISION: I beheld a crowd worshipping a golden bull which stood upon a pedestal. The bull asked, "Where did you lose yourself, woman? " I answered, "I could not pass the giant until I had drunk of the goblet." The bull said, "From that goblet you shall forever renew your strength. Drink again." So I drank from a goblet which had been left upon the pedestal as a libation. When I had done so the bull descended and lay down beside me.

166

This is apparently the Mithraic bull God — or the golden calf: a reference, of course, to Apis, the Egyptian bull God. The fact that he is golden would suggest the worship of the sun bull, which is extremely archaic. It belongs to the period between two and four thousand B.C. and no one would expect it to appear in the heavenly city which should be a place of perfect consciousness. If the bull is still there, of course she can't stand the white city upon the world mountain. The heavenly Jerusalem, the city of God, or the city of the Self, naturally has nothing to do with such a very chthonic, archaic cult, You see this simply points to the fact that something in her of a very earthy nature is resisting the idea of the white city. Now what would you say of a person who had such a vision?

Answer: I think she would be unequally developed.

Dr. Jung: Yes, there is an enormous gap between her far-reaching introverted intuition and her real situation. This goblet containing the life-giving substance, the blood or the wine, emphasizes the cult of the bull and suggests something in complete contradiction to the idea of a heavenly city. . . . What is strengthened in her when she drinks the bull's blood — that libation?

Answer: The chthonic side of her nature, the instinctual side.

Dr. Jung: In other words, everything that characterized the cult of Dionysos, who was a bull, mind you. The Thracian form of Dionysos was Zagreus; he is called Dionysos Zagreus. The legend is that he was chased by the Titans and transformed himself into all sorts of animals in order to escape them. Finally they caught him in the form of a bull and tore him to shreds and put him into a caldron and feasted on him; but Zeus, suddenly discovering what they had done, rescued a part of him, the still-living heart, and sewed it into his thigh. That is one version; the other is that he ate it; in either case Zeus gave him rebirth. . . . Zagreus is the most typical form of the dismembered God, the dismembered chthonic powers, and he also symbolizes fertilization and the sacrificial death. . . .

So this bull advises our patient to drink from the goblet of life, which takes her entirely away from the white city — it is not yet the time for the city. . . . Nobody goes into the heavenly Jerusalem with his body, and she is not yet dead; therefore she had better live on the earth and drink of the wine of life. If she lives her life, in time she will be able to reach the heavenly condition, but not yet. The intuitive type very often forgets this; when he sees through his telescope the top of the distant mountain, he assumes that he is already there; his intuition — his telescope — takes him there; but he is miles away, four or five thousand meters below the top, and the whole work of climbing has still to be done.

One discovers now the useful role of the giant and understands why he was so unshakeable; he wanted to keep her here in this life until she could fly past him as a ghost. It also explains the Holy Ghost bird that sucked the giant's lifeblood till he was depleted and collapsed. The idea is that the ghost can overcome the giant, but a living human being cannot; as long as she is in a body she cannot pass the giant, but if she transforms into a spirit she can pass him easily. To the body, that abode she is looking for is obviously an impossible place, so the apparition of the bull is a sort of compensation to an intuitive attempt to shrink from life, to funk life.

The Bull Lies Down Beside Her

When she has drunk of the goblet the bull descends from his pedestal and lies down beside her. . . . The divine power is now domesticated, and it becomes domesticated through what?

Answer: Acceptance. She drank again which meant that she accepted life.

Dr. Jung: Yes, by the acceptance of life as it is this divine power becomes domesticated. Is it not a peculiar idea?

Answer: No, for in a way it is assimilated.

Dr. Jung: How can you assimilate a divine power?

Answer: Very much as the Titans did Zagreus.

Dr. Jung: Well, I would say, just as we are able to eat the Host, we are able to eat the God. Eating the Gods was a royal prerogative of the Pharaohs, the idea has become the most familiar religious rite, the Communion. . . . That really started from the totemic meals, where the totem animal was eaten, and in the course of thousands of years, it degenerated into the idea of eating the God in a more ordinary form. Then at later stages it developed into the idea of killing and eating the king, and the killing of kings led naturally to the Christian legend of killing the Son of God. There the two things came together, eating the totem animal and killing the king; Christ is the king that is killed, therefore Iesus Nazarenus Rex Judaeorum, INRI, is on all crucifixes, and then he is eaten. An old cannibalistic idea becomes the central idea of the Communion. . . . The God is not only killed, he is also distributed among the crowd and assimilated. . . .

The whole complex of legends is very mysterious, but this analogous phantasy elucidates it. You see, by drinking the wine, by accepting the earthly life as it is, she overcomes the divine power that is in the instincts. That is, the instincts have an overwhelming strength, but only if one opposes them. If one accepts life as it comes, one is with them, then one doesn't feel the impact of a resistance. It is like traveling in a balloon in a hurricane: as long as one is going with the wind, one hardly feels it; one can strike a match and light a cigarette, or a candle will burn steadily; but if a balloon should try to go against the impact of the storm, it would be torn into shreds in no time. Or it is like a boat on a swift river: if it goes with the current, it is quite easy, but against the current it is hard pulling. So if one accepts the instincts of life, there is no trouble; it is like paradise, even when a bull settles down beside one; but if it should not be a paradise, if one knows too much, one is up against the instincts and there is trouble.

That is why so many people dream of bulls, of a wild bull chasing them perhaps, and it is always when they are up against an instinct — whatever it may be. It is not always sexuality. People assume when they dream of being persecuted by a bull that it is repressed sexuality but this is by no means true. When one sins against one's collective instinct, for instance, against one's adaptation to collective conditions, one may be persecuted by a bull representing the herd instinct. The bull may even represent the police.

So here, when the bull comes down from the pedestal, its instinctual earthly power is no longer divine; that is, it is not necessary for it to be divine, it doesn't claim her worship because she has now accepted it, it becomes simply a part of her life and there is nothing divine about it. We may now assume that something will become the divine principle, or that the divine principle will take another form.

VISION (cont.): Upon the pedestal a green tree shot up. In the tree were many birds. I lifted my hands to them, and they descended upon me.

The bull is now succeeded by a tree, and that means what? . . . Well, first the bull is the divine principle and there she accepts it, drinks the blood, and becomes a friend of the bull. She is now just a cow, an animal. This idea was often expressed in ancient cults. For instance, the followers of Artemis called themselves *arctoi* (bears) because the bear was one of her hunting animals. Then in the Mithraic cult, the initiates were divided into four separate classes or degrees [the lowest of which were called lions and eagles]. . . . In practically every religion there are such hierarchies, but the animal designations would be only in the very old cults. So this woman would be a divine cow, which explains her identification before with Isis, the moon-Goddess who, as Hathor, was crowned with crescent-shaped cowhorns. . . .

169

The Many Birds

I don't know whether you can fully appreciate the real meaning of such an analogy. You see, it is a matter, as I keep repeating, not of the ego in this woman's psychology, but of the non-ego; it is the non-ego with which she is concerned. We are dealing with an impersonal psyche, not her personal psychology; it is the development — or the transformation, one could say — of her unconscious, but she is not that unconscious. The unconscious comes to her and it is her task to behave toward it — to do whatever is necessary — so that it may become transformed through her conscious attitude. It is as if she had the sacred task of changing a certain part of the unconscious — a sort of mission, one could say — the task of domesticating or transforming the unconscious. And what she sees in these visions is a part of that great work, which is done in her and through her to transform the blind powers of the collective unconscious into something conscious, something like man — or like unto man. But it never becomes man himself; it transcends man.

Here we see an important stage of the transformation of the impersonal psyche that is going on in this woman: she accepts the divine power of the instincts in the form of the bull and so she necessarily becomes a cow. She is quite glad to accept her identity with Isis, to have the crescent upon her head, and to say to the giant, "Now behold me." But she would not have assumed that to say, "Now behold me, I am a cow," would have made much impression upon him — although it probably would have made more than just being a Goddess. As a matter of fact it is the same. If one has a feeling for animals and looks into the eyes of a cow, one sees that it has a peculiar sad expression. We project our melancholy into the eyes of animals and we have reason to feel sad because we see there nothing but an animal. On the other hand, that "nothing but" is also a great thing. One actually does behold something divine in the eyes of the animal, for one sees there the expression of the creative will and the creative spirit. So, in being a cow, she would be just as the archaic woman was — not only an animal, but also a sharer of divinity.

Comment: A cow has the quality of docility.

Dr. Jung: Yes, it is not only accepting the fact of being a cow, but also becoming docile like a cow, which is a higher form of the same idea; to the Chinese, cowlike docility is the way of Tao. Therefore the acceptance of cowlike docility, which to every modern woman is a most loathsome idea, is nevertheless the nearest way to perfection. This woman's acceptance, through partaking of the blood or the wine, has led her into the animal condition, into the rhythm of the animal kingdom. But the bull is succeeded by the tree. So now the only thing that is still divine to her, that means strength — standing by her and compensating her — is the plant, the tree. And this symbolizes an entirely different principle from the animal. . . .

[Plant life as symbolizing the principle of spiritual life and growth was taken up by Dr. Jung earlier in this series of seminars. A great part of the excerpts in Part Three dealt with this subject. Here he recalls what was said there. — Ed.]

Our patient seems to be invoking the birds that live in the branches of the tree for now they descend upon her. What would the birds be?

Answer: Her intuitions.

Dr. Jung: Yes, but why intuitions? Is there another idea?

Suggestion: Would they not be more the representatives of the Holy Ghost?

Dr. Jung: Many little Holy Ghosts! I think that would be depreciating the Holy Ghost a bit; if there are so many little editions, he loses his uniqueness.

Suggestion: Messengers, as it were?

Dr. Jung: I think that is a bit too nice, they might be very ordinary birds. She says, "I lifted up my hands to them and they descended upon me." Do you remember that famous man in the Jardin des Tuileries with the sparrows? He holds out crumbs to them and they descend upon him but there is nothing of the Holy Ghost there. And you have often seen pictures where pigeons are lighting upon women but we do not assume that they are Holy Ghosts; we have rather a carnal worldly idea about them, for those white pigeons are what?

Answer: Symbols of peace?

Dr. Jung: Oh, Mr. Ford was the main originator of that peace idea — the famous ship with the white doves.

Suggestion: They are the birds of Venus.

Dr. Jung: Yes, the dove is the bird of Astarte, the Goddess of love — it is a very unholy bird. I remember a woman who was living at the Hotel Sonne in Küsnacht once complained about the very indecent behavior of the pigeons there; she discovered why they were called the birds of Venus. They are really very erotic. So it is funny that such a bird should be the Holy Ghost; it shows something very interesting about female nature, also a bit of the hidden story of the Holy Ghost, originally called Sophia. Sophia is the Greek word for wisdom, and in the early church the Holy Ghost was understood to be Sophia, the female corresponding to the male God, the wife of God, and the mother of the Redeemer. Later on that view was designated as heresy, but there are still traces of it. And one is the dove.

Now that figure of wisdom is a maternal figure; it is the highest form of the anima, one could say — the spiritual woman, or the universal mother; yet according to Gnostic teaching, Sophia was the last to take form in a rather scandalous series of women. . . . There were four stages in that series. Chawwa, or Eve, the primordial earthy mother, is the first; the second is Helen of Troy — as you know she was a woman with a pretty bad reputation, but symbolically she is the second stage of the universal mother. The third stage is Mary, the Mother of God. That is most shocking. The church hated the idea and so it was repressed. . . . Yet that story has been preserved in the old Gnostic fragments, and it can be interpreted as the true and unadulterated development of the anima. The first form of a man's anima is his mother, Eve, the mother of all human beings; and the series culminates in Sophia. It is a Western form of the Kundalini Yoga.[8]

. . . Now our patient is moving somewhere between Helen and Mary, but in the opposite sense; she has not developed up from Eve but is really coming down. The situation is reversed; she is coming down because our civilization only goes about as far down as Mary, and below that it is all unconscious; we imagine that everything is in heaven and has no roots in the earth. And because things don't have roots in the earth they have no sap, they are dried up with living; but through analysis, or through opening up the gates of Hades, the sap begins to rise again. . . . It is as if all the canals were filled up with the original liquid; when the contact with the earth is re-established, the blood comes up, the sap rises and fills the remotest branches of the tree once more. Certainly that tree must be living because it is alive with birds, and they are symbols, winged beings, which since time immemorial have meant psychic facts, what one calls thoughts or ideas or intuitions. Anything that has to do with the mind has an air quality. As fishes are always contents of the sea, the unconscious, so birds are the contents of the mind or the spirit or the air — mental facts.

The tree is the same that we encountered in a former vision. There she was transformed into a tree, she was identical with it, whilst here it appears as a detached vision. This is the tree of yoga, the natural growth of the relationship between the conscious and the unconscious — or the tree of knowledge, of wisdom, which naturally contains thoughts. So as soon as her development reaches the stage of the tree, it begins to function through the birds — the results of the life of the tree. This vision ends with the statement that she is now filled with thoughts. But we don't know what thoughts.

Many Men Marching

VISION: I beheld many men marching; I stood with other people beside
the road watching them pass. They cried in a loud voice, "We are the way."
Then I entered into the ranks of the marching men. They led me up on a
high mountain. There they dissolved and I stood alone in the snow.

Do you see the continuity with the vision before?

Answer: They are like the many birds.

Dr. Jung: Yes, many birds or many thoughts are here many men; and
many men means of course the animus, who is, as you know, a multitude.
... [But] it makes a great difference whether the thoughts appear in the form
of birds or in the form of men. ...

Remark: The opposite sex is constellated.

Dr. Jung: Yes, there is attraction. When things are represented as having
the opposite sex, then there will be attraction; so the thoughts will be attrac-
tive. For as long as they are birds there is very little psychical rapport; they
are very shy and at any time may fly away. But when birds take on human
forms, particularly of the opposite sex, it means that a union is possible. The
unconscious uses that symbolism to express the idea of union or reconciliation, just as the so-called sexual transference is used by the unconscious as
a bridge. Where there is a great gap between the analyst and the patient a
sexual transference appears in order to bridge the gulf; this transference disappears as a compulsory phenomenon as soon as the rapport is established.

Here, the birds appearing in the forms of men have lost their original
strangeness and they approach her. At first she merely watches them, then
she leaves the people by the road and joins their ranks. ... The thoughts
being characterized as a multitude of men, however, probably means that
she is not able to control them. ... Moreover it looks like a parade, a most
collective movement in the mind, almost a thought system. They would
probably be part of a big army, or they might be men representing a powerful, collective public institution; that is, a definite impersonal power which
assimilates her rather than the other way about.

Such things may happen in the mind; people are afraid of the unconscious
because they feel instinctively that there are trains of thought of a strange
collective nature, not personal, which may catch them and carry them away.
Since she cannot control that animus, that body of men, they can leave her
whenever they choose to do so. In this case they dissolve when she has
reached the top of the mountain and leave her alone in the snow. What has
happened?

Answer: She is quite cold and absolutely alone.

Dr. Jung: Well, it is synonomous: to be cold and alone are the same. For being in the herd, or being surrounded by human beings, always has about it something of that very remote time when we were monkeys sitting on a branch close together. That is why people often feel particularly well in a crowd, especially when they are pressed together — it reminds them of those days. It is not only because of a gregarious instinct but for the physical warmth itself. Most people don't ordinarily admit this peculiarity, but it is an animal instinct to like the physical warmth of other hairy bodies. . . . So being left alone on top of a mountain, isolated in the snow, simply means absence of any human contact, means that she is deprived of animal warmth. Naturally, the animus is apt to lead a woman to an unhuman region where no human warmth is provided, because the animus is not human. . . .

[To understand why this vision comes to her now, we must go back to her inability to stand the white city, and to the vision of the bull and the drinking of the blood, the libation, that came just before. – Ed.]

Bull worship is always an earthy cult and astrologically the bull is an earthly sign; Taurus is the house in which Venus dwells. So she has been down on the level of the earth, partaking of the wine of the earth, the libation poured out to the bull. Then at the end of that vision the yoga tree appeared, from which we may conclude that she was in the *mulādhāra* center, in the roots of the tree. In other words, she was in the sphere of the instincts, in communion with the flesh; she was the divine cow, docile to the intimations of the Gods of nature. . . . So the fact that she is next led up by the animus to isolation on the mountain is a compensatory reaction. . . . Now we shall see what is going to happen next.

The Lion Appears

VISION: A lion appeared to me and I asked, "Why am I here, O lion? " The lion answered, "Because you have taken the way."

This brings us back to the fact that the marching men were all shouting, "We are the way." What does that mean?

Answer: It is just the collective way.

Dr. Jung: Yes, that was not her way, it was the way of the crowd. . . . Those marching men were shouting a system of opinions that claimed to be the way. We know it well. But when it comes to a culmination, such a system of thoughts simply disappears and one finds oneself left high and dry in an unpleasant situation. . . . In this particular case she is to be criticized for following the suggestion of the men. They led her out of the human atmosphere, and it was a mistake for her to be led by them at all. Now the lion comes in as a sort of compensation for the system of thoughts. The lion would represent the instincts. However, a symbol like that should never be designated by such an exceedingly vague word — God knows what we mean by instincts. It is better to follow the intimation of the unconscious and try to characterize the symbol. Why not an eagle or a snake or some other animal? Why just a lion?

Question: Has it anything to do with two different forms of ritual succeeding each other; first a bull belonging to the Magna Mater cult and then the lion in the Mithraic cult?

Dr. Jung: There is an old astrological connection between the bull and the Mother. . . . The bull in astrology is, as I said, the *domicilium Veneris.* The cult of Attis belongs to that great group of Mother cults, Attis was very much the son of the Great Mother; and in that cult the *taurobolium*, an initiation ceremony, was celebrated in the place where the cathedral of St. Peter now stands in Rome. The initiate or candidate was put into a hole in the ground, which was covered with a grating, and on top of that grating the bull was sacrificed; his throat was cut and the initiate underneath smeared himself with the blood which poured down through the grating; it represented the blood of birth, and so of rebirth, baptism. Then the initiate was taken out and fed with milk and given new white garments, he was treated as *quasi modo genitus*, the newborn one, because he was twice born; now he had a soul, he had access to the Gods. So the bull is very much connected with the cult of the Magna Mater.

Mithraism is really one of these cults too. . . . Like Attis, Mithras is the dying and resurrecting God because he himself is the bull; the meaning of the famous bull sacrifice of the Mithraic cult was the sacrifice of man's bulllike passions, or lack of discipline. . . .

The lion does, however, play a curious role in Mithraism, an indecisive, merely symbolical role. . . . In the representations of the bull sacrifice, of the altar stone where the God kills the bull, the lion appears somewhere below the sacrificial scene; it has nothing to do with the ritual above. Sometimes the lion is opposite a serpent with an amphora between them, and it looks as if they were competing as to which would get at the vessel first. Astrologically the lion is the highest position of the sun, the month after the summer solstice, the end of July and the beginning of August, fiery, dry, and terribly hot; the serpent on the other side is cold and humid, a nocturnal

175

creature that creeps in the dark. So there is the pair of opposites again. In one Mithraic representation, the amphora is standing on the ground with a flame rising from it and the lion is in the air above, as if he were just precipitating himself into it. The vessel is the female symbol, the vessel of rebirth, or the *uterus ecclesiae*, so the lion is obviously making for rebirth in the fire.

The vessel is also called the *krater*, coming from the Greek verb *keránnymi*, to mix; it was originally the vessel in which wine and water were mixed. We use the word for the crater of a volcano which holds the fiery liquid lava. The original idea was probably a vessel used in the secret rites occasionally, containing fire or perhaps burning oil, in which magic transformation took place; it was a sort of alchemical melting pot. Possibly the Mithraic lion precipitating himself into the fire of the *krater* was an alchemistic symbol. The idea of plunging into the crater for rebirth is very old. Empedocles, a Greek philosopher, was said to have ended his life in the crater of Aetna; when he became old he threw himself into the flames of the crater in order to be united with the Gods, to be reborn out of the crater of death as a God. We know that the main purpose in those old cults was to be reborn as a God. . . .

As was mentioned before, the members of a certain class or degree in the Mithraic cult were called lions (*leontes*); probably they were those who had not yet undergone trial by fire, who were still to be made over in the *krater*. That is only a conjecture but in all these ancient cults there were the lower degrees, from which people progressed to others, and each time they had to pass through the caldron, through a rebirth ritual, so that they were reborn numbers of times. . . .

Now, obviously, when a modern patient dreams of a lion or produces a picture of a lion, it does not mean any particular lion, it is mythological; therefore we are justified in assuming that the lion in this vision has the generally prevailing meaning of a principle, which is fiery and strong and noble, and that, unlike the lion in the zoo who is anything but royal, it has all the old mythological qualities.

Comment: The lion is just the contrary of the cold snow.

Dr. Jung: That is true. The lion is passionate, fiery, dangerous, and it is exceedingly male. The Chinese Yang principle expresses the quality of the lion; that concept has been really formulated in China but I know of no Western expression that conveys the idea exactly. Of course, the lion does not exist in our philosophical literature but in our unconscious it does exist, and we ought to have a suitable word for it. . . . However, to explain the lion here as the opposite of the serpent in the terms of Chinese philosophy is rather too general an interpretation. . . .

But there is still another aspect of the lion as a symbolic animal. He is the symbol of power. The British lion would be an example. You see him in every issue of *Punch.* The power of imperial Rome was symbolized by a lion; those columns on top of crouching lions at the entrance to Norman churches signify the Christian church built upon, or victorious over, the power of paganism. . . . And the lion as a symbol of power in astrology comes from the fact that it is the sign for the hottest time of the year, when the power of the sun-God, the ruler of heaven, is at its height. Also the lion has been understood to be the strongest animal, excepting the elephant, and to Western people he was much better known than the elephant, which is possibly the reason why he was considered the royal animal. . . .

The lion expressing the idea of power is really the oldest form of the symbol. Many primitive tribes called the chief the lion of the tribe – the Lion of Judah, for example, means the great man of Judah . . . and the kings of Babylonia and Assyria were represented as lion-killers, that is, as stronger than lions, super-lions; so a king wore a lion's skin, just as the King of Abyssinia still wears a crown made from a lion's mane, in order to express his supreme power. You see the lion is really born into us with that meaning.

[Here Dr. Jung interrupted his interpretation to show some pictures from a medieval book about alchemy which also dealt with a combination of lion, bird, and tree symbolism. To perceive the close parallel to the patient's material in these pictures one has only to recall how, after she had partaken of the wine and so entered into communion with the earth, a tree grew up from the pedestal where the bull had stood, and the birds appeared, followed by the symbolic lion.

The first picture (*Figure 1*) shows a tree growing from the head of a naked woman. There is also an eagle on her head and birds are flying up and down around her. She stands on an alchemistic oven, which on either side supports contrivances for distilling a volatile substance, spirit, from crude matter. Their appearance suggests a sex analogy, so apparently the alchemistic process that takes place below in the earth is a sort of sexual process. – Ed.]

Here the birds rise and fall in a peculiar movement which is not indicated in our visions yet, but the picture is nevertheless a close analogy to our situation. On the left of the woman's figure is the symbol of the sun, on the right the moon, referring to the union of male and female (actually, to that alchemistic process), and the accompanying text says that on the left the sun-birds are dying the white death, and on the right the moon-birds are dying the black death.

This idea has also been represented by a tree shedding its leaves, the leaves falling down on the right and the left, and then the process beginning again.

Figure 1
Reproduced in *Psychology and Alchemy*, CW 12.

Figure 2
Originally, like Figure 1, from Hieronymus Reusner's
Pandora, Basel, 1588 (1st edition 1582).

A patient of mine once drew a strange picture which is another parallel. Below is a vessel in which a fire burns with bluish flames, and out of those flames, like the trunk of a tree, there grows a bright column which branches out into a beautiful cascade of light; this then comes down into the fire which flares out again to meet it. That is the circular process, the tree growing out of the fire, then shedding leaves that fall down and feed the fire so that it starts up again. . . . It is a symbolic formula, which one also finds expressed in the antique philosophy of Greece,[9] where it is said that the bull is the serpent's father and the serpent is the bull's father — they are father to each other.

Or one can reverse the idea; the bull generates the serpent and the serpent generates the bull. It is an eternal process which goes on in a cycle. And that is obviously the process that takes place in the unconscious when there is no intervention from consciousness to interrupt it. The birds would fly up and fall down to earth again forever, if man's consciousness did not interfere. The unconscious processes revolve in this mysterious cycle: they rise, they develop, they flourish; they decay, they die, and are swallowed up into chaos; then from chaos they rise again.

One sees the same movement in the dreams of insane people. I have observed series of dreams which worked up sometimes to great beauty, so that one thought something must be going to happen, but then it all decayed and fell back into chaos — until it started up again.

That is the regular way in which the unconscious is brought to consciousness. In certain cases of analysis one sees very clearly how the significance of the nightly dreams rises and rises, and the patient can almost grasp it; but then he does not take it into consciousness, so the thing fades back to chaos and it is as if nothing had happened; but then it starts once more. . . . Heraclitus expressed this long ago in another form; he said that the soul becomes water, then earth, and then water again; and after that, it becomes the fire of the empyrean, it is in the upper spaces with the Gods. He also said that when a man drinks too much wine the soul becomes humid and returns to earth. So he described the rhythm of the soul: it is always changing, below and above.

The eagle on the woman's head in the picture is a very particular bird in alchemy: he is usually on top of the whole thing as if he were the inexpressible fruit. Apparently the fruit was meant to be a winged being; it suggests the old Babylonian symbolism. On Babylonian seal cylinders one finds representations of the tree of life, usually with two figures of worshipers, one on either side; and out of the tree rises the winged-disk symbol, a circle with

a cross. Now, curiously enough, that is a symbol of individuation, and individuation is the realization of the individual pattern, the *entelechia*. That is the
inexpressible fruit of the tree. So individuation should come from this process.
But if consciousness does not interfere, the fruit never appears, the birds simply
go on rising and falling again. You see this is a very psychological picture. As
is well known, one goes through many strange stages in the course of analysis;
all sorts of birds fly up; one has all sorts of phantasies. But each time in the
end, alas, all the birds come down and it is a sad disappointment. One thinks,
"It was nothing, a mere phantasy"; everything is dead and one is back at the
beginning once more. Then up grows the tree again, and the birds appear; one
thinks, "Ah, now"; but it is the same story all over. One is led astray by the
phantasies, and does not concentrate on the inexpressible fruit of the tree.

[In the second alchemical picture (*Figure 2*) only the top branches of the tree are to be
seen at the center, emerging from behind a protective surrounding wall. Above them the
birds still fly up and down, up and down; but now the lion appears in the foreground
twice: on the left he is as naturally, on the right with his paws cut off. The text beneath
reads: *"Whoever drinks the blood of the lion and behaves accordingly, whoever burns his
father's body into ashes by means of the glowing fire and then pours the blessed water
into the ashes, will produce from it an ointment that heals all sickness,"* and so on. – Ed.]

Will Power and Inflation

Now the idea of conscious intervention comes up. The alchemistic idea
was that the natural process would continue to go on if man did not interfere. But here man interferes; he cuts off the paws of the lion, he burns up
the body of his father and pours the blessed water into the ashes; and that
produces the ointment, the philosopher's stone, what the early Christian
church called the *pharmakon athanasias*, the medicine of immortality.

This text is very interesting. The lion obviously represents the will to
power, which is identical with the royalty of man, in that man's will is a
weapon which he superimposes upon nature. That is the difference between
man and animal. The animal is obedient, pious, he obeys the laws of nature;
but he can *only* obey the laws of nature, his power extends only that far; for
the animal's power is not his own, it is the power of nature manifesting itself
through him. But man has real power because, in his disobedience to nature,
he has succeeded in wresting away, or abstracting, a certain amount of energy
from nature, and has made of it his own will power. The danger lies in the
fact that this was originally animal power which may still assert itself and run
away with him. He has stolen something from the Gods, and is therefore
punished by them, as in the myth of Prometheus.

181

The possession of will power causes a sort of inflation, a *hybris*, which gives too much value to the conscious side. . . . Man's will then carries him away as can be seen in our present cultural conditions — where the machines we have invented become our masters. . . . His will becomes his God, and it is a terrible God which runs away with him like a lion running away with its prey. That is why one should cut off the paws of the lion.

The idea of burning up the father's body has a specific mystical connotation, but psychologically it means the destruction of the things that have been. The father's body is the condition that prevailed before the present condition, the bull is our father, and it must be sacrificed in order that we may liberate ourselves; that is, we have to sacrifice the past to illumine the future. . . . If we can make that change, if we can destroy the body of the father, if we can cut off the paws of the lion, we can produce the medicine of life eternal; that is, we can help life to go on. . . .

Question: In connection with the lion you spoke of the Yang principle and now also of human will power. In this case doesn't that mean that the lion represents the animus power? The procession of men led the patient to the mountain top where they left her alone in the cold to face the lion, in other words, a concentration of their own energy.

Dr. Jung: The logic of this question is sound. It is true that after the bull sacrifice, the patient was led by those marching men up to the top of the mountain and left there alone in the snow, and we said that this was a form of animus. So many collective thoughts naturally led her, as a compensation, out of communion with the earth, out of the warmth of the blood into the cold snow, just to the opposite extreme.

You see whenever a woman does something which seems to be wrong [going too far one way or another] so that she is extremely perplexed, then the animus is sure to come in and express some traditional opinion — and up or down she goes accordingly. That is what has happened in this case, so now she is faced with the lion, an instinctive power which is apparently the essence of the animus, and which also represents will power — inasmuch as one is the victim of one's will power. That is to say, the animus-thought that one is in a humiliated condition when down on the earth has a certain power, and in following it one asserts power over the powers of the earth. It is as if one were free to say, "I don't want this communion with the earth, it is too barbarous and primitive. Therefore I am lifting myself out of it." That is will to power.

But the real question is: "Should I stay close to the earth, or may I assume the power to lift myself above the laws of the blood and up onto a mountain

182

top? " On one hand it is will to power that has brought her up there but on the other hand no one can say that that is wrong; because we have a certain amount of freedom of choice, we can say, "I don't want to touch the earth, I prefer to stay in heaven." Only, of course, it would not be pleasant to stay there long! When she arrived in the heavenly city she couldn't stand it and returned to earth; but now she has gone back, as it were, to the mountain top. You see, she has that much choice, but in either case it is due to an involuntary swinging to and fro; first she is led by the unconscious down to earth, and then suddenly she is lifted up again by that instinctive force which is behind the animus. For the animus is based on instinctive force; all these forces have been liberated by man quite instinctively. No matter whether one lives the life of the body, or whether one suppresses the principle of the body and becomes a spirit, one's way of life has been evolved along the lines laid down by instinctive forces. At first men were the laws of human nature, they were the forces themselves; only later did they give names to these forces, and only very much later did they think of the laws as moral or philsophical principles.

For instance, the repression of sex, which we hear so much about in our times, is by no means the modern invention of certain well- or evilly-intentioned people. It is a phenomenon of nature, nature herself forces people to it; the interference of other instincts produces such repression. . . . It is a very natural reaction that this woman should be forced out of the earth almost before she went into it; it is a reaction of the historical powers within her that lift her automatically out of the hole into which she fell.

There we see the eternal up and down movement of the unconscious. . . . Something presses her down into the earth, and then something else comes and lifts her out of it. The lion is an expression of that principle. According to my idea it is best to understand the lion as a sort of philosophical principle formulating the rise of the wave, the positive part of it; that is what I meant when I linked it up with Yang; then the going down of the wave would be the Yin principle.

Because You Have Taken the Way

VISION (cont.): Then a bird came to me and I said to the bird: "Why am I here in the eternal snows? I desire warmth." The bird answered: "Follow me." I did so and the bird took me to the sphinx in the desert.

The lion is the beginning of a new development in the vision. . . . our patient is just reaching out into the next stage of transformation which is characterized by the lion. That is, she has the will to get out of her former humiliated condition and so she rises, and when she is quite alone she meets the lion, thus becoming aware of her royal will power which has lifted her out of participation with the earth and led her to that height. She asks him: "Why am I here? " — meaning, in this particular isolation. The lion replies, "Because you have taken the way." This answer shows, one might say, a connection between her instincts and her quest. She does not understand what it was that lifted her up, or what brought her down again, but she feels intuitively that it must have something to do with the instincts. And the lion gives the correct answer: "Because she has taken the way." . . . You see the lion obviously refers to something like a decision in her, the decision to take the way. . . . How do you understand that?

Answer: Was it the decision to drink the blood?

Dr. Jung: Yes, but that decision is only a part of the whole procedure; it was long before that that she began to take the way. The real start was quite in the beginning when she decided to watch the visions; that was her acceptance. She had dreams in the beginning in which the unconscious came nearer and nearer to her, and finally it began to develop a certain autonomous activity. When it became perceptible and she began to see it as an objective factor, she decided to continue to observe it. It offered a sort of hypothesis of how to live. For, as you remember . . . she did not know what to do with her life or how to continue it, she had run up against an impossible problem. So she said to herself, "I might follow that road."

The visions are the road, and she has naturally gotten more and more into the real swing of it — into that eternal up and down, which is a specific quality of the unconscious. That is why the lion answered that she was up in the snow because she had taken the way.

And then she asks the bird, "Why am I here in the eternal snows? I desire warmth." She has just come from the blood and it is already too cold, *she* wants now to return, she is already identical with the rhythm. The bird says, "Follow me," and leads her right down from the eternal snow into the hot desert, and there she comes to the sphinx [see Part Six]. A part of the descent is accomplished but you will see that it will go further.

So her life now begins slowly to function in that strange rhythm, while before it was level or a straight line. When she saw something in the distance which seemed to be good she made for it. That is the modern way of living; we decide in our minds that a thing is good and go for it, instead of living in the way that nature intends us to live — in that oscillating way. We say, that is the goal, and make a straight line for it, but what nature wants us to do is to move with a snake-like motion. Therefore the snake symbolism in the unconscious of those people who live in a straight line. People living in town never see a snake but they all dream of snakes, and particularly those who live in a straight line have dreams and fears about snakes because the unconscious wants them to move in the natural snake way. So the snake is the symbol of the great wisdom of nature, for the too direct way is not the best way; the crooked way, the detour, is the shortest way.

PART SIX

The Sphinx and the Tree

What is the sphinx? . . . We must always ask ourselves what such a monster consists of. If it consists of animal parts only, we know it is a conglomeration of conflicting instincts that are forced together. If it is both human and animal, it is a combination of the animal and human parts of man. The sphinx is a combination of animal and human and, inasmuch as the monster is mythological, it is not very real, it cannot live as an autonomous being. An animal with a human head is an impossibility, therefore it means an attempt to bring humanity and the animal kingdom together, a sort of provisional attempt at a reconciliation between animal and man.

Hitherto in the visions this union has not taken place; there have been various animals and birds but this woman herself has always been a detached human being. You have seen that the rhythm of the unconscious influences her, yet she is at variance with it; she cannot accept it and still wonders why it does not move in a straight line like a human being. Evidently she is not at one with the animals, so the unconscious makes at least an attempt at a union, and this is symbolized by the sphinx. One might also say that in this case the animal is about to change into a human being, as it already has a human head, or vice versa that a human being is about to change into an animal. But we must understand more about the symbolism of the sphinx. . . .

Question: Is it not a guardian of the dead? It is always connected with pyramids which are graves.

Dr. Jung: It is near the pyramids, but we don't know that it served in any burial ceremony, although it may have. The sphinx is really a sort of dragon — the animal devouring the animal — so it may be a symbol of the great enigma, death. If we were able to solve the riddle of life we would live on eternally, but since we cannot solve that riddle of the sphinx, it will devour us. And there is something else. . . . The sphinx is a religious object, there are a temple and an altar between the paws in front; this shows that it is not only a chthonic dragon or a devouring monster, it is also a spiritual fact. What strange spirit may be contained in the sphinx we do not know, but perhaps we shall find out more about it in the further elucidation of these

[From the lectures given between December 16, 1931, and February 10, 1932 (*Spring* 1965).]

186

visions. We had better leave the question now, since it is of a nature which can only be understood when that union between man and the lost instincts has been established. Probably it has to do with the wisdom of the serpent.

VISION: Now our patient very boldly took her stand before the sphinx and said: "Render unto me your secret."

What would you say about this remark?
Answer: That it was very impertinent.
Dr. Jung: Yes. We may assume that she is in a state of inflation.
Suggestion: It is part of the lion's characteristics.
Dr. Jung: But there is another reason too. . . . When a person is inflated like a balloon it is a compensation. It means that he is confronted with something disagreeable that he would rather not touch, that he would prefer to look down upon. But the sad thing is that no balloon can remain always in heaven. It must descend. . . . Our patient is trying to get out of something. That is why she assumes this God-like attitude. Then she says:

VISION (cont.): The eyes of the sphinx opened. I saw that they were green, and I beheld therein a tree. The branches of the tree reached up into the white snow. The roots of the tree reached down into a stream of blood beneath the earth.

Here is the tree again. We last saw the tree on the pedestal where the bull had stood before. And now she sees it in the eyes of the sphinx. What do you make of this?
Answer: It is a combination of the flow of blood and the tree of a still earlier vision [*illus. 9*].
Dr. Jung: That is true. The tree is a combination of, or at least a bridge between, the things above and the things below. The general theme here seems to be to connect those opposites, blood and spirit, warmth and cold. The attempt was made to find that union in the sphinx on the level of the human being and the animal, but now in its eyes she sees the tree, which seems to be a very real and better connection.

Here we must speak again of the general aspects of the tree. . . . Plants are entirely rooted in the earth, helpless victims or absolutely at one with the basic laws of nature. Animals have the faculty of moving away and seeking their own place; they are literally less attached to the laws of the earth. And the life of man is detached to a very high degree; we have produced an artificial world for ourselves that is very far from the laws of nature and has an entirely different rhythm. Therefore the plant demonstrates a principle of life that is far closer to the laws of the earth than even the animal. Now that is what our patient sees in the eyes of the sphinx, and the sphinx is now no longer a temple or monument in the desert, made of stone; it is a living being. What does one see in the eyes of the living being?

Answer: The soul.

Dr. Jung: Yes. So the tree is really the soul of the sphinx, and it is what solves the riddle of the sphinx. It is the union of opposites which, in a way, has been interrupted in animal and human life. . . . Man's best attempt is the sphinx and that is a monster, but the plant is humble. . . . It is not always running toward some goal, devouring whatever seems good; it grows very silently and in absolute submission to the laws of the earth. Yet a tree may grow to a very great height. Therefore the tree appears as a symbol wherever spiritual development is needed to reconcile opposites or settle a conflict.

Suggestion: Do you remember the question that the sphinx asked Oedipus about man's way of moving in youth, in adult life, and in old age?

Dr. Jung: Yes. It refers to human life in general; first to the course of life — youth, maturity, and old age — then to particular movements, to the ability to move. For to primitive men movement is always the symbol of life . . . life is detachment from the soil, exactly the opposite of plant life. But the riddle of the sphinx and the crux of our problem is that the merely animal principle in our life has to be compensated by a different way of living, and the plant symbolizes that because it is the only example we have. . . . When one follows up the symbolism, understands the problem of our patient, and remembers the former occasions on which the tree has appeared, one sees that it is invariably the symbol of the way she should take in order to reconcile the pairs of opposites, and to settle the impossible problem with which she is still confronted in life. . . .

Comment: You said the patient questioned the sphinx in an impertinent way, but it seems to work well because the sphinx opens her eyes and shows her secret.

Dr. Jung: That is perfectly true, it works, and it is not easy to explain why. One would assume otherwise. What do you think about it?

Answer: Because it is the right way.

Dr. Jung: To deal with what? What is the sphinx psychologically?

Answer: The unconscious.

Dr. Jung: Exactly. . . . In such a phantasy one must assume the role to which one seems to be assigned. One cannot entertain any social relations with the sphinx, so it has nothing to do with the outside world. All we have to explain is why she takes such an important tone. But it is right because it is her role. She has to play it until someone pricks her balloon and then she will collapse. Now the vision continues:

VISION (cont.): The sphinx spoke, saying, "Woman, the way is two-fold." Then the eyes closed. I besought the sphinx again to speak to me but it remained silent. I leaned against it wondering.

That is a very cryptic reply. The sphinx evidently alludes to the lion's remark that she has taken the way. . . .

Comment: The opposites are there to be lived.

Dr. Jung: Exactly. . . . One has to live in the two extremes; like the snake, up and down, right and left. One cannot take the road of life without taking both sides of it because one side alone would lead to a standstill; if one wants to live one must endure the opposites because the way is two-fold.

Obviously this woman does not understand the deep meaning of that answer. You must remember that when she had these visions she was not aware at all of what I am telling you now. There was such a flood of them, one every other day at least, that it would have taken an enormous amount of time to analyze them with her, and she had dreams and conscious problems besides. So it was impossible to deal with these phantasies to any extent, and although she felt that they were somehow important, she did not understand what they meant. Therefore when she says: "I leaned against the sphinx wondering," it is merely a statement of fact. She was puzzled.

[A snake now leads her to a deep black cavern where she beholds the mummy of an ancient king encrusted with gold. There is a parallel here with her first view of the yoga tree after her immersion in the stream of blood. From the blood she arose at that time to the sun, in the form of a tree, and later descended for initiation to the Great Mother in the earth (Part Three). Here again we have the tree rising out of the blood, followed by her descent – through the sphinx, a symbol of the mother, who gives birth in the beginning and also, as the sarcophagus (*sarx*, meaning flesh, and *phagein*, to eat), devours life in the end. But now she finds the mummy of a king. – Ed.]

The Mummy of an Ancient King

Our patient has already been initiated by the Great Mother into the female kingdom, both spiritually and physically, but there was no Great Father so it was a parthenogenesis, a birth from a virgin. That the Great Father was not present was naturally a grave omission, and really what has troubled her ever since. That is why she now has to descend again to find what she lost or did not realize. This time the ancient king whom she discovers symbolizes not the human father but the divine father, the father of mankind, a sort of Creator. . . . But this father is dead, he is a mummy.

Here again is an Egyptian connotation, for she knows something about Egyptian mythology. . . . The God that is chiefly worshiped in the form of a mummy is Osiris. As the king of the underworld, he attained his greatest power only through his death. You remember . . . he was dismembered by Set and put together by Mother Isis, but he was a ghost and, in particular, his phallus was lacking. However, he was able to generate as a ghost — spiritually. . . .

This strange myth shows a tendency in the unconscious mind to dethrone the obvious God of the world — the visible principle of existence, that is — and to substitute for it a spiritual principle, sometimes a principle of the underworld that can only thrive safely in darkness and secrecy, hidden away from the eye of the sun and having really more to do with the moon. This is because the spirit of man is not masculine, it belongs to the mother, to the unconscious female side. Man wishes this were not true and is always trying to make something intellectual and masculine of the spirit. But the spirit in its original form is always female, it comes from the Great Mother. . . .

The idea is that Osiris only became a spirit by dying, that one must die in order to become free or develop spirit. This is the essential principle of the Christian religion; only through death can one obtain immortality, either through a figurative death or a real death. . . . The ancient dead king whom she meets now is a mummy and has not yet been transformed into the spiritual principle, but he is like Osiris. This part of the vision is concerned with the resurrection of the dead . . . and that the mummy is covered with gold indicates its very precious royal character. Looking at the coffin, she continues:

VISION: Slowly it opened and I heard a voice saying, "Unwrap the linen winding sheet." I did so, and there appeared a strange creature half animal, half man. (This is a man, mind you, not a woman, like the sphinx [and she describes him later as looking like a faun].) "Who are you? " I asked. It answered, "I am he who dwells beneath the sphinx itself. Though you wind me with linen you cannot kill me for I am within you where I grow."

Obviously this is a principle that she has tried to keep under restraint. She has herself given service to the corpse, winding it in long linen mummy bandages. She is in the role of Mother Isis, who brought death to the God, but is now giving him decent burial and preparing him for a new life. This binding with bandages has something to do with the binding or dressing of a little child. Also the mummy case is a sort of maternal form. That is why

190

one sometimes finds representations of the Great Mother inside of the sarcophagus; at the bottom or the lower part of the wooden sarcophagus a woman is painted with outstretched arms, holding the sun. So the dead man is really lying in the mother. The Etruscans had a similar rite; the ashes of the dead were poured into an amphora and put inside the clay statue of the mother. And the Christians in medieval times put their dead in holy ground inside the church, as the mother, in order to give them a chance of resurrection into eternal life.

So here that strange being, half-human, half-animal, that Osiris man, is buried in the mother and prepared for final resurrection. And this is the moment of resurrection. Of course nobody would expect the mummy to be half-animal and half-man. . . . That Osiris looked so is an entirely new idea. This is a representation of the spirit as it appears to a woman in its genuine living form, she sees it as half animal and half man. . . . Now to what sort of mind would such an animus point?

Answer: The natural mind.

Dr. Jung: Yes. The so-called natural mind which says absolutely straight and ruthless things.

VISION (cont.): I saw that in one hand he held a staff and in the other hand a bowl. I looked into the bowl and saw reflected my own face. It was black and about my head was a white halo. I said, "This the sphinx has told me. The way is two-fold."

You see that figure now has attributes. . . . She painted the staff in the form of a *crux ansata*, but it looks like a shepherd's staff. It means guidance; one often finds the staff in the Old Testament — in the Psalms and also in the prophetic books — as meaning a guide. . . . God provides a reliable staff on which one may lean. So that gives the natural mind the quality of the leader, the *poimen* or shepherd. Then she looked into the bowl which reflected her face. One is rather astonished that a bowl should be a mirror, but since it is obviously functioning here as both, we may be sure that two functions come together in this symbol. What would the mirror indicate?

Answer: Self-examination.

Dr. Jung: The understanding or knowledge of herself. Generally a mirror symbolizes the mind or intellect. Schopenhauer uses that metaphor. He says that the intellect holds a mirror up to the blind primordial will so that it may recognize itself and deny itself when it realizes what it is, namely, a blind groping urge which leads only to suffering. Understanding the blindness of its own purpose, it will deny itself. Thus the world comes to an end for the individual who recognizes the illusion of the world. [Of course] this is also the Eastern idea. . . . So the mirror is obviously a function of self-knowledge. But what is the bowl?

Answer: The two symbols together would perhaps suggest the Yin and the Yang.

Dr. Jung: That is true. The bowl would be the female and the staff the male form, which means a union of opposites; the male and female are together in this *poimen*. It also means neither male nor female. That is expressed in what is called the Gospel according to the Egyptians, cited by Clement of Rome in the conversation between Jesus and Salome. Salome asks Jesus when the prophecies will be fulfilled and Jesus says, "When ye have trampled on the garment of shame, and when the two become one, and the male with the female is neither male nor female . . ."[10] . . . .

The unrecognizable and incomprehensible thing can only be expressed by a paradox; when we cannot understand a thing in its essence, when we cannot grasp it by means of reason, we describe it in such a form. . . .

The union of male and female in this figure, then, simply means beyond sex; it is neither male nor female, it is something incomprehensible. That is, the natural mind is no longer subject to a sexual point of view, it is neither a man's nor a woman's point of view, it is the point of view just beyond, and that accounts for its divinity. What is beyond the human is animal and divine, and neither animal nor divine. That is why we have animal symbols for the divine, the Holy Ghost as a dove, for instance; all the antique Gods had their animal counterparts. So the natural mind is not a function of man; it is a part of nature, the mind of trees, rocks, water, clouds, or winds, and so ruthless, so absolutely beyond man that it hardly takes him into account. One almost feels that the utterances of the natural mind have an almost animal ruthlessness, along with a strange kind of superiority that reaches far beyond man. It contains a fundamental truth that makes it superior, and because of that superiority it is also divine. . . .

Now we must assume that this patient has a particular capacity for realizing the so-called natural mind. This figure of Osiris, or Pan, expresses it. What does it mean that he shows her in the mirror that her face is black, that she looks like a Negro?

Question: Is it an allusion to the black Messiah [*illus. 13*]?

Dr. Jung: Yes, to the Negro who said to her twice, "Now you are wedded to me." That was an assertion of a very close union, which means that the blackness has gone into her, she has become black. And if you take the color as symbolical, what does it indicate?

Answer: Is it not the color of Yin?

Dr. Jung: Yes, it is the color of the earth. . . . She is now extremely feminine and very much on the Yin side; her face is black because she is nothing but earth. . . . Yet she has a white halo.

Question: Does that mean that light comes out of darkness?

Dr. Jung: Under certain conditions. . . . It is true that the day comes out of the night, but it is not so certain that the absence of light produces light. This is again a paradox. We must assume that the black and the white exist simultaneously. Then the halo means that she is a saint, but a black saint; that she is saintly in her blackness. . . .

When one is at one pole the other pole is naturally constellated. In that sense it can be said that night always produces day. It is from her extreme position that the white light comes, the halo, which gives an appearance of saintliness to her Yin attitude.

Comment: The black face and the white halo give the idea of a pair of opposites within her.

Dr. Jung: Yes, but the opposites would not have appeared if she had not become absolutely black; it was because she went to one extreme that the other became constellated. . . . Otherwise the white would not have appeared, and she would have remained gray. If one is not capable of going to one extreme, one can never constellate or produce the other extreme. That is why it is said in the Scriptures, "So because thou art lukewarm, and neither hot nor cold, I will spew thee out of my mouth. . . ." (Rev. 3:16)

[The strange spirit now disappears after dashing the bowl to the ground and a goat, not a snake, leads her back to the surface. Dr. Jung explains that now that she has acquired the "natural mind," both animals give her better guidance than the animus figures she used to follow. It was natural to be led by a snake going down and now to follow a goat going upward, since goats are always suppose to mount very high. – Ed.]

You remember when the strange Pan figure first appeared, she asked him who he was, and he replied, "I am he who dwells beneath the sphinx itself." Now when he disappears, we can see that it is as if he has become a part of her, as if the rebirth has taken place within her. What does it mean that the natural mind, or the God-man, who was at first outside as he always has been, is now inside? Does the fact that he had to be born outside before he could become an inside thing explain the necessity of the rebirth ritual? What is the psychological meaning of this?

Answer: This part of her was projected before, now it is assimilated.

Anima and Animus as Psychological Functions

Dr. Jung: Yes. Now it is no longer projected. It is the animus that has always been outside of her. Psychologically, projection has been the ordinary state of affairs since the beginning of the world. But now comes the great moment of rebirth, when she assimilates the animus and begins to understand that it is a psychological function. For the first time in history the animus is appearing now as a human function. Before this the anima and animus have never been part of human psychology, they were always projected. That is why I said once that it looked to me as if the human mind had grown out of external objects all over the world. It is as if our consciousness had really started with the stars, not in the brain, and as if we had just begun to assimilate these psychological facts in our time. In the Middle Ages, when a man discovered an anima, he got the thing arrested, and the judge had her burned as a witch. Or perhaps a woman discovered an animus, and that man was doomed to become a saint, or a savior, or a great medicine man.

Medicine men are made by projection. Many become leaders quite against their own intention, they are forced into it because the role of leader is projected upon them. The poor fellows become the victims of other people's expectations. Only now, through the analytic process, do the anima and animus, which were always outside before, begin to appear transformed into psychological functions. . . .

But it is very difficult to see the natural mind . . . as an integral part of one's own psyche. You see the more we assimilate such functions, the more we grow doubtful of the existence of a human mind or psyche. We have had to assimilate so many things that I am afraid it may have stretched the framework of our mental capacity too far. . . . We have been eating the Gods and there is danger of our getting too full and exploding. . . . That accounts for our inflation nowadays; our size has increased enormously because we are housing the upper and lower Gods. Human consciousness has become almost divine, and people believe that we are really on top of the world. Instead of doubting more and more about our own identity, we really think we are Venus and Mars and the whole astrological heavens.

We should *dis*identify. We should *not* identify with those grand powers which were once great Gods worshiped in temples. In the past, a man who was possessed by an uncontrollable emotion was always thought of as being possessed, and nobody was mistaken enough to think otherwise; he was just a poor sad victim. But now if a man is angry, we make him responsible.

Primitive people would be afraid to do that, they would wait until the spirit had left him. And on a higher plane the analyst must do the same thing; when a patient gets out of control, one must say, "Now just wait. You are possessed by an evil spirit, a thought that is blinding you. We will wait till the storm has blown over." I don't make him identify with his anger, because he has to learn that he is not necessarily identical with his emotions. Not one of us would make anyone responsible for a thunderstorm, and it is equally impossible to make anyone responsible for his psyche. Only when we learn that the soul or psyche is really a world with its own laws, like the world in which we live and move, do we get down to our natural proportions. As long as we identify with our psyche, we are just megalomaniacs and things will go very badly with us. . . . Now let us continue to the next vision.

The Gargoyle Appears

VISION: I beheld a Gothic cathedral with high spires. A great religious procession was entering the church chanting a Te Deum. A small grotesque animal like a gargoyle kept clutching at the gold robe of the priest. The priest tried to kick it away but could not. I entered the cathedral with the procession. The priest ascended the steps to the altar and lifted on high the sacred chalice. As he did so small animals and frogs leapt forth from it.

Here is a new situation. We have been moving in an antique and heathen atmosphere, and now suddenly comes the Christian motif. That is most natural. When one has been deeply immersed in heathendom, by the law of contrast the opposite becomes constellated. . . .

Comment: Perhaps the Christian cathedral appears here only to show that it is not right for her, because the gargoyle enters at the same time.

Dr. Jung: The gargoyle shows that someone is still playing the devil's part, but the Christian setting is constellated by the blackness of her face . . . her unconditioned acceptance of an antique, chthonic point of view. ([But] paganism is not necessarily chthonic, it can be spiritual just as well. But to us it usually has a chthonic character when it occurs in such unconscious visions, because whatever antiquity has produced of spiritual matter has been assimilated by Christianity. . . . But the chthonic elements of paganism were excluded and suppressed and therefore they are in the unconscious: nearly all unconscious products are saturated with chthonic qualities or allusions.) Then up comes the historical reaction. . . . And when does one sing the Te Deum?

Answer: To express thankfulness.

Dr. Jung: It is usually part of a rite to celebrate a particular accomplishment, a victory for instance, so it is a sort of thanksgiving – *Te Deum lauda-mus*. It is part of any moment that celebrates the triumph of the church; or the solemn entrance of a cardinal or the Pope. It always signifies a culmination of some kind; it may be the culmination of the rite itself. Here it means the triumph of the Christian church. And in this moment, which expresses the extreme opposite to what the blackness of her face represents, the grotesque little animal like a gargoyle appears. You have seen those figures on Gothic churches. They frequently form the waterspouts, and the Gothic seats of the choirs are often beautifully decorated with little gnomes and dwarfs, and frogs and lizards, all sorts of funny creatures. Such grotesque animals represent the chthonic roots and are therefore supposed to live in caves or amongst the roots of trees; they are the animals of darkness, of the depths of the earth, and they are always a bit comical – in vivid contrast to the world of light. Where does that idea come from?

Answer: They interrupt the Gothic line upward to the clouds.

Dr. Jung: Yes. The Gothic line, that wonderful elevation, that uplifting effect, is naturally interrupted by these mocking spirits. . . . One also finds them in poetry, in the second part of Faust grotesque beings appear, the *Lemuri*. Here they are the evil ghosts of the dead, whom the devil calls upon to dig Faust's grave. . . . Such figures can be seen in Egypt too. The chthonic God Bes is an archetypal figure; he is an exceedingly grotesque little dwarf but he is also the teacher of Horus, just as Mimir is the teacher of Siegfried. So the most grotesque appearance is associated with wisdom. It has been pointed out many times that the bust of Socrates looks like a faun or like Silenus; even to the people of antiquity he appeared grotesquely ugly, yet he was the father of wisdom.

Comment: One finds the same idea among primitive peoples. After very serious rituals, some North American Indians wear grotesque masks.

Dr. Jung: Yes. . . . Sometimes there is a special group within an Indian tribe, whose particular task is to ridicule the Gods. They are the clowns of the Gods and they are called the "delight makers." [11] In the Catholic Church, as late as the thirteenth century, a mock mass was celebrated, in which vulgar and obscene songs were sung as the responses, in order once a year to interrupt the solemn hierarchic structure of the Church. . . .

Comment: Kings used to have jesters who were deformed.

Dr. Jung: They were often very important personages, as well as the source of the greatest wisdom the king was ever likely to hear. . . .

These examples show that chthonic wisdom has always been associated with grotesque form. And it is not only legend; it is a fact that the dwarf is especially wise. That is because a dwarf, or a person otherwise deformed or mutilated, is usually very ambitious — he achieves a compensatory development on another side — like Wayland, the blacksmith, whose tendons were severed, and Vulcan, the God of the blacksmiths, who had lame feet. And the seer is often blind, Melampus, for instance, the famous seer of antiquity. Probably the first intellectuals, in a time when men were chiefly warriors, were those who had to stay at home on account of being crippled, either crippled from birth or incapacitated through disease. Moreover, dwarfish or mutilated persons always cast a spell because they have something strange in their eyes; one often recognizes them from a peculiar expression of the face although one does not know that they are mutilated. And you know how children react with such people, they are afraid of them. . . .

When the priest as he stepped up to the altar was attacked by that gargoyle, it meant that the chthonic factor was asserting itself; though it seemed to be completely overcome by the spiritual quality of the Gothic mentality, it was not repressed but began to disturb the ceremony. The little creature kept clutching at the gold robes of the priest, who tried to rid himself of this pagan factor, but could not. Then when the priest lifted the sacred chalice in the ritual small animals and frogs jumped out. . . .

It is quite possible that the patient is here alluding to something that she has read, as is often the case in such visions. Moreover, it is probable that she has seen in my *Psychology of the Unconscious* [12] the reproduction of a very famous picture of St. John by Quentin Matsys. St. John is often represented with a chalice, but this picture is unusual in that there is a little *(Illus. 15)* dragon with feet and wings in the chalice. This refers to a legend that St. John was given a goblet of poisoned wine but caused the poison to disappear by making the sign of the cross. Probably it is a so-called explanatory legend, as legends are often invented to explain something otherwise inexplicable. But it really does not explain this picture, for if there had been a real snake in the goblet St. John would have seen it. Therefore the snake must symbolize the poison. And when he takes away the power of the poison, the virtue of the drug, why should a snake or dragon rise from the goblet? . . . Probably this has to do with antique symbolism; in early Christianity many motifs were taken over from antique illustrations or ways of thinking. . . . So the chalice in the vision may originally have looked different, like the chalice with the snake.

Chalice
with snake.

The Serpent as a Soul Daimon

The serpent was the sacred animal of Aesculapius, the God of doctors, who had a famous clinic for all diseases at Epidaurus. A huge serpent was kept there, and in the time of the great pestilence when Diocletian was emperor they brought the serpent — it was not mythical but a real snake — from Epidaurus to Rome as a sort of apotropaic charm. Probably the chalice has something to do with that serpent. You see the idea of the antique symbol is that the bowl or goblet contains the medicine, but in order to make the medicine powerful, to give it mana and true healing virtue, a drop of poison is needed, the addition of the serpent. One might say that the serpent was the familiar daimon of Aesculapius. And Aesculapius was a sort of God-hero. He was the mediator — a pagan Christ, a Messiah figure really — and he had, as all those old heroes had, the soul of a serpent. In Northern mythology it was said that one could recognize the hero by the fact that he had snake's eyes. . . . This was not in any way derogatory, it simply denoted his divine character. . . .

So the serpent is a soul daimon, and the idea is that when the doctor prepares his medicine it is human work — it is quite nice, perfectly all right — but it has no virtue until the doctor's soul daimon puts at least a drop of poison into it; then it works, then there is magic power in it. That is an extremely modern conception. When the doctor's medicine is nothing but routine, when he draws it from a textbook on pharmacology . . . there is no juice in it, it lacks the real thing; but when the soul daimon is in it, it works. Then there is a special sort of *participation mystique*: the serpent, as a soul, represents the lower strata of the human personality, the cold-blooded animal, the animal of the darkness, of the spinal cord and the solar plexus.

From time immemorial the solar plexus has been associated with the sympathetic nervous system; the word sympathetic, meaning suffering with, comes from the Greek *sympatheia* (*syn*-, together, with, and *pathos*, feeling, suffering). Paradoxically — since it has no sense organs or brain, and is represented by a cold-blooded animal, the serpent — it is through the sympathetic nervous system that we feel the most. Our experience of *participation mystique* comes through this inner psychical system, deep in the unconscious. It is as if we were connected with everyone else through this hypochondriacal region. In books by old German physicians, like Justinus Kerner, or in Passavant's book about magnetism, the sympathetic system plays a great part and particularly the hypochondriacal region, which is the triangle just above the stomach in front of the solar plexus. Kerner's patient, the famous seeress of Prevorst, gave special importance to this region; anything that she wanted to read or understand or get into sympathetic contact with, she would place on this most sensitive spot.

Now applied to our symbolism that would mean that the doctor's medicine is good or helpful only if the serpent has put a drop of sympathy into it — of *participation mystique* — and you can understand the extraordinary wisdom in that. Why St. John should be equipped with such a symbol we can only speculate; it was St. Luke who was said to have been a doctor. The Christian interpretation, however, is quite simple: the chalice contains the wine or the blood, it is the *pharmakon athanasias*, the medicine of immortality, and the wine is not good and strong unless it is the blood of Christ. But it only becomes the blood of Christ by the grace of God; that is, through the *intercessus divinus* in the sacrament, in the rite of transubstantiation. So Christ would appear in the form of the serpent.

That Christ was the healing serpent is a Gnostic idea.[13] His blood is the essence of his life, and the healing poison for the world. Only when Christ puts that magic drop of his essence into the chalice does the wine become the blood, only then does it become magic, the medicine of immortality. . . . Curiously enough, there is no trouble in identifying the dragon or serpent with Christ, even within the Christian iconography; for what one usually sees in the chalice is the Host like the rising sun, and the Host is the body of Christ — it is Christ in the chalice. So when one finds the dragon or the serpent there, one can be quite certain that it means Christ. The Gnostic interpretation was taken over, more or less unconsciously, by the early church. . . . [For although the church persecuted the Gnostics as heretics] it absorbed as much, if not more, from the heresies as from antiquity.

The Frogs and Little Animals

Now where do the frogs and other little animals that leap from the chalice come from, psychologically speaking? We must see where these symbols start, for there is a sort of transformation here, with a beginning and an end. This is not merely a disconnected series of pictures; there is an inner causal *enchaînement* of the facts.

Answer: They come from the chthonic element which was in her, then went into the gargoyle, and from there to the serpent.

Dr. Jung: Yes. The gargoyle is the serpent. It keeps clutching at the priest's robes, he cannot get rid of it, and it comes into the sacred ceremony too. The gargoyle creeps into the chalice and reappears transformed — though not much transformed, because the frog and other small animals are very similar. Probably there is also in the back of the patient's mind that picture in

The Psychology of the Unconscious which shows the little winged dragon, like a gargoyle, coming out of the chalice. These creatures are like the gargoyle too, but less grotesque — presumably just cold-blooded little animals. The only thing she really saw clearly was a frog jumping out. . . . The frog also appears in alchemy in the form of a toad — they did not pay much attention to small zoological differences in those days; so we can lump them together and call them by one name. . . . [In alchemy] the toad drinks milk from the breasts of the Virgin. And there is a fountain in Nürnberg where the water pours from the breasts of women into the mouths of frogs. Also, the toad is a medieval symbol of the womb. Then there is the beautiful fairy tale of the frog and the princess:

> The princess was playing with a golden ball which fell into a well where she could not recover it. But in the well there was a frog who said he would bring it up if she would promise to fulfill three conditions: that he should sit at her table, that he should eat from her dish, and that he should sleep in her bed. She promised everything because she was so grieved by the loss of her ball. So the frog brought it back, but then, of course, she wanted to forget the conditions, and he had to keep reminding her of her promises. Each time she obeyed with reluctance because the frog was so terribly slippery and cold and repulsive, and each demand was worse than the last. To be in the same room, yes, but to eat at the same table and from the same dish! Then the last condition, that the frog should sleep in her little bed, was simply unheard of; she would not allow it. Nevertheless the frog forced himself into her bed, whereupon she seized him and threw him against the wall. In that instant the frog fell away and Prince Charming came forth.

The golden ball is the sun which represents our libido. When the libido of the princess runs away, the poor girl has a depression, she loses her joy in life. She doesn't know where it has gone and wants to recover it. Then the voice from the depths says that if she will fulfill those conditions she will get back her delight in living. In other words, she must assimilate something cold and repulsive, and if she is able to do so, she will recover her joy, her prince will appear.

This is an eternal truth and at the same time a piece of wisdom that has very practical applications. I have to say pretty much the same thing three or four times a day. There is great religious symbolism in this too: the sun, the light of day disappears; our highest value — for the golden ball is our highest value — disappears into darkness, and we don't know what to do. We are left in utter darkness, the sadness of despair. Then we hear the voices of the depths, and they make conditions that we don't like at all.

But if we can fulfill the conditions, the light of divinity will return, the superman. For Prince Charming is always a superior man, a paragon of virtue, and he represents man's renewal, his own resurrection.

The idea here is similar; that is, the frogs which appear do not mean a defilement for the sacred chalice, they mean the healing substance or healing symbol that emanates from the womb of the chalice. That is the connection between the Virgin and the chalice: the Virgin is the vessel, the *vas insigne devotionis*, as she is called in the Lorettian Litany, the excellent vase of devotion into which the devotion of believers is poured. And the Virgin is at the same time the astrological sign Virgo, meaning the earth; so the earth is the cup, the receiving or conceiving vessel from which the saving symbol issues. On the one hand, the Virgin produces the Prince Charming, the superior man, the beautiful youth, a sort of mediator of pagan quality (since fairy tales are thoroughly pagan), or she produces the beloved spiritual king, Christ. On the other hand, the Virgin gives birth to, or nourishes, the toad or the frog.

So the frog is a peculiar symbol. If you think of the transformation of the frog into Prince Charming and of the frogs fed by the milk of the Virgin . . . you realize that this is simply another analogy; the frog is an animal symbol of the child.

Suggestion: It is the thing that Nietzsche could not accept.

Dr. Jung: The "ugliest man" in *Thus Spake Zarathustra* was the thing he could not accept. Like this patient, Nietzsche went back to the Dionysian experience, and the idea of the "ugliest man" followed from that; then, after many detours — a serpent-like movement of the symbolism — the book ends with the idea of the superman. He refused to accept the other side because it was too repulsive, and because it became associated with his phobia. (He suffered from the idea that he had to swallow a frog or a toad, and whenever he saw one he felt a compulsory inclination to swallow it.) This appeared in a dream that he had of a toad sitting on his hand; it referred to his syphilitic infection which he really could not accept. That was where he clashed with the earth, where the earth got him down. But this is a side question.

But the general meaning of the frog is pretty clear. . . . It symbolizes a transitory stage . . . [and it represents] very definite beings — children, of course. Perhaps you have never realized that the frog is nature's first attempt to produce a creature like man, an animal with two legs, two hands, and no tail. But when mothers bathe their children they call them little frogs or tadpoles in the water; also a dwarfish child or guttersnipe is called a little toad. And here in Switzerland we say that a "flapper" is a little toad too. So the frog is a sort of child; it is a childish attempt of nature to produce something like man on the level of the cold-blooded animals; it is a cold-blooded little man. The frog in the fairy tale could be called a kind of embryonic man in whom the beautiful prince is not yet recognizable. This fairy tale is in a way very profound. . . .

Man as He Is: The Stone Rejected by the Builders

You see the deeper idea is that the frog prince is man. Man as he is is the frog form of the superior man to come, of the beautiful being that is in man but that has not yet revealed itself. We are the repulsive, ugly husks surrounding the golden kernel, the divine soul of man. This little fairy tale is really a great myth, a sort of initiation myth; perhaps it derives from, or is the source of, the ancient myth that man, by violent intervention, can break through the husk, can become the superior being.

So when the frog appears, in dreams or visions or fairy tales, it means man in his chthonic aspect, his "nothing but" aspect; our consciousness of what man is, of being human, is the frog; it means man viewed as a merely biological being. But that is only the outer shell of something very much more beautiful and perfect inside, the shell that will be broken and cast off, either by death when the beautiful man is liberated or through the intervention of a mystical rite in initiation. That is the reason why in certain African tribes, the members of the tribe who refuse to be put through the cruel initiation tests are called animals by the others. They have not been liberated from the husk of the animal. They are still cold-blooded frogs living only partly on land – that is, still partly immersed in the primeval unconscious condition – and they have not yet attained the warmth of the divine sunlike being. As a warm-blooded animal, man is on a higher level, he is more sunlike. That explains why the inner man is always understood to be the sun of heaven, or son of the sun.

Here, then, the frog appears from the chalice like the mediating and healing serpent and it expresses the same function; it is a healing symbol. And this means that man as he is is a healing symbol, that he is the thing that has not been accepted, the thing that has been suppressed or avoided. Man as he is is the stone rejected by the builders that becomes the head of the corner (Mark 12:10); he is the tender plant, that grows in dry and sterile soil where no one would expect any life to appear, fulfilling the messianic prophecies of Isaiah (53:1-3).

But the frog, symbolizing man as he is, only attains to the dignity of a

202

healing symbol when it is compensatory; that is, when it meets an audience — individual or public — that identifies with the superior inner man. For if we, in the form of frogs, identify with the beautiful Prince Charming, we necessarily suffer from inflation; then we are one-sided and unnatural, because we cannot possibly be that superior man. Nietzsche, who tried to be, overdid it completely, and was threatened with the ugliest man. That is the reason why he broke down, and the reason why we break down when we assume a superiority that is not ours. But it is redeeming and healing for us to accept ourselves as we are, instead of always wanting things to be different. We are constantly saying: "He would be very nice, if he were not so-and-so," or: "I could really accept myself, if I were not what I am." . . . But wisdom begins when we take things as they are; otherwise we get nowhere, we simply become inflated balloons with no feet on the earth. Only by agreeing with facts as they are can we live on earth in our bodies, only then can we thrive. . . . It is unfair to our friends and unfair to ourselves to assume that human beings can become supermen. The thing that is ugly and repulsive is precisely what leads to redemption: the princess got her Prince Charming out of the skin of the frog.

So the idea in this vision is that the medicine of redemption which issues from the sacred chalice is merely man as he is, incomplete, a first attempt of nature to make on the cold-blooded level the warm-blooded man to be. And why should man be the last idea of the Creator? . . . So many things in his structure and disposition are utterly foolish and unsuitable, not only in his body, but also in his mind. It is quite possible that those who live in the distant future, say a hundred thousand years from now, will look back at us, as we look at the pithecanthropus, and say: "That was not man, that was a beast!" Yet the pithecanthropus, if he thought at all, may also have assumed that he was on top of creation.

We recognize this and out of a world-wide sense of inferiority, identify with what is most beautiful. We have glimpses of it and think that we have already reached it, that we are really good, for instance. But we are not good. . . . Look at our ideas and our conditions. Everything is desperately embryonic, and we are just beginning to be aware of it. . . . We are like a swarm of tadpoles; each tadpole wants to do something, but because the tadpoles are a mob none of them can; for a mob has no brain, the psychologies of the so-called leaders and of the mob are identical.

Man is in an exceedingly embryonic state, and the superior man can never develop when the tadpoles decide they are not tadpoles but something much more wonderful, when they deny that they have tails and fins, when the frogs pretend that they have warm blood and beautiful singing voices. First we must accept the fact of ourselves, what we are; then we can develop. In accepting ourselves in our embryonic condition we receive ourselves, as a mother receives a child in her womb where it is fed and develops. If we can really accept ourselves, we can feed and develop ourselves; to expect anything else is like expecting a cast-off child to thrive. So when in this vision the frog issues from the chalice instead of the serpent, it means that the frog is here the redeeming symbol. . . . Not the perfection of man but his imperfection is what is meant.

The Advent of the Antichrist

VISION (cont.): The priest knelt, chanting: "Forgive us, O Lord, for we have sinned." A snake with a black hood over its head silently glided up the steps to the altar and wound itself upon the cross. I went up to the snake and asked it why it was there. The snake answered: "I am he who has taken the place of Christ."

(Illus. 16)   The patient made a picture of this snake.

We have been saying that the frog is in a way a redeeming symbol, but here there was not one frog, there were many. . . . The multitude suggests a multitude of human beings; one might say that just as a multitude of frogs issue from a pool after transformation from the tadpole stage, so symbols issue from the chalice for many people, and for the individual inasmuch as he is part of a multitude. Then when everyone has accepted his individual imperfection, the serpent appears and coils itself into the place of the re-
(Illus. 17) deemer, meaning that the serpent is the equivalent of the redeemer.

This is again the extraordinary Gnostic idea of Jesus as the serpent in paradise, which was considered heretical and utterly rejected by the early Church. But it never really died, it has come up again and again. It is the same as the Kundalini serpent, and the Kundalini is identical with the *agathodaimon*, the serpent of Egypt and of the later Hellenistic syncretism in the first centuries before and after Christ. Moreover, the serpent is the Antichrist, the brother of Jesus, according to a legend that reaches back to the first century. The Antichrist was expected to appear soon after Jesus, in the rather immediate future, because it was then understood that Jesus would return before the last of his disciples, or his living witnesses, had died, and it was assumed that his brother, the serpent, would come before his return.

The legend is that the Antichrist was also born in Palestine, worked miracles in Jerusalem, did everything in exact analogy to the life of Christ, but that all of it was evil, black magic. This shows that in those days the idea of the Christian savior was felt to be checked within by a contrary power.

... The chthonic reality, insofar as it was opposed to the spiritual effort that men were then making — the attempt of Christianity to spiritualize itself — had necessarily to be diabolical. . . .

The Antichrist legend was therefore a true expression of the spirit of that time. It was also expressed in the symbolism of astrology, for that was the beginning of the time of the Fishes. According to the actual shape of the constellation of the Fishes [which differs from the astrological sign], one fish is upright and the other fish is horizontal, and between is the *commissura*, a sort of string from tail to tail. (Note that the vertical and horizontal lines indicate a cross.) The upright one would be the Christian fish and the horizontal one the Antichristian fish. Therefore Christ was called *Ichthys*. He is the one rising to heaven, the head pointing upward to the summit, while the Antichrist never leaves the earth, he is the ugliest man, the Devil.

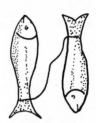

Astrological sign.

So this Christian psychology belongs to the time of the Fishes and we are still there [in 1932], but our present psychology is nearing the head of the horizontal fish. This second fish, unlike the traditional astrological symbol, does not head in exactly the opposite direction; the Antichrist is not contradictory, it is only horizontal, and it is not clear why this fish should be so evil. It is only evil because it does not rise to heaven, it remains on earth.

Astronomical sign.

As the spring point has moved from the first fish to the second, the redeeming symbol has developed further and further away from the spiritual hero, and man's humanity, his chthonic aspect, has been increasingly emphasized. It was in the middle of the *commissura* in the year 1500, the time of the Renaissance, followed by the Reformation. It entered the tail of the horizontal fish in about 1720 at the time when the French Enlightenment began, which led to the overthrow of Christianity in Paris and the enthronement of the Goddess Reason instead. The dividing line is right in the middle of the *commissura*; since then we have had the Humanists and an entirely new point of view.

It is as if the tremendous heights of the Gothic times were collapsing, sinking down to earth, and as if man were reaching outward, instead of up to heaven like the first fish. Energy was no longer heaped up but extended horizontally. That was the time of the great voyages and the great discoveries, of the growth of natural science, when man became all important.

Now we have developed so far along these lines that there is nothing but man. The heavens have become entirely depopulated . . . all the hierarchies of angels and archangels, and God himself, have entered man . . . and man is left entirely alone with a tremendous inflation.

Earlier I quoted a passage from Synesius, Bishop of Edessa, who really was half heathen, and also a poet. He said that the *spiritus phantasticus*, which is actually human imagination, can even enter divinity (and St. Paul says exactly the same: that through thinking we can know God), but if it does, it will have to sustain, or suffer, the divine punishment which is dismemberment — the human mind will be dismembered. And that is a destructive process, the dismemberment of all that was heaped up in the first fish, the whole spiritual point of view dismembered by our extraordinary horizontal extension. . . . Man has covered the earth, and everything on it is subservient to him, but we are still under the influence of the first fish and have not accepted it yet. We hover like spirits over the earth and above ourselves.

But now we have to accept ourselves. The complete acceptance of man as he is appears to be the necessary conclusion of the age of the Fishes. Since he thinks himself divine and behaves as if he were divine, he must assimilate himself, become acquainted with himself. And to become acquainted with oneself is a terrible shock. . . .

The acceptance of man as he is is the psychological or, if you prefer to call it so, the spiritual or religious problem of today; it is what we are up against now. But the vision says that when that happens the serpent will take the place of the redeemer on the cross. That means that the Antichrist, what we think of as the principle of evil, will be the redeeming symbol. Then a cycle will be completed and we shall be back where they were in the first century A.D. when they discovered the serpent was really the redeemer. After that something new may begin.

She Looks in the Golden Disk

VISION (cont.): I went out of the cathedral and knelt on the stones of the square before a golden disk upon the ground. I asked the disk why the snake had taken the place of Christ upon the cross. Then I looked in the disk and I saw my face reflected there. My eyes were green, my lips were scarlet, and my hair was wreathed with grape leaves. I returned to the cathedral and I said to the snake: "Now I understand."

The first important point is the square with the golden disk on the ground. Do you remember anything about that?

Answer: It was the pool of gold in the roots of the tree.

Answer: She passed God's face and then came to the pool of gold.

Answer: It was like the sun above and the sun below.

Dr. Jung: The sun above has been the symbol of a spiritual deity since time immemorial. . . . But that pool of gold characterized a very concrete value, not a spiritual value. It was the face of God, as it were, but materialized in the form of gold. . . . In this vision the golden disk has the meaning of matter versus spirit. The gold is really meant as the concrete substance; it is not only emblematic, it is the actual valuable material, which now takes on an almost spiritual value. It is substituted for the spiritual value because the spirit is as if exhausted; in these visions there is a new consideration of matter as a sort of religious object.

This is entirely strange to our Christian mentality. We cannot conceive of matter as a spiritual entity, or imagine that it could have a spiritual connotation or a spiritual value. It seems an absolute paradox. But when one studies Hindu philosophy, one sees that matter, as the opposite of spirit, is really much the same thing. . . . For spirit to them is what they call *cit*, or consciousness, meaning a universal consciousness which is not to be defined by any specific contents; it is a detached, all-pervading, ever-present consciousness. And when that consciousness creates an idea, they say it is expressed as concrete matter; so matter is the concrete defined thought of the deity or of the *cit*; when *cit* becomes specific it is matter. . . . In other words, when the universal consciousness – or you can call it Brahman . . . produces a definite thought, then it is matter. . . .

When this woman looks into the disk of gold and sees herself in a different guise, she suddenly understands why the snake went up on the cross. What is her new aspect? How is she transformed?

Answer: Now she has a Dionysian appearance, and her eyes are green.

Dr. Jung: Exactly, the wreath of grape leaves on her head is Dionysian. And the great God Pan had green eyes in the picture that she painted of him. So now she recognizes herself as a nature-like being, for Pan was the God of nature according to the late interpretation. . . .

There is a very symbolical legend which seems to refer to an actual fact [that in late antiquity a rumor spread throughout the Greek islands that Pan was dead]. Taken as a symptom of the mentality of those days, this would mean that the unconscious felt the necessity of informing the people that great Pan had died, that that principle had come to an end — and it really was the time when Pan, as the deity of nature, came to an end.

Now in our time again, after the reign of the spirit, something similar is happening. In *Thus Spake Zarathustra* Nietzsche says: "God is dead." It is the same but now it means that the spiritual God has come to an end. And the unconscious reacts immediately, bringing up the symbols of Pan once more. . . . Mirrored in the golden disk, in the material creation of her own hands, this patient is Pan-like, she is a nature-being. And inasmuch as she is a nature-being she is the exact replica of the deity; through her identity with nature she experiences her identity with the Creator. We might assume that we would feel identity with the Creator only through spirituality, but our extreme cultivation of the spirit has made us feel our difference from the deity. We are filled with the idea of extreme sinfulness, so how could we identify with the deity? Rather, it seems to us an extraordinary impertinence on the part of the mystics to insist upon their identity with God. And it was really only the later mystics who dared to do so.

The best example of it is that most mystical and most childlike poet, Angelus Silesius. In a very naive way he confessed his identity with the deity, but he could only do so in a more or less somnambulistic condition. . . . He was overcome by the vision, and unable to live up to it, to assimilate the tremendous truth he had discovered. . . . [In him] one sees that even without any particular persecution it may kill a man to undergo such a change in his religious convictions.

There is a change like that going on in the case of this woman. When she sees herself as a nature-being, she can understand why the healing snake has once more become the symbol of the redeemer, of the healing one, the *Soter*, the *Heiland*. It is the daimon of Aesculapius, the nature form of the healer. . . . . The serpent, or the dragon, is the other side of the hero, because the truth is that they are two aspects of the same thing. As the Bhrigu Upanishad puts it: "I am the food; I am the eater." [14] Or: I am the hero and the dragon. So, seen from the human point of view, Aesculapius was a semi-divine man; seen from the point of view of nature, he was a serpent. His essential quality was nonhuman, it was superhuman and therefore symbolized by an animal figure.

One might almost say that at a time in history when people look at things from a human point of view the Gods become human; and when they look at the world from the standpoint of nature, material forms or animal forms

208

appear. So, after this recognition, when the patient returns to the cathedral and tells the snake that she understands, something of this sort may be meant.

Married by a Witch

VISION: I beheld many men riding by on horseback carrying white streaming banners. They wore helmets. As they rode past they tore off their helmets and threw them to the ground. I picked one up and inside I saw engraved these words: Wear this helmet if you would shield yourself from the world. I threw the helmet down and walked on. I saw one of the riders dismount from his horse and stand before the ghost of an old woman. In front of the ghost was a caldron seething with fire. I joined the man and we stood together. The old woman said: "I will wed you with fire." She threw fire upon us.

These men riding by on horseback are obviously soldiers. What does that suggest?

Answer: The collective animus.

Dr. Jung: Yes. It is the motif that we have encountered many times before: always when some new enterprise that she cannot face becomes necessary, the animus precedes her, either alone or as a multitude. . . . These soldiers suggest an enterprising mood. . . . There is something triumphant about it. . . . Usually the animus is a collective opinion, and collective opinion would be likely to be against her, but that is only the negative animus. . . . As the involuntary function of the mind the animus is not necessarily negative; sometimes it is very positive. . . . So the fact that these soldiers throw their helmets down on the ground might be a rather friendly action, and the inscription inside the one she picked up might be to her advantage . . . suggesting that she take the necessary precautions against the world by covering her head with a helmet. Now why precisely that?

Answer: Is it because she now has such a Dionysian look?

Dr. Jung: Yes. If she should go out into the world with green eyes, scarlet lips, and vine leaves in her hair, she would not look as she should. It would be disreputable to go out with Pan's eyes. No one must suspect that one is a natural being. . . . Don't forget that the medieval devil was represented with horns and a tail, just like Pan. It is dangerous to set out into the world as a nature-being. Her animus is giving her sound advice when he tells her to cover her head, to hide it, because that is what the world will most certainly beat upon. But she does not realize what she is up against. [Like the soldiers] she throws the helmet down and is going to face the music without protecting herself, which is rather over-courageous. It would be better to keep perfectly

quiet about the whole situation . . . [but] the animus mood takes the form
of a sort of belligerent attitude; like coming out with an absurd statement
in order to fight for it, as if the fight were for Jerusalem.

Then one of the riders dismounts as though coming to her aid. That is,
a part of the group of animus figures condenses or concretizes into one man,
and when the animus becomes one, it is most probably projected into a real
man. . . . In this case she sees him standing before the ghost of an old woman
who is evidently a witch because there is a caldron on the fire and that always suggests a witch. Expressed psychologically, the animus is now turning
to the unconscious; the ghost indicates the unconscious; the collective unconscious is the ghost world, and the witch is a figure of the collective unconscious. This woman was going out to face the world, but since her animus turns in toward the collective unconscious, she has to stay with him.
It is her reckless procedure that has caused the animus to dismount; instead
of going further he turns right back to the unconscious. Now who would
the witch be?

Answer: She is the shadow.

Dr. Jung: Yes. Of course, it is rather baffling that our patient should suddenly be represented by an old woman, but it is entirely logical on account
of the fact that she was proceeding so recklessly. She is too young, therefore the old woman appears within as compensation. One sees that in dreams:
when the conscious attitude is too infantile, too immature, an old woman
appears as a compensating figure. . . . So the old woman is really her shadow.

Here again her subjective condition is enacted before her eyes. . . . As that
green-eyed, scarlet-lipped aspect of herself . . . she goes to the side of the man,
and the old woman throws fire on them as they stand before the caldron.
She is not her own shadow here because she is in a magic ceremonial. The
old woman is her shadow, and she is the figure standing between the conscious and the unconscious; in that position she is very much herself, detached
from the shadow as well as from ego consciousness. Now what does the caldron suggest? . . . Whenever it appears it indicates the alchemistic process, the
process of transformation. So what should be transformed? . . .

Answer: Her belligerent attitude.

Dr. Jung: Her recklessness in stepping out into the world as a maenad, a
female Pan. That won't do at all, that is too nonsensical. And now the ceremonial; why does the old woman say: "I will wed you with fire"?

Answer: She wants the patient to marry her animus.

Dr. Jung: And the psychological reasons for that? First of all, the animus
should not normally be connected with the shadow because then there are

210

two against one: the shadow plus the animus against consciousness. That is too much; consciousness either breaks away and goes wild, or succumbs to the prevailing unconsciousness and is wiped out. Then an animus possession takes place. She should be related to the animus, just as she should be the proprietor of her own shadow.

You see, people who do not possess and are not aware of their inferior shadow side, may appear to be marvelously good people, one can discover no flaw in them, they are white as milk. They tell you themselves that nothing is wrong with them; everyone else is wrong, but never they. Yet because they deny their shadow, such people are absolutely possessed by devils; the women are all eaten up by the animus. Strengthened by that excellent nourishment, he grows so strong that he is able to possess consciousness, to rule it. In such a case the connection between the animus and the shadow should be broken, and here it is even broken by the shadow.

When you see your own inferior side you can detach from the anima or animus, but as long as you don't see it, you haven't a chance. So what the witch does is very useful; she tries to wed the animus with the conscious self by throwing fire at them, a sort of smelting procedure.

The Shadow

Question: How does it happen that the shadow assumes such a positive role? Has the shadow become tired of the animus? . . .

Dr. Jung: The shadow has done nothing really . . . the patient herself has acquired an active attitude. She shows herself in a very masculine role, even throwing down the helmet that the animus has offered her for protection. As a result one of the riders dismounts and comes to her side; in other words, she forces the animus down to herself; she detaches the animus from the shadow, thus making the shadow into a ghost, an unreal thing, yet with the positive quality of fire. A witch can be a witch whether she is real or a ghost, she can throw fire on them, and the question is whether the fire is positive. My supposition would be that it is destructive ill will. . . .

One must make a difference between the shadow and the personal unconscious. . . . The Freudian concept of the unconscious is the personal unconscious alone, inasmuch as Freud assumes that, practically speaking, the existence of the unconscious is based on repressions. This, at least, is his main working hypothesis. According to his idea, the unconscious exists only as a function of the conscious, it has no virtue of its own, no existence of its own. He assumes that if one changes one's conscious personal attitude, one will no longer have an unconscious; that if his interpretation of neurotic symbolism were generally known, neurotics would be cured, that they have neuroses only because they do not know what it is all about. Say a man has an incest complex; as soon as he knows it he will no longer be neurotic. But that is wrong because it is based to begin with on the idea that the neurosis is caused by repressions, which Freud simply takes for granted; he is convinced that one will necessarily be well again if one knows the contents of one's repressions. But this is not true.

It looks like hairsplitting when I try to explain the subtle difference between his concept of the personal unconscious and what I would call the shadow . . . but it is very important to know it for practical reasons. For the shadow is a normal and natural fact, while the Freudian unconscious, or the personal unconscious, is not necessarily a normal natural fact; it is to a certain extent a cultural fact. When you ask people what their shadow is, they are likely to tell you what they repress; that is, their conscious assumption of the nature of their shadow. But you must realize that such an assumption does not necessarily coincide with the reality. We usually make the mistake of assuming that the shadow is coincident with our repressions, we explain it in those terms. But while this may be so, it is not necessarily so. The real evil in people is often quite different, they repress something which is perhaps not even evil, it is only a mistake, an illusion.

I will tell you a case. A man came to me and told me among other things that he was a homosexual. He didn't look so and I get rather suspicious when people assure me that they have sexual peculiarities, so I asked him whether he had had a Freudian analysis, and found that he had — for some months. Then I said, "Now tell me, have you had love affairs with boys? " "Oh, no," he said, quite upset, "it is not as bad as that." "But of what does your homosexuality consist? Do you have phantasies about boys, do you like them better than girls? " "Oh, no, I have always been in love with girls. When the analyst told me I was homosexual I was shocked, I didn't know it." "But how did the analyst know since you did not know? " "It came as a great surprise; I once dreamed that I was sleeping with someone who I thought was a woman and it turned out to be a boy. I woke up terribly shocked."

Now of course, one can dream anything, one can dream that one is sleeping with an animal, but that does not prove that one is a sexual pervert, it is simply a symbol. But those people take it quite literally, and are convinced that it is sexual, which just isn't true. That symbolism does not come from a repression; the repression theory is not necessarily an eternal truth, it is a *point de vue*, gives an *aperçu*. . . .

The personal unconscious is in a way coincident with the shadow, yet it also may be like a film of illusion, a sort of assumption about the evil nature of the shadow. For although the shadow is the negative of the conscious personality, it may be much more decent and have many more positive qualities than the conscious. Many people live their dark side consciously, their conscious life is the shadow life. . . . They go about falling into one hole after another, and if you ask them about their shadow, they inform you that they are murderers, cutthroats, and gamblers, everything that is wrong, while in reality they are entirely decent folk; if one takes away that film of illusion about their shadow, one discovers them to be eighty percent pure gold, perfectly nice people. (There is always a sort of hidden Christ complex in such an attitude; also that infantile principle: "It serves you right when you hurt me.") . . . So the film of illusion which we have about our shadow is not to be taken as the shadow; to find out what the shadow really is, is sometimes quite a task. . . .

Here we are not speaking of such assumptions, but of the shadow as it ordinarily is in reality, namely, the unconscious part of the personality — and that is an exceedingly real thing. To say the shadow is merely the absence of light is like the famous definition which optimistic people give of evil — that it is nothing but the absence of good, only a mistake. But when one sees how things develop in the world, one sees that the devil is really in them, that there is abysmal evil at work. One cannot explain the destructive tendency in the world as the mere absence of good or as a mistake made in something originally good. People say that at bottom man is good, but that is not true; one might as well say the opposite. . . .

And so our shadow really exists. It is as evil as we are positive and constructive in consciousness. . . . I mean the more desperately we try to be good and wonderful and perfect, the more the shadow develops a definite will to be black and evil and destructive. People cannot see that; they are always striving to be marvelous, then they discover terrible destructive things happening which they cannot understand. They may deny that such things have anything to do with them or, if they admit them, take them for natural afflictions, or try to minimize them and shift the responsibility somewhere else. The fact is that if one tries beyond one's capacity to be perfect, the shadow descends to hell and becomes the devil. For it is just as sinful from the standpoint of nature and of truth to be above oneself as to be below oneself. . . .

Now you ask whether this old woman, the shadow who is throwing fire on the patient and her animus, is behaving in a positive way, doing something good for the whole psyche. That is not so simple. We must remember the text here: the patient sees one of the riders standing before the ghost of an

213

old woman, and in front of the ghost is a caldron seething with fire. And as we said, the caldron shows the old woman is a witch. There is nothing very positive about that. Moreover she is not even a real witch, she is the ghost of a witch, which makes it still more negative, it is very spooky. . . . That fire comes from the unconscious side, it is a telluric fire from the bowels of the earth. . . . So evidently the shadow did not become positive, despite the fact that she weds the patient to the animus.

Wedded to the Animus

But this union of the patient and her animus creates a different situation, of course; she is now separated from the shadow, or in opposition to it, and yet wedded to the animus. This means that she now has an immediate connection with the collective unconscious; it provides a chance for the collective unconscious to blend with the conscious, the two can unite and produce a new condition naturally. For the conscious world and the unconscious world are the principle pair of opposites; when the two come together, it is as if man and woman were coming together, like the union of male and female, of light and darkness. Then a birth will take place.

That is why in alchemy . . . the philosophers' stone is characteristically represented as a reconciliation of opposites – that is, of Yang and Yin. And for this woman being wedded to the animus would mean a union of Yang and Yin which would settle the conflict in her between the two worlds, the light world and the dark world, the visible world and the invisible world. It would be the beginning – or the anticipation, at least – of Tao. That is only a psychological condition, of course; in this case it is a mere intuition, one would seek in vain for symptoms of Tao in her external life, or even in her general feeling about herself. The way to establish Tao is only indicated here. If Tao were really established, everything would fall into place; there would be no conflict requiring soldiers and helmets and other means of protection.

VISION (cont.): A flame shot up from the head of the man and from my breast shot a flame, also. Then the old woman said: "Go forth and see what you can find." We walked away.

The fire of Eros bursts from her heart, and the fire of Logos from his head. The unconscious involuntary mind of the woman is aflame and blends with her woman's heart, the Eros. Now she should be equipped, one would suppose. But going out into the world so carelessly shows a lack of feeling consideration; if she had a differentiated Eros function and were not altogether possessed by the animus, she would instantly see that such a performance could not succeed. If she realized her own feeling, she could not appear as a nature-being like Pan, because love after all has something to do with kindness. In most cases, I admit, it isn't concerned with kindness, it is just a hellish possession, but love *should* have to do with kindness — I am pleading for love.

In the East, where they know as little about that kind of love as we do, they have a beautiful symbol for it in Kwannon, the Goddess of Kindness. She gives nourishment to all living beings, even to the evil spirits in hell, and to do so she must go down to hell; but it would frighten the devils if she were to appear there in her heavenly form and, as the Goddess of Kindness, she cannot permit that to happen; so, having such an extraordinary regard for the feelings of the devils, she transforms herself into an evil spirit and takes the food down in that guise. There is a beautiful traditional painting where she is represented in hell as a devil among the devils, giving them food; but there is a fine thread going up from her head to a heavenly being above, who is herself in all her splendid finery. That is the psychological attitude which real love suggests. . . .

But to bring about the union of opposites in our patient it is first of all necessary that the principle of Yang as well as of Yin should be active in her psychology. She must contain the principle of light and not lose consciousness and understanding; on the other hand, she must also have the power of darkness; that is, the flame in her breast.

Similar things have been hinted at before, when dark influences got at her and when her animus turned into the dark principle, as in the Negro. Here it is in the form of the Eros flame shooting from her heart, and the Logos flame coming from the man's head. Those flames are unholy and have to do with the fires of hell rather than warmth and light. They show the intensity of the dark purpose. And the old witch says: "Go forth and see what you can find," which is not exactly a blessing. It would mean that further on they will encounter tremendous obstacles, for now they have to deal with the very immediate, formidable resistance of the earth.

VISION (cont.): The white banner of the men trailed on the ground. We came to a forest and there beheld a snakelike dragon. In its mouth it held a knife. The man wrenched the knife from the dragon and tearing out its teeth threw the teeth behind him. We walked on and soon came to a block of ice. I said: "Within that ice is a beautiful red jewel. How shall we melt the ice to obtain the jewel? " The man answered: "Only your body will melt it." So I lay on the ice which melted away. I gave the jewel to the man who put it upon his breast. As we walked on in the darkness we saw before us in the sky the streaming lights of the aurora borealis.

This is a typical situation, the hero and his lady on a quest. A dragon is apt to appear, or they will get into a dark forest, or something of the sort. And now the adventures on the road to the distant goal begin. The dragon holds a knife in his mouth, which is rather unusual. There is no mythological parallel, but she has read *The Psychology of the Unconscious* and has probably seen there an early Christian legend about a dragon who lived in a cave and to whom virgins were sacrificed.[15] An early Christian saint made his way into the cave and destroyed the dragon which, he discovered, was a mechanical contrivance. Its tongue was a projecting sword, and the women were hurled down upon the sword, right into the tail of the dragon. Our patient is probably referring to that dragon, having adopted it because the symbolism was an apt expression of her particular case. For what would the dragon with a sword in its mouth represent?

Answer: Animus opinions?

Dr. Jung: The dragon is an engulfing, enveloping, or devouring monster, I think it means here a multitude, a collectivity. And the tongue, which is sharp like a knife, would be gossip, slander, public criticism or depreciation, anything that kills. So we might call this dragon another form of the animus. Yet we should not exaggerate the use of the term animus, so we had better say that the dragon is here collective opinion, which is not necessarily represented by the animus, because it is also an external fact. . . .

She has to face that. So the man, who is her mind, wrenches the sword — or the knife — from the dragon, and tearing out its teeth, throws them behind him, meaning that her mind takes the sting out of the gossip. You see in analysis one naturally has to deal with gossip all the time, and one finds that there is usually a sting in it because it contains an element of truth. Moreover, it stings because, inasmuch as we are collective, we also have collective opinions; so when we hear the same thing outside which we already have inside, it stings us in the back, we are momentarily overcome and our thought fails us. Therefore I usually say to anyone who is wounded by gossip: "Now let us think about it. What has really happened, and what does it matter? "
. . . You see thinking is a Logos activity which discriminates between things, while a woman who has nothing but the Eros attitude is related to the things that sting, and is stung again and again. She has absolutely no weapon against it because her Eros principle always tries to establish a relationship to it; but if she begins to think, that makes a space between it and herself; then she is relatively safe. So here our patient has to learn to disarm gossip and wounding remarks in the way that a man arrives at his own convictions, that is, independently of public opinion. . . .

The Jewel in the Ice

VISION (cont.): We walked on and soon came to a block of ice. I said: "Within that ice is a beautiful red jewel. How shall we melt the ice to obtain the jewel? " The man answered: "Only your body will melt it." So I lay on the ice which melted away. I gave the jewel to the man who put it upon his breast.

What is this block of ice with the red jewel in it? You see the symbolism here emphasizes the importance of the body. When a woman is wedded to the animus, she is usually lifted up into a mental sphere where she is only concerned with spiritual things, as if everything could be done by a spiritual attitude. But that is the wrong kind of spirituality, because there is a secret joy behind it at having escaped the awkward problem of the body. And this vision says that only the warmth of the body will melt the ice which contains the red jewel. A certain influence of the animus which would otherwise lift her too far into the spiritual sphere is counteracted here by the emphasis on the body, on the fact that the ice cannot be melted without it, that the body plays a decisive part in her further progress. Now obviously a great deal depends upon the interpretation of that red jewel.

It is the heart or the blood; it is warmth of feeling, and a jewel of that substance could be called love. As the heart is a red jewel, I think we are safe in assuming that this jewel means the treasure or jewel of life, here surrounded by ice. For if one is lifted into the upper strata of the atmosphere, there everything is frozen, even the heart may grow cold in a woman just on account of the animus.

For when women begin to think they often dismiss the heart altogether, and when the animus rules alone, it often seems as if the world contained no feeling at all or anything resembling Eros. The animus statement is always peculiarly beside the mark because it is made in an absolutely unfeeling way. So this vision confirms what we have seen before, that through her contact with the animus she becomes disembodied and cold, her heart is in the block of ice.

But the human heart has to do with the body, it is not made of air, and she can obtain the jewel only by using her body to melt the ice, for the heat, that flame, is in the body, and it comes from the dark side. If she should try to be wonderful and perfect, her shadow would contain the flames of hell, but she herself would not contain them. She would be a pure block of ice, she would have a red flaming heart inside but its warmth would reach no one. And warm rays from anyone else's heart would have to pass through

217

that ice to reach hers, but the ice would annihilate them, they would die down completely. The existence of a heart in ice means nothing, it has to reach a fellow being.

Ideals are nice and wonderful, but they can transform a person into an abstract ghost emanating no warmth at all. . . . A drop of hell-fire is absolutely indicated. It is always there, but if one disregards the body, one disregards that drop of hell-fire and it doesn't work.

This is not my invention, the idea comes from an old Jewish legend about Jezer Horra who is the evil spirit of passion. The story is that there was a very wise and pious man who saw that all the sins of the world were caused by this evil spirit. So being a pious man and therefore on very good terms with God he went to the roof of his house one evening and prayed to God to remove the evil spirit of passion from the world. God granted the request, and the pious man thanked him and was very glad and went down into the world now redeemed from the evil spirit. But when he went into his rose garden, though the roses were as beautiful as ever, he could not enjoy the beauty and the perfume; they seemed very ordinary and their perfume was somehow not right. He said to himself: "There must be something wrong with me," and bethought himself of a wonderful old wine in his cellar; so he descended into the cellar to fetch it, and it was the same wine but it had no taste, there was no kick in it. Then he remembered that he had a beautiful young wife in his harem, so he went and kissed her but it meant nothing. He was quite desperate till the idea occurred to him that it might have to do with Jezer Horra. So he went up to the roof and prayed to God, beseeching him to let Jezer Horra out into the world again. And because he was a pious man God let out the spirit of passion, and since then it has been in the world.

You see that is the drop of hell-fire, the flame, and without it no ice can be melted. There will be no warmth, heart will not touch heart, and no fire will be kindled.

Well, this woman succeeds in melting the ice, and then she gives the jewel to the man, who puts it on his breast. That is, the animus now reaches her heart, there is a union between the animus and feeling. He is no longer merely the Logos function, he contains feeling which is a tremendous asset. For then the woman's thought, her conception of things, is no longer a mere abstraction; it is adapted and adjusted through feeling values, which correct the mistakes of the animus.

VISION (cont.): As we walked on in the darkness we saw before us in the sky the streaming lights of the aurora borealis.

218

What does that indicate?

Answer: Is not the aurora borealis the light of the earth itself?

Dr. Jung: No. It is electrons coming down from space. Therefore it is closely connected with magnetic storms; when there is a thunderstorm, the aurora borealis is often to be seen at the same time, but it really comes from the cosmic spaces. That fits in particularly well here because the situation is now very earthly, the Logos is now connected with the feeling, with that drop of hell-fire in her heart, so she is entirely on the earth and in darkness. Then comes the vision of light from the cosmic spaces. Now what is that light psychologically?

Answer: The light of Tao.

Suggestion: Is it the constellation of the Yang again, having accepted the Yin?

Dr. Jung: Yes. This last part of the vision contains a full recognition of the Yin, and of the essential psychology of a woman. Then comes the cosmic phenomenon, in other words, an illumination, an enlightenment which is only possible when one is in the depths of darkness. Then only can that unearthly light be seen. The aurora borealis is particularly impressive because it occurs in the almost interminable winter nights of the arctic countries; it is an exceedingly brilliant phenomenon of almost metaphysical beauty, a very spiritual and mystic light.

PART SEVEN

Natural Spirit and Christian Spirit

Today we start a new series of visions. In the beginning she finds herself again in a cathedral. That the movement of this series should start in a spiritual setting was prepared for by the aurora borealis, an apparition from above, as she was coming from below, with which the last series ended. But what kind of spirit would you expect in a cathedral?

Answer: A Christian spirit.

Dr. Jung: Obviously, and that does not fit in with the aurora borealis, which is the natural spirit, a cosmic sort of spirit. We have encountered this conflict between the cosmic spirit of nature and the Christian spirit before. Do you remember an example?

Answer: Pan.

Dr. Jung: Yes, the God Pan is a nature spirit, a sort of philosophical nature God. Originally he was a local field deity . . . a God of the meadows and the woods. . . . The word panic comes from Pan. He went about whistling or playing his pipe and frightening the shepherds. Their fear was like the fear of the stampeding herd. Occasionally herds stampede for no obvious reason, as if the cattle were frightened by something. In the midst of nature the same thing occasionally happens to us; we are suddenly gripped by terror without knowing why. Sometimes the place is particularly lonely and uncanny, at other times we cannot say why we are seized by an animal fear. It is the great God Pan who causes terror, causes panic. Later, through a transformation in the meaning of the name, this nature demon became a great philosophical God. The Greek word *pâs* means all, the whole, and *pan*, the neuter, means the universe; that meaning became attached to the God – he became the universal nature spirit.

This nature spirit was opposed by the Christian spirit. The early Christians of the first centuries repudiated nature worship of any description; nature was not to be looked at or admired. But the antique religions worshipped nature intensely, particularly Mithraism. That is why Mithraeums are always found in lovely places – near springs in the woods, or in natural grottoes and caves. . . . It was a beautiful form of worship, and the most

[From the lectures given between February 17 and March 9, 1932 (*Spring* 1966).]

formidable enemy of Christianity; for the Christian spirit had to combat the natural joy we feel in nature. Christians said that this was the temptation of the devil, that natural beauty lured men to the beauties of the flesh and made them dull in spirit.

It is true that contact with nature makes men more or less unconscious; so in that respect nature's influence is hostile. Primitive people when they are exposed to intense natural influences simply become unconscious. And that happens still; people go to the woods and mountains nowadays in order to become unconscious; it is a great relief to identify with nature after the strain of conscious city living. But it may be overdone and have a bad effect, it may make people too primitive.

I have seen several cases in which the influence of nature had to be combatted, cases of people who were always avoiding issues by going off into nature and forgetting themselves completely, using nature as a sort of dope. That's how it was in the beginning of Christianity, in the Middle Ages, and very much later too. Nature had to be cursed as unholy in order to make men aware of the power and importance of the spirit. That was because the great God Pan was not really dead, the spell was still there.

Of course the Christian spirit is not to be rejected entirely; when too much nature overwhelms people, they lose what the Christians gained by repudiating it. The Christian spirit is the Western attempt — still very modest — to deny the flesh; it is a stage on the road that the East has already traveled, toward the denial of reality. The early Christian argument was that the flesh is transitory, while the spirit is eternal; that the flesh vanishes like grass, while the spirit lives on in eternity. This is the beginning of the idea that reality is not what it seems to be, that it is an illusion.

Our patient suffers from the same conflict. When she is confronted with a natural manifestation of the spirit, there is always the danger that she will come under the influence of Pan and fall into an unconscious condition. That panic terror of nature, you see, does not come from nature itself but from the nature of man; it is the fear of being overcome by the unconscious, the terror of going crazy in solitude. Her vision of the aurora borealis was a manifestation of the spirit of nature, and if she can now avoid what might be called the aesthetic aspect of that phenomenon, if she can look at it and understand it without losing herself in it, then she will be maintaining a spiritual attitude toward it. But if the aesthetic quality of the vision overcomes her that will mean that she has lost consciousness and deserves to fall into a panic; then she needs to be Christian.

This explains why the aurora borealis immediately constellates the

221

Christian spirit; a cathedral means a refuge, in it she is sheltered from the demons of nature. For nothing natural is allowed in the church; animals are never permitted to enter it. Everything that is used in the ritual has to be denaturalized. The water used in the baptismal font, the wax of the candles, and even the incense must be purified, denaturalized, before they are used. This denaturalizing of things seems extraordinary, yet human nature needs it to come to a spiritual point of view. When one is already denaturalized, however, there is no use carrying it further; then the problem becomes like that of teaching a horse to get on without oats, the day one succeeds he dies.

So the return to nature becomes a problem. It should not be a regression; one should not sink below the Christian accomplishment, the seeing of the flesh as illusory; rather, one should keep the Christian view and return to nature with it as a safe-guard. Otherwise one would fall into the demonism of primitive times and the whole intervening development would come to nothing. That has been this woman's danger, it is why she returns to the problem of Christian spirituality whenever she touches on the natural spirit. But now there is a difference: she has come to a manifestation of the natural spirit that is beyond the denaturalization of Christianity, so that if she returns to Christianity now it is a regression. And such a regression, you may be sure, will have to be worked on again; it will have to be transformed into a new attempt to approach the spirit of nature in a conscious way.

"From My Womb I Bring Forth Suffering"

The next vision tells a very coherent story, so I will give it all at once:

VISION: I was in a cathedral. I saw a dark Christ on the crucifix and beneath the crucifix the weeping Mother of Christ. I said to her: "Why do you weep, O mater dolorosa?" She answered: "Before this he was with me. Now he is up there upon the cross. Something has broken between us." Then I took her by the hand and led her away saying: "Woman, why are you afraid to stand alone?" We stood there together facing the dying Christ who turned his face toward us and gazed upon us. Then he spoke saying: "O you two women who have created me, behold me now. Did you create me only to be crucified?" I answered Christ: "Yes, from my womb I bring forth suffering. I will create you again with my body and again you will be crucified." When he heard these words the eyes of Christ closed. He turned his head away. Then the mother of Christ wailed in a loud voice: "You shall not speak such words." She called in a great crowd who stood about menacing me. I drew a veil over my face and went forth from the church. The angry crowd called: "You have spoken words no one shall speak." I made my way through the winding streets of the town and came at last to the

banks of a stream. Here I knelt down and lifting my veil I bathed my face
in the water. A swan came toward me and in a basket I saw a new born babe.

This vision contains the reconstruction of her rapport with the nature
spirit. In it regression is transformed into progress. She is obviously identified, or parallel, with the mother of Christ, as may be seen from the words:
"We stood facing the dying Christ." Then she talks with Christ as if she
were the mother and he says: ". . . you two women who have created me."
Only Mary created him, but it seems as if the patient were a second Mary,
as if she were assimilated into the story, and she answers him: "Yes, from
my womb I bring forth suffering, I will create you again. . ." Do you understand this?

Answer: Her conflict is constellated between the spirit and nature, for
Mary is nature and she complains in the beginning that something has come
between Christ and herself. Also, is the Christ not black?

Dr. Jung: She does not say black but dark. The dark Christ means obscure, dim, referring perhaps to the antiquity of the wood. I think it is
better here to take Mary . . . in her medieval Christian significance, rather
than as identical with the earth. You see, Mary does not agree with the
patient. She says: "You should not speak such words." She calls in the
menacing crowd and disavows the patient, she does not want to be identified with her. She does not want to know that she has brought Christ into
the world only to be crucified. She brought him forth assuming it was for
a happy and successful life, not for a cruel death. . . . In contradistinction
to Mary, the patient says that she brought him forth for suffering and that
if she should do it a second time, it would be again for crucifixion.

She is apparently perfectly conscious . . . far more conscious than Mary
. . . and almost ruthless, very unsentimental. Now how would you interpret
this? What about the way she takes the place of Mary, as if she were going
to create a Christ, as if she were Mary herself? . . . In the Catholic Church
it would be exceedingly blasphemous for anyone to identify with Mary.

Suggestion: Is it not the collective idea about mothers that they should
suffer?

Dr. Jung: That children are always children of sorrow is certainly true,
it is the eternal fate. The suffering of the world is continued through the
fact that mothers have children; every woman who has a child is continuing
the suffering of the world. It is a very conscious point of view, very mature,
to say: I am bringing forth this child for the suffering of the world. . . .

Comment: It seems as if she had assimilated the Christian or medieval
point of view about Mary, as if she had Mary within herself.

Dr. Jung: Yes, we see progress here. She has obviously attained a certain consciousness in that she is able to say: There is nothing particularly divine in Mary, we are all like Mary in bringing forth children who will suffer, it is even our purpose to do so. It is better to assume that one will procreate suffering than the eternal lie that everyone will be happy. A mature consciousness cannot assume such nonsense. So here she takes the initiative, she talks to Christ as if he were her son, and in putting herself in the place of Mary, she is practically putting herself in the place of Christ. Christ is the symbol of the man who shoulders the cross, who goes to his death with a deliberate consciousness, a clear conscious vision that things must be as they are, and that one must accept one's individual suffering. And when she says she is bringing him forth a second time, it means that she is doing so for the same end; she is then doing what Christ did when he deliberately went to his cruel death.

What is described here is really the assimilation of medieval Christian psychology. That is, the medieval man — who is still living in great numbers today — considered Christ the redeemer, and thought of the life of Christ as a divine mystery. But modern man sees that it is by no means unique, that it is ordinary human life — the life of a person who deliberately and consciously accepts his own fate, accepts what he is. Any man who accepts his individual pattern and his individual condition in the same way that Christ did would be Christ's brother, he would be a Christ himself. Probably he would not be crucified. He might be hanged, or shot, or die of an ordinary disease or some other kind of suffering. . . . But he would come to his end asserting that a life such as his had to be. And when he accepts himself in this way, as Christ accepted his life, he fulfills the condition of human life. After that [the external] Christ is no longer necessary to him. Christ came into the world to fulfill the will of the Father; and inasmuch as he did so, he is the son of the Father, he is the visible manifestation of God, and as such he dies. Hence that allusion in the New Testament: "Ye are gods." (John 10:34)

You see Christ made desperate attempts to teach his disciples that they should *not* imitate him, that they should live their own lives, that only then would they be like him. But they did not understand: they took him for God, and his life for a divine mystery which they were very glad to leave to him; they preferred to hide behind him, to organize a church where such events as Christ never happened. Nobody tried to live his own life, as Christ lived his. . . .

Now in this passage it becomes evident that our patient has intuitively attained to such maturity of character that she can place herself beside the mother of God and take the situation into her own hands; she is willing and conscious enough to accept the facts of life, namely, that the woman who has children has made up her mind to continue the illusion and the suffering of the world. And with that understanding, she can go out of the church. . . .

Now we have the symbol of the veil again. You remember that appeared in one of the earlier visions. . . . There the veil covered the back of her head and was meant to cover her unconscious. Here she is hiding her face, which means that as a conspicuous social individual, it is necessary for her to hide herself; her taking the veil now has to do with her renouncing the respectable role. So she goes out of the church and finds herself confronted with the hostile crowd. Naturally anyone who is courageous enough to live his own life in an individual way finds himself in the same awkward situation as other Christ-like people, all the martyrs and saints who have been tortured and killed because they were at variance with their collective surroundings.

Next she comes to the stream, which is nature, and she kneels down beside it because it is now an object of worship to her. She is conscious enough, has suffered enough, to endure the influence of nature, to be able to worship nature consciously. I don't mean to convey the impression that the patient had attained this much maturity in reality; this is merely an intuitive anticipation.

Then the swan comes to her. What is the swan? . . .

Suggestion: Was it not a symbol of Aphrodite?

Dr. Jung: We have the scandalous story of Leda, and . . . the swan is a bit connected with that. . . . The swan is a different kind of spirit, it seldom flies but prefers to live between the water and the air. So it is the symbol of the two elements, something between the water, the unconscious, and the air or light of consciousness; it is more chthonic than the dove. Then in a basket, which the swan apparently brought, she saw a new born babe. What is that?·

Answer: A new birth.

Dr. Jung: Yes, a new attempt, as if she were a new born babe. It is like Christ being raised up again, born anew, when the voice said: "Thou art my Son; this day have I begotten thee." (Hebrews 1:5)

Comment: Is not the fact that the swan brings the child a parallel to the Holy Ghost as a dove?

Dr. Jung: Yes, in medieval art the Holy Ghost is often represented as a dove bringing the infant Christ. . . .

Now I hope the main idea of this vision is clear because it is of fundamental importance. It is really the logical continuation of the Protestant idea.

225

As you know, the Protestant Church, as an institution of intercession between man and God, has been slowly but very decidedly splitting up; it is already split into more than four hundred denominations, and finally everyone will be his own church. . . . Christ was alone with the divinity, and anyone who lives his life like Christ is alone with his God, he is his own church.

Question: What does the stream in the vision mean?

Dr. Jung: A stream always means natural life, the waters of life, and crossing the stream of life is a very important motif. In dreams of modern people one often finds the same motif expressed in other symbols; a high tension wire, for example, instead of the stream of water. . . .

Question: If a person has assimilated that stream of natural power to a certain point — enough to reach another stage of conscious development — would you say that he is then one with the God?

Dr. Jung: No, *alone* with the God.

Question: But does that not really mean that you have simply reached another layer, or level, completely surrounded by another stream from which you have to disidentify? Are you not still part of a vast layer of non-understanding?

Dr. Jung: Naturally. You always have to be, otherwise you would be God himself. The point is that you should assimilate yourself, and not project half of yourself into other people or institutions. Of course you are far from being perfect, or perfectly conscious. And if you become integrated you may be as unconscious as you were before, only you will no longer project yourself; that is the difference. One should never think of man as able to reach perfection, he can only aim at completion. And completion would be a necessary and indispensable condition, if there were any question of perfection at all. For how can you perfect a thing that is incomplete? First make it complete, then see what it is . . . then polish it up, if you have the time and the breath left. . . . Now we will go on.

The Volcano and the Oasis

VISION: I stood on the edge of a volcano. I looked into the crater and saw a sea of boiling fire. Dead bodies were cast up and fell back again. A great cross of smoke with the Egyptian symbol of life above it arose, hovered in the air and vanished.

Now that the babe has been brought to her on the stream of life by the swan (symbolizing the Holy Ghost in a natural form) . . . one would expect to find her in a redeemed condition. Instead she is on the edge of a volcano about to erupt. It is obviously a most dangerous place, and this is a most

226

critical moment. But the rapid enantiodromia that takes place here expresses a profound truth. . . . You see she removed herself from her collective world and left a vacuum there. Now the empty space is sucking everything in. It is a catastrophe like an explosion. . . .

This truth has been recognized in many places in many different forms. [There is a Hindu myth of treasures obtained from the sea.] Among these is Mâni, which means the jewel in Sanskrit. Mâni is the title of Buddha in Mahayana Buddhism, and the famous Tibetan prayer: *Ôm Mâni Padme Hûm*, means: O, the Jewel in the Lotus. . . . Now when the [jewel and the other] treasures are brought to the surface in the myth, one would assume that everything would be right, but a destructive poison wells up from the sea which threatens to destroy the world. That is an example of this rapid enantiodromia. . . . Similarly after the birth of Apollo the terrible dragon Python attempted to swallow him. And Christ was no sooner born than he narrowly escaped being killed by Herod's mass murder of the infant boys. Then when the woman in Revelations brings forth a man child to rule all the nations, there is a dragon waiting to devour him. . . . So, after rebirth comes the void, emptiness, disappointment, destruction, and the question is how to deal with it. That is the content of this vision. Dead bodies have been cast up and have fallen back again; that is destruction, people have been killed.

And then a cross appears in the smoke above the crater. The Christian cross means sacrifice, but this is the *crux ansata*, the cross with the loop on top, the Egyptian symbol of life. This sign means that the crater is not only destructive; the *crux ansata*, also called the *ankh*, always denotes life, either given by the Gods to the Pharaohs or by the Pharaohs to the Gods; there are representations of both. . . . The smoke from a volcano actually does make such a figure; in fine weather the hot air rises until it cools, and expands into a sort of mushroom shape; then if the form is made a little more abstract it becomes the *crux ansata*.

So the crater here is the crater of life. The sign shows that it does not mean extinction. This crater is like a baptismal font; it is like a crater in the old mystical sense of the word, namely, a vessel in which different constituents are mixed to create a new being. . . . Its positive meaning is the mixing bowl. . . .

VISION (cont.): The fire in the crater died down and instead of fire I beheld a beautiful green oasis.

Suddenly a complete transformation has occurred, another enantiodromia. The destructive volcano has turned into a lovely bit of fertile land, the very symbol of life. But what happened to change it? All we saw was the cross of smoke; but there must be a key to unlock this mysterious transformation.

Answer: She did not identify with the situation, and that kept her above it.

Dr. Jung: What would have happened otherwise?

Answer: She would have gone back to the unconscious. She would have been destroyed.

Dr. Jung: But how would she have been destroyed? In what specific form?

Answer: By going crazy, I think. Usually when a thing goes up in flames it is a symbol of insanity.

Dr. Jung: A psychosis may very well be described that way. In a case of dementia praecox the first outbreak of the disease is sometimes linked up with cosmic visions of earthquakes and other things that correspond to the phenomena observable in a crater. The patient may fall into a tremendous emotional upheaval; the flames of passion bursting forth are like volcanic forces, like a chaotic, fiery, boiling lava welling up from the bowels of the earth. In psychological terms they would be insanity, an outburst of madness. . . .

The hopeful feature here is that our patient has not identified with the crater, she is not the crater herself nor is the crater inside her; she is standing outside on the edge and looking at it. This detachment is a sign of maturity in her. . . . If we look at destruction in a detached way, not allowing our emotions to participate in it, we can see that it has a positive side, that something new may come out of it. That is why the scene suddenly changes and becomes a beautiful green oasis.

VISION (cont.): I descended into the crater and walked through verdant grass. I beheld a woman drawing water from a well. On her head she wore the Kybele jewel. She looked at me and said: "You are a stranger here." I answered: "Yes, will you teach me? " She asked: "Have you strength to descend to the very bottom of this well from which I draw water? " Then I saw that there were stairs leading down into the well and I began to descend, down and down. At length I reached the bottom.

The funnel of the crater, where the fire and smoke and lava pour out, is now the shaft of a well into which she can descend, a place where water can be drawn. And the woman she meets there wears the Kybele jewel — you know Kybele was a Goddess of Asia Minor, another form of Astarte or Ishtar, the Goddess of love. And what jewel is this?

Answer: The jewel that was in the ice, a red jewel.

Dr. Jung: Yes, and that was a heart, so it is presumably the same here, because the heart is the symbol of love, and this is the jewel of Kybele, the Goddess of love. And the woman? . . . We must assume since she is wearing the jewel that she is either Kybele herself or a high priestess of Kybele; also she must live there by magic — no ordinary person could live in a place like that which was sometimes a volcano.

We can find an analogy for this symbolism in H. Rider Haggard's *She*. "She," who was the daughter of a priest of Isis, descended as a high priestess into the crater of life. There she achieved relative immortality by allowing the pillar of life to pass through her body. . . .

That the patient was unconsciously reminded of the symbolism in *She* is suggested by the fact that the *ankh*, the Egyptian sign of life, turns up here; but it is not a direct and conscious influence, it is hidden in the meaning. This analogy indicates that the descent into the volcano is not only a psychological rebirth mystery but something more, because relative immortality means divinity. You may remember that "She" often appears as a divine person, despite very mortal traits of character. In this way Rider Haggard conceived of something like a Greek Goddess. . . .

The Greek deities could be explained from either aspect; they were peculiarly divine and at the same time peculiarly human. This conception seems rather strange to us but it was not at all strange to antiquity; there is even a suggestion of it in the idea of Christ. Christ was in a way an ordinary human being; he could have had all the imperfections of a human being, and probably had them, but on the other side he was a God. . . .

Now in this vision we encounter the same curious mentality. The woman our patient meets is a Goddess, or a figure like "She." This is due to the fact, as I have said before, that all of these visions move in an antique atmosphere, the atmosphere out of which Christianity emerged; so they are on the one hand Christian and on the other hand pagan. It is as if a layer of the antique mind, dating from about 100 B.C. to 100 A.D., is being brought to the surface again; we find many typically antique modes of thought or conceptions of things. . . .

The fact that this woman at the bottom of the crater is a Goddess, or at all events a person of competence and authority, is proved by the patient's attitude. She asks the woman to teach her, showing that she at once recognizes her superiority, and the woman answers by questioning whether she will have the strength to descend to the very bottom of the well.

229

Encoiled by a Serpent

So now the patient will be going down again into the unconscious, but deeper still. At length she reaches the bottom.

VISION (cont.): There upon the ground I saw a man and a woman lying as if in the womb and about them was coiled a snake.

I will show you her picture of it:

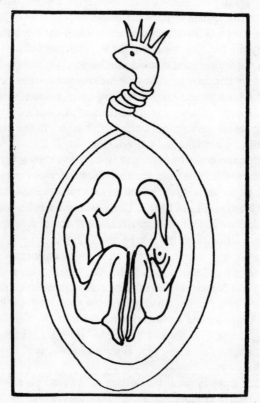

Man and woman encoiled by a snake.
(Rendering by Janet F. Jones.)

Notice the embryonic position of the bodies. Who are these people? What do you think of this strange discovery at the bottom of the well?

Answer: It is a rebirth, a completer one. Until now either a boy or a girl was reborn, but here it is the whole man.

Suggestion: They might be Shiva and Shakti. And this might be the Kundalini serpent before it stirs.

Dr. Jung: Yes, so that canal or shaft she is coming down would be the *shushumna*, the canal through which the Kundalini rises. Here we have a most remarkable fact: that *she is coming down.* Here one sees the tremendous difference between India and the West. . . . She is already up above, and what she must establish is below, she must come down from above. . . . So you see the great mistake that people make when they imitate the Eastern Yoga practices, for they serve a need which is not ours; it is the worst mistake for us to get higher and higher. What we ought to do is to establish the *connection* between above and below. But we take eagerly to the Yoga practice which, of course, does not work . . . because our need is just the contrary one. . . . I never have seen a case [of Yoga practice] that was not applied with the wrong purpose of getting still more on top — to acquire more power or more control, either of their own body, or of other people, or of the world. . . .

In the Kundalini system the God is represented as the fertilizing linga, encoiled by Shakti in the form of the Kundalini serpent. But here we have simply a man and a woman encoiled by a snake; we are uncertain whether they are Shiva and Shakti. Let us see how the snake functions. She says:

VISION (cont.): When I appeared the serpent came toward me and said: "You too will I coil about." I said: "But I am alone." Then the snake coiled itself about my body and put its head close to my face. I saw that it had a crown upon its head and rings of gold around its body. I looked into the eyes of the snake and putting my arms about it I said: "Serpent, you are beautiful to me." Then the serpent fell away. I ascended the well.

This shows that the active element down there is the serpent; the man and woman don't function at all, they are just dormant. That the serpent is divine is evident from the gold rings and the crown. Such decorations add emphasis to a symbol, so this must be a very unusual serpent. It is the divinity here and the man and woman do not have that quality. If we were in India they would be Shiva and Shakti, but since this is a Western mind they are not. Here the emphasis is on the serpent, and it is doing to her exactly what it did to the couple. What is the meaning of this?

Answer: Are they not just an example?

Dr. Jung: The patient says, "But I am alone," as if the serpent would then reply, O, well, in that case I won't coil around you because I am only coiling around couples. But lo and behold, the serpent coils about her as if she were a couple.

Question: Is it coiling about the male and female parts of herself? There are always these two parts to begin with and they are still in her now.

Dr. Jung: We may assume that that pair have been there since the beginning of time, a sort of eternal symbol of what the serpent coiling about an image of the male and female really means. As such it would be a suggestion that wholeness comes from compression by the coils of the snake, that the male and female are united into one by that embrace. This is only obvious symbolically.

You see the essential function of the crater, its magic life-giving quality, is expressed in the serpent lying at the bottom of it; whoever the snake coils about is made whole, the male and the female come together there. Something of the same sort is hinted at in *She*, when Ayesha tries to make Leo enter the pillar of fire with her. . . . One is also reminded of the rite in the Eleusinian mysteries in which the initiate had to kiss a snake; that meant a kind of union. And there was another rite representing union in which a golden snake was passed into the collar and down under the garments of the initiate, then taken out below; this symbolized complete penetration by the divine serpent. It was assumed that the initiate was thus begotten or generated as a twice-born man, and obtained immortality. . . .

So this ceremony at the bottom of the well is the union of the divine principle, represented by the serpent, with the patient. . . . She is for a moment in the God's possession. . . .

Trusting the Serpent

The ceremony is making her whole . . . but she is doing nothing herself. Usually she is quite active, but here she is passive and the serpent is the active one.

Suggestion: Doesn't this have to do with accepting the divine principle? The part about being asleep in the womb might be connected with faith in the divine principle. Can you connect the snake with the river of life?

Dr. Jung: You are on the right track. The particular point of this symbolism is her passive attitude; she is equivalent to that couple, dormant as if in the womb, meaning that she surrenders herself completely to the strange milieu down below. And when she is absolutely inactive, the unconscious assumes the activity — acting for her or upon her — and that is shown by the serpent coiling about her. She is here quietly undergoing the effect of

232

the unconscious. Don't forget that this series of visions began with the danger of psychosis, the volcano, and now she is trusting herself completely to the volcano's activities. This is emphasized by her gesture when she puts her arms about the serpent and says: "You are beautiful to me" – not horrid, or terrifying, but beautiful.

Her acceptance of the serpent shows that she is making friends with the element which threatened to completely destroy her before. When she achieves this she will experience a very peculiar effect. That is why I mentioned the parallel with the Eleusinian mysteries where the initiate had to kiss the snake, which was loathesome and terrifying. This was done because it meant union with the serpent and that meant the entrance of the God. The God entered the body of the initiate who was then called *entheos*, meaning God within. One of the titles of Dionysos was *Enkolpios*, meaning "in the vagina." Dionysos enters initiates as if he were the phallus and each initiate were a vagina. He is then contained in the initiates, his followers, and as such he is called *Enkolpios*.

From this sequence we see that the madness which threatened our patient was really a panic caused by the immediate vicinity of the God. . . . If one identifies with such emotion, one is simply blasted to bits and the connection with the God does not come off. But if one can detach oneself from this panic, if one can stand it, one can go down into it, and then the God enters the initiate. That is why the patient is shown here in a passive attitude, surrendering completely, and accepting the activity of the unconscious that coils about her like a serpent. This is a terrible moment in itself: nothing could be more terrible than to be attacked by a python – one might die of fear. And without lifting a finger she has to endure that supreme moment when fear itself, the serpent, coils about her. Now if she is capable of doing that, she will be able to stand fear, and thereby gain many advantages. For it is a supreme moment when one can stand the onslaught of such a panic, and that is how she might be able to overcome the danger which was threatening her in the beginning. Is that clear?

You see, if she were capable of realizing this vision, she would acquire a kind of magical protection; everyone else might be upset but it would be as if the serpent were coiled around her and she would never again be profoundly upset. Things could still reach her, but she would be at a depth deeper than the deepest emotion.

VISION (cont.): I ascended from the well. The sky became dark with heavy clouds. Skeletons on horseback galloped by. (Again a sort of mad vision suggesting panic.) The clouds turned to smoke and streams of boiling water began to flow past me. I knew that the eruption had again begun. I sought to escape from the crater but could find no way to the rim. Then I called out that I was lost and would be burned alive. The crescent moon swung down low to me. I caught it with my hands and it lifted me out. I walked down the side of the volcano, and came to a village in the valley. I said to the people: "What do you call the mountain? " They answered: "The Great Mother.". I said: "But your Great Mother is a destroyer." They answered: "She only smokes." I said: "See my clothes are charred and torn with the fire." They answered: "You went too near. We only behold our Great Mother from our valley here below."

Here we have an interpretation of the volcano. It is called the Great Mother, and if one doesn't go too near, one won't be burned. Our patient went too near. . . . But you see what she gained through her experience with the snake; she is now apparently on very good terms with the moon, so that it helps her out of the embarassing situation of being at the bottom of an active volcano. But where did she get a connection with the crescent moon?

Answer: From the Goddess in the well.

Dr. Jung: Yes, Kybele is the moon, the crescent is her emblem. . . . That Luna herself should descend to take our patient out of danger is very fantastic symbolism, but psychologically it means that her complete surrender to the unconscious powers has made them into her friends; now the unconscious functions helpfully and produces a miracle in her favor. The Western mind never accepts the possibility that the unconscious can be anything but a terrible nuisance, that it can do anything more than cause neuroses of the stomach or the heart, or give bad dreams; it never assumes that the unconscious behaves intelligently. . . . [But] it is really true that if one improves one's relation to the unconscious, it shows itself to be a helpful power; then it has an activity of its own, gives helpful dreams, and at times really produces little miracles. . . .

The Normal People

Now who are the people who live in the village at the foot of the mountain?

Answer: Those who repress their emotions.

Dr. Jung: I don't think they repress their emotions especially. They are very hopeful people who never go too near the fire, just ordinary people to whom the world means nothing in particular. To them that mountain is entirely harmless, it is called the Great Mother only because it is rather bulky in form; and the volcanic activity counts for nothing. It is the old grandmother smoking her pipe; naturally one gets burned if one goes too close,

"We never go there." You see they are the ordinary people who find nothing in the world to marvel at, to them the whole history of the world is a "just so" story. This patient was astonished that such people could be, that they were allowed to exist without getting neurotic. But I remember telling her: "You should not be astonished, for in a way you are a crank. You are different from other people, outside of the usual order, so you have certain peculiar experiences; that is why you have to know more about the inside of the mountain." Other people don't know about it because they encounter nothing in their lives that forces them to know about it: they live in an everyday world where nothing extraordinary happens.

Naturally there would be a danger if one were to say: Yes, I admit I am a crank but I am a very divine crank. That would be a great mistake, for we live in these villages of normal people, and even being a divine crank doesn't go well with ordinary existence. There is absolutely no reason for any inflation, and it is better to keep all this away from the so-called normal people, because it wouldn't be understood in any event. Now we come to the next series of visions:

VISION: I stood on the shores of the water. A fish cast itself out of the water at my feet. I picked it up, put my hand in its mouth and drew forth a black rough stone. I rubbed the stone against my breast and it turned to amber. Within the amber I saw a face of suffering. I put the amber in my robe against my breast and walked away.

What is this? One must always keep in mind the end of the vision before to gain a clue for deciphering the next one. She has just come from the village of the normal people, where the world is a "just so" story, so now she is probably quite bewildered and doesn't know whether they are crazy or she is crazy. . . . That is the situation in which the new phantasy begins.

Comment: The fish brings her a stone that will turn into a jewel again, so she realizes that she herself has not been one of the ordinary people, that she has indeed won something. . . .

Dr. Jung: But it must have been lost since the fish brings it back. How was it lost?

Answer: After she had been with the ordinary people for a while she lost her belief in those experiences.

Dr. Jung: Exactly, that is what happens. People may have the most extraordinary experiences in the course of analysis, but when they go out into the world they forget about them. The further they get away from that mountain the less impressive it seems; it just smokes, so they forget their experience. What they have gained is lost, like the ring of Polycrates, which would have been lost in the ocean if the fish had not brought it back. Under the influence of these village people the woman has lost her precious experience, which really is a treasure if kept in consciousness as such.

So she stands, rather forlornly, on the shore of the great waters and the fish brings her the jewel again. But this time it is a rough black stone and does not look like a jewel at all; it looks like any stone, one would never notice it. Apparently the blackness comes from the volcano, and she doesn't see that it is a jewel until she has rubbed it against her breast and filled it with her own libido again; however, when she begins to realize what it is she puts it against her heart, and the jewel *is* the heart. It turns to a precious substance, amber. And how does amber differ from the rough black stone?

Answer: It is transparent, and occasionally little plants and insects can be seen in it, floating about as if in water.

Dr. Jung: Yes, amber is a very preservative substance; the most tender algae and the most delicate organs of microscopic insects can be preserved in it. Reminiscences of millions of years ago are marvellously preserved in amber.

The Amber

And there she sees the suffering face. What is that?

Answer: Her own.

Dr. Jung: It might be her own, the memory of her own suffering. We shall see. She says:

VISION (cont.): Then I felt the amber beating with a strong pulse and I felt tired and lay down on the ground. There the amber beat like a great heart and soon the ground and the trees about me beat also. I began to feel the pulsation everywhere.

This amber symbolizes the red jewel or the heart that we saw before in the ice. . . . But it is a very peculiar heart in that it is beating not only in herself but also outside, it fills the surroundings with its pulsation. . . . It is as if the heart were a part of nature; she cannot distinguish whether the heart or all of nature is pulsating. It is a sort of synchronistic phenomenon.

Suggestion: Is it not like the Chinese concept of Tao, the life force, the life energy?

Dr. Jung: The realization of Tao has this quality of being in synchronistic relation with everything else; it is as if the same stream of events, or the same stream of life, goes through everything, so that everything has, as it were, the same rhythm, the same meaning.

Suggestion: Another analogy might be what the mystical Mohammedans describe in Sufism — a transcendental essence, a feeling of the heart actually, in which all of outer reality is reflected.

Dr. Jung: Yes, it is the general mystical experience, the coincidence of the individual condition with the universe, so that the two become indistinguishable. This moment in the vision is such a realization of Tao.

The symbolism is most unusual; I have never seen the experience couched in such terms, but this is an excellent way of putting it. Yet, you must realize, the experience is indescribable, it cannot be defined. Tao is incomprehensible. Not by the greatest effort of our minds can we imagine a condition of complete coincidence or harmony between two incommensurable things. Our subjective condition seems the exact opposite of an objective condition.

This incomprehensibility of Tao is allied to the fact that the mind is unable to understand, or consciousness to grasp, anything that is not disparate, not made distinct. Only by means of discrimination can we be conscious, whereas Tao might be formulated as the condition of things before consciousness. So to speak of the consciousness of Tao is paradoxical. Tao is a sort of semi-consciousness — almost unconsciousness. That is why Tao is the beginning of things, the mother of everything, and also the crowning effect of everything; it is the beginning and the end. But that is what we call the unconscious, where ego consciousness simply comes to an end. We cannot go further into the meaning of such an experience here. We can however discuss how such a psychological experience is connected with the flow of the visions. . . . It would be valuable to know how such a central experience could be brought about.

Suggestion: Was it because the inhabitants of the village made her feel quite alone? That she is now connected with the universe might be a compensation for the feeling of loneliness.

Dr. Jung: That is true. She was first threatened with immediate destruction by the volcano, then rescued in a miraculous way. . . . She had had a tremendous experience . . . and the world in which she arrived depreciated it. . . . She got out of heat into cold, with absolutely nothing in between, no mediation. But here she rescues something from the experience — the amber. It is so small that she can conceal it in her bosom and carry it with her, yet when she contemplates it, she gets into Tao. The amber is the middle condition, it symbolizes Tao. . . . On this side it is a piece of amber, on the other, it is the great mystery. . . . [This talisman, or lapis, is a token made] of understandable commonsense material . . . she can wear it as a jewel and people will say: You have a nice thing there. And she will reply: Yes, although

237

as a matter of fact, it is quite cheap, it is just a piece of amber. . . . But there is something about it, known only to herself, which will have a magical effect upon her. Now concerning the face of suffering that appeared in the amber:

VISION (cont.): I felt that I must free the face inside the amber but I could not.

Where does that face come from?

Answer: The making of such a stone is always connected with great suffering.

Dr. Jung: That is really the idea; she cannot come into the possession of the lapis without suffering. It means individuation, which can only be attained through sacrifice. The memory of suffering makes a stone particularly precious; a jewel which does not remind one of much suffering, many fears, hardly has a value, because good things soon lose their glamor, while the memory of suffering has a much stronger grip upon our minds.

The Imprisoned Animus

VISION (cont.): Many snakes appeared, looked at the amber and glided away. A bull came and licked the amber but it remained the same. Then I knew that only my blood spilled on it would break the amber. So I cut my breast and blood fell upon the amber which vanished. In its place there stood a man bound with thongs and pierced with many arrows. I drew the arrows forth as gently as I could and freed him of his fetters.

So this is the face of suffering that was imprisoned in the stone. Formerly she had to melt the ice with the warmth of her body, and here she goes through the same kind of performance, spilling her blood upon the amber which means a sacrifice, in order to liberate this unknown man from within the stone. You see, when the stone was made, a man was included in it — and you will remember the man and woman encoiled by the snake — so this is her masculine counterpart who has been locked in the stone.

Comment: It is the animus.

Dr. Jung: And obviously the positive animus, because he appears here as an absolute masculine counterpart. That also explains the great suffering; it is the fettering of her masculinity that has caused the suffering. But how did it happen that her animus was fettered, caught in the stone?

Answer: The other side of her nature had come up, the Yin side.

Dr. Jung: And that meant the undoing of the animus. We have to differentiate between the two aspects of the animus: in his real form he is a hero, there is something divine about him; but in this woman's case we usually have had to deal with a very unreal form of animus, an opinionating substitute, for she was beset with animus devils. Through the process of transformation that took place in these visions, however, her mind — what she called her mind — became imprisoned in the earth — in the female, the mother, the upcoming Yin material; thus her animus was slowly suppressed. She no longer had opinions about things as she assumed they should be, but gave the material a chance to speak for itself. So things began to happen to her, thoughts came to her. . . . An unreal negative animus attitude [such as she had before] prevents the accurate perception of psychological facts; it is always putting an opinion in place of actual perception. . . . But now she had learned to experience things objectively, to see what really happens, and learning that has imprisoned her animus.

The motif of imprisoning the animus has its counterpart in masculine psychology in the imprisonment of the anima, but naturally that is different insofar as it concerns emotions and moods. When a man is able to distinguish between the objective situation and his mood, when he no longer allows his mood to blindfold his mind, but can acknowledge that it is peculiar and set it apart, that is the beginning of the imprisonment of the anima. After a while he will be able to say to his mood: You have no right to exist, I will put you in a test tube to be analyzed. Of course that means a great sacrifice . . . to bottle up the anima requires a superhuman effort, so I recognize what an extraordinary accomplishment it is for a woman to put the animus aside . . . for analysis.

In alchemy the procedure is to begin by putting something into a test tube, or into a caldron; similarly the animus or anima is imprisoned for the purpose of transformation. This is a real process of sublimation — there is no sublimation of sex; that is imaginary — this is a transformation, not of sex, but of forms, of experiences. Through imprisonment the animus is stripped of his world and undergoes a change. If a thing is in a sealed test tube external influences are excluded; it is not disturbed and neither does it disturb the surroundings, because nothing can get into the test tube and nothing can get out. When the animus cannot get out into the atmosphere he has no object. Then he has time to transform.

You see, in this transformation it is essential to take objects away from those animus or anima devils. They only become concerned with objects when you allow yourself to be self-indulgent. *Concupiscentia* is the term for that in the church — St. Augustine spoke particularly strongly about it; the word is *convoitise* in French, *Begehrlichkeit* in German, or desire in English. On this subject the great religions come together. The fire of desirousness is the element that must be fought against in Brahmanism, in Buddhism, in Tantrism, in Manicheanism, in Christianity. It is also important in psychology.

When you indulge in desirousness, whether your desire turns toward heaven or hell, you give the animus or the anima an object; then it comes out into the world instead of staying inside in its place. What should be a nighttime thing comes out in daylight, and what belongs under your feet is on top of you. But if you can say: Yes, I desire it and I shall try to get it but I do not have to have it, if I decide to renounce, I can renounce it; then there is no chance for the animus or anima. Otherwise you are governed by your desires, you are possessed. A woman may be possessed by a real man, but only because of an animus projection; in the same way a man may be possessed by a real woman through an anima projection.

So it boils down to your own subjective condition, to your indulgence in your desires. But if you have put your animus or anima into a bottle you are free of possession, even though you may be having a bad time inside, because when your devil has a bad time you have a bad time. . . . Of course he will rumble around in your entrails, but after a while you will see that it was right [to bottle him up]. You will slowly become quiet and change. Then you will discover that there is a stone growing in the bottle, the amber or the lapis. This solidification or crystallization means that your way of dealing with the situation has become habitual; insofar as self-control, or non-indulgence, has become a habit, it is a stone. The more it becomes a habit, the harder, the stronger, that stone will be; when that attitude becomes a *fait accompli*, the stone will be a diamond.

Question: Have you ever seen such a diamond? Has any patient ever reached the diamond?

Dr. Jung: You must never ask such questions — whether we have seen a savior or a holy virgin. It is absolutely certain that we have not . . . [but] perhaps one day somebody will possess a diamond. When one talks of such things one does not possess them; and when one possesses them, why talk?

Now the real animus comes out of the stone — and he should not be bottled up. Keeping the animus in a test tube is a temporary expedient. It must be done until one is safe, until nothing is left of the old *concupiscentia*, or the evil spirit will take possession again. But if one is fairly safe, and the stone has been made, one can open it and let the new animus appear. Then one can see what he does, how he behaves.

In this case the man who comes out is bound with thongs and pierced with arrows, and that is quite comprehensible, it is the result of what she has already done. She *had* to fetter the animus to suppress his opinionating

about things and find out what they really were. . . . [She had to] tie him
down to arrive at an immediate experience. You see the animus is like a film
between reality and a woman's mind. . . . [He is] like a mist before her eyes.
. . . An enormous effort . . . and careful systematic self-education is needed
to penetrate that mist. The reason the man is pierced by arrows as well as
bound by thongs is that arrows move swiftly and penetrate. They are like
thoughts, like shafts of light or of insight that penetrate the animus veil.
Our patient has succeeded here in penetrating . . . the mirage between herself and reality — for this is the real animus. . . . He has been wounded, for
one has to be rough with the animus, to use force. You must not forget
that to be possessed by the animus or the anima was the original condition
of man. We were all possessed, we were slaves, and . . . we don't know to
what extent we are still possessed; it is probable that our liberation is very
relative.

So the suppression of the animus or anima is an act of extreme violence
and cruelty. . . . And naturally the animus gets quite sore in the process and
has to be made whole afterwards. [That is why she is pulling the arrows out.]
All those attempts to tie him down have caused wounds that have to be relieved. It is as if she now had to make the animus conscious of the fact that
he is healed and different.

After she has freed him of his fetters:

VISION (cont.): He ran with great fleetness away from me until he came to
a great precipice. Then he called like Icarus: "I will fly." I answered: "And
like Icarus you will be killed." Slowly and with great sorrow he walked back
toward me and knelt down beside me.

The animus is trying to resume his former position in the world of objects,
he wants to jump into space again and fill it with illusions. He wants to reach
the impossible, the sun. But she tells him: Not a chance for you to go flying
about creating more illusions. No opinionating here. So he lies down obed-
iently beside her. . . . This is a very grand moment in her visions . . . it is an
enormous achievement to be able to say to the animus: *Couche toi.* . . . But
what now? What is the situation of a woman with an obedient animus, or
of a man in control of his anima?

Answer: They have to take full responsibility.

Dr. Jung: Exactly, and to be forced to take responsibility for oneself is
a most awkward and loathesome situation. That is what one is afraid of,
why one doesn't want to see things. It is better not to know what is going
on in the next room for then one is not responsible; one can deceive oneself

and say one does not know the reason for what has happened. . . . People say: "I did not know what he was going to do. How could I be responsible?" Of course they could have known if they had wanted to. But things look so much easier when one doesn't see through them; they run more or less smoothly, and then if such and such a thing happens one can always say it just happened by chance. But when one sees, it becomes altogether too clear how one has prearranged the whole show. So the moment the animus obeys her this woman has to assume responsibility; she has to live with open eyes. We don't know what the trouble will be but we can be sure that if she controls her animus she will get into an exceedingly difficult situation; she will be put to a test. . . .

Now we begin a new series of visions.

VISION: I was descending many steps into the black earth until I came at last to a catacomb where lay many dead.

We are again on a voyage into Hades. How does this situation arise from the former one?

Answer: Is it not connected with the precipice at the end of the last vision?

Dr. Jung: The precipice suggests a drop, a descent. . . . The graves are Hades, or the underworld, the place of shadows; and the Hermes Psychopompos, the leader of souls, is leading . . . to the dwelling place of the dead. . . . In *She*, the anima dwells in the tombs surrounded by mummies; the corpse of her former Greek lover, Kallikrates, keeps She in the tomb. One finds a similar idea in Benoît's *Atlantide*: Antinea the queen lives where she has a huge mausoleum of all her former lovers. . . .

VISION (cont.): I passed them by until I came to a dead man whose flesh was red. He was very beautiful and I thought he was an Indian.

. . . You see the other animus, the man bound with thongs, has disappeared and his place is taken by this very different figure; it is as if she was returning to the beginning of her visions, where a Red Indian on horseback led her to her initiatory adventures. Now she discovers him again, as a beautiful corpse-like figure, but the flesh is red, which means that he is alive although dormant. It is interesting that he should resuscitate just when she discovers a positive animus. For the Indian is a positive, not an injurious, animus, he would adapt her to the American soil. The realization of Indian values by an American is an asset, not a liability. The Red Indian has great qualities despite the fact that he is primitive. To be primitive is no argument against having values.

(Moreover, the American is peculiarly placed between the West and the Far East, which gives a very peculiar quality, particularly to the Western American. The farther one goes West the more one finds that indescribable something, and when one comes across a Chinaman or something Chinese there, one gets a feeling that it fits, that it clicks somehow. In California the conditions of life are so very peculiar that one could expect, in the course of thousands and thousands of years, an entirely new species of man to be shaped. I should not wonder if the influence of the Far East would play a big role there. If there were no immigration laws [1932], the far West of America would be Mongoloid. If anything should happen to America, if she should decay perhaps, surely that whole side of the country would become Mongoloid. And it might become so through the spirit of the Far East, which would be a most logical compensation for the peculiar temperament and mentality of the Californian. American mentality in general, which is characterized by incredible extraversion, can only be compensated by the earth-like passivity, the apathy almost, of the Eastern attitude of mind. The American is really calling for it, so I should not wonder at all if it happened.)

VISION (cont.): From his neck I took a necklace of teeth and walked on carrying it in my hand.

What would this mean?
Answer: That she took his mana perhaps.
Dr. Jung: Yes, teeth are usually amulets, a protection against the evil eye or the perils of the soul. This is another variation of the jewel theme.

VISION (cont.): A dwarf followed me and tried to snatch the necklace away but I held it firmly. I came to a fire of blue flame and I held the teeth in the fire. The teeth changed to blood red jewels which burned my hand.

The dwarf is a figure we have already encountered several times. It is an impish form of animus. This is probably an abortive (dwarfed) attempt of the animus to turn negative and take the talisman away from her. . . . You see, when a man controls his anima, or a woman her animus, they are doing something that no one ever dreamed of doing before; because mankind has always been possessed. When you dare to free yourself, you get into a new order of things, and that means a challenge to the old order, so you no sooner rid yourself of one devil than all the other devils are against you . . . trying to bring you back into the fold of Mother Nature. . . .

If a man makes a modest attempt at controlling his anima, he will at once be forced into a situation where he is tested to the limit . . . and it is the same with a woman; every devil available for miles around will do his best to get at her animus. [Again] it is as if a vacuum had been created and everything rushes in to fill it. That is why people who attempt to control these figures get into new situations that almost force them back to their former state; it works quite automatically. So now, essentially because she made such an attempt, there is the possibility that she will get into a trying situation, into something too difficult for her, too much for her to carry.

For one should realize that one risks an unusual loneliness in controlling the animus or the anima. This is because a *participation mystique* is created by not controlling them; when one allows a piece of one's self to wander about and be projected into other people, it gives one a feeling of being connected. And most connections in the world are of this sort. *Participation mystique* provides this appearance of a connection, but it is never a real connection, it is never a relationship; it only gives one the feeling of being a sheep in the flock. And that is, of course, something; for if you disqualify yourself as a sheep, then you are necessarily out of the flock, and you have to suffer a certain loneliness. Yet then you have a chance to reestablish a connection, and this time it can be a conscious relationship which is far more satisfactory.

Participation mystique gives one a peculiar unconsciousness; in a way it functions like the mother, carrying one along in unconsciousness. Sometimes it is nice and sometimes not at all so, but as a rule people prefer it because the average man gets frightened when he has to do anything he cannot share with his world; he is afraid to be alone, to think anything other people don't think, or to feel anything other people don't feel. One comes up against man's gregarious instinct as soon as one tries to transcend ordinary consciousness.

It is because of some such difficulty that an Indian turns up now, and the Indian is not quite alive. Yet he has the potentiality of life, and if he assumes a leading role, we shall know that she has given up her responsibility and is submitting to the animus again. So it is important to see what happens next. When she takes the necklace of teeth from the Indian's neck and walks on, it shows that she does not make a regression here, that she does not submit to the animus. On the contrary she takes the talisman from him. . . .

This necklace of teeth is the power of the animus; that is, his capacity to put his teeth into a thing. It is a fearful weapon, but if she is going to be responsible for herself, she will need it to give her the aggressiveness and courage of the animus. And what about the dwarf who tried to snatch it from her hand?

Answer: He would be one of the devils you spoke of.

244

Dr. Jung: Yes. . . . The dwarf is always a subordinate creative power in the unconscious that may be helpful and bring things up from the unconscious, or harmful and steal them away. Then its effect is like a momentary eclipse of consciousness during which power and decision suddenly disappear. That often happens. For instance, after long struggles and deliberation, you make up your mind about something and think: Now that is settled; then comes a moment of unconsciousness and the whole thing is gone; it has disappeared as suddenly as if snatched away by an evil power . . . the dwarf has snatched it.

Then our patient went on to say that she came to a fire with blue flames and held the teeth in the fire, whereupon the teeth changed to blood red jewels which burned her hand. Why does she hold them in the fire?

Answer: She is spiritualizing them.

Dr. Jung: The blue flame would be good for that purpose, blue is the color ordinarily used to express the spirit. But why should the teeth be spiritualized? . . .

Suggestion: In the beginning the Indian was leading her, he had her feeling, she was not in control of it, and that gave him the power.

Dr. Jung: Quite so, but now he is no longer in control of her feeling. She holds his power – the teeth.

Suggestion: And that is a spiritual power, unlike anything she has had before.

Question: But why do the teeth turn into red jewels?

Dr. Jung: That is what I am asking you. . . . The teeth certainly mean negative feeling, hatred or hostility rather than love; while the red jewel – which always refers to the heart – would mean love. So this is a pair of opposites. You might say that the aggressiveness or hostility of the teeth of the animus is transformed here into a feeling of love. But doesn't that seem peculiar?

Comment: It happens all the time if you can hold on long enough.

Dr. Jung: And often if you don't hold on it happens, it already means that! When a woman makes an animus attack on a man, it means that the animus is busily using all the negative arguments he can lay his hands on against that man because he has become so extremely important to her feeling. Turn the thing around, you see, and up comes the positive feeling, the heart. . . . An animus attack is usually a substitute for positive feeling . . . when a woman does not take responsibility for her feeling, when she doesn't look out for it consciously, the animus consumes it; then he becomes powerful and may devour her or any other innocent prey. But here that feeling is symbolized by a red jewel, so there must be something more to this than could be expressed by a warm living heart. To what does the jewel point?

Question: Is it something more durable and valuable than the usual feeling?

Question: Is it like the diamond at the center of an Eastern mandala?

Dr. Jung: This precious stone has to do with the center of the mandala; there is in it the idea of the crystal again, and this time it happens to be red. A gem is a truly unchanging thing, one might say an almost eternal thing, and being starlike in character, it is the equivalent of a star. So it refers to the center of the mandala, it refers to the Self, which appears in the feeling here. Naturally when the animus possesses that, he has an almost mystical power, he is surrounded by the taboo of something almost divine. . . . If a primitive man breaks his taboo, he will die; he feels so lonely and outcast that he prefers to die. It is the same with the animus and anima, they are living taboos; if we violate them we are likely to find ourselves in the devil of a lot of trouble; it takes tremendous strength to control the animus and anima. That explains why having the strength to do so is usually symbolized as possession of a precious talisman — an apotropaic charm to ward off the evil that comes from violating the taboo. Then our patient said that the jewels burned her hand. Why is that?

Answer: Because there is so much libido in them.

Dr. Jung: But it is hardly possible that her libido would be sufficient to heat the jewels to the point of burning her hand. The body could not produce so much heat.

Question: Is it not like the stones in the white city which hurt her feet?

Dr. Jung: Just so. In the white city there was such a glare that she could not stand it, and now she is in a similar situation. These red jewels are not as insupportably bright as the white city was, but they are so unnaturally hot that they are almost more than she can deal with. . . . Now why are they so hot? And why was the city so glaring?

Answer: Because a human being cannot stand it.

Dr. Jung: Exactly. It is not human in itself, and so human beings cannot stand it. That accounts for the taboo; such taboos exist because there are things in us that we just cannot endure, they are too much. I know people who simply cannot see certain things because they are unable to stand them . . . and they must not see them. There are things which must not happen. . . . If you have insurmountable resistances, don't even make an attempt to break them down; you might violate a taboo, and not be able to stand the realization. Stay with the feasible things. This woman did not force herself to remain in

246

the white city. It was better for her to return, and then after a while be led on to another test. Here it is the test of the red jewels. If she can stand it, we shall know that she can break the animus taboo. She will be able to hold her own jewel. Hitherto the animus has had to carry it, she could not stand the burning pain.

Comment: It is difficult to know when to go on and when to withdraw.

Dr. Jung: No, that is not at all difficult. I tell you, when you come any-where near such heat you cannot touch it, you simply turn tail instinctively. When you are up against the inaccessible thing, you know it. . . . Of course, people are often so blissfully unconscious that they think they have never encountered such a thing, but that is just animus mist. If they would open their eyes a bit they would know that they had encountered the living taboo — whether in the form of an insight or understanding that would have been impossible; or as a feeling, an emotion, an adventure that was untouchable.

Comment: I suppose the patient did not realize that she was up against a test in this case. But if she had realized it, would she have had to go back to the unconscious to get more strength to meet it?

Dr. Jung: I do not know what her conscious situation was. . . . But if she had realized this was a test she would surely have done her best to hold on. . . . If you are hanging on for life, you will exert yourself more than when you are just holding onto your umbrella; when you are hanging to the edge of a roof over a six story drop, you will find additional strength to hold on. So it is often a question as to whether people realize their situation or not; if they realize its importance they will put all their reserves of strength into it. You see the conscious realization of their situation is the only reinforce-ment they get. . . .

Comment: Her consciousness seems to have progressed.

Dr. Jung: Decidedly. Even if she does not consciously know what is hap-pening in this vision, the vision shows that she has acquired more strength, more consciousness as a person, because now she can carry the thing through. She can hold on to the stone. As you realize, these things are very subtle but of the greatest practical importance. They are symbolic of the funda-mental decisions that take place *inside* human beings — and those are the im-portant decisions.

§

CW – *Collected Works of C.G. Jung* (Bollingen Series XX), trans. R.F.C. Hull, ed. H. Read, M. Fordham, G. Adler, Wm. McGuire, Princeton, N.J.: Princeton University Press; London: Routledge and Kegan Paul.

1. The mandalas referred to here appeared originally in *The Secret of the Golden Flower* (C.G. Jung and Richard Wilhelm, London: Kegan Paul, 1931; New York: Harcourt Brace, 1931). They are now to be found, together with a number of others, in *The Archetypes and the Collective Unconscious*, CW 9, i, in connection with "Concerning Mandala Symbolism," §§627ff.

2. A Tibetan mandala resembling the one described here but having 12 thunderbolts instead of 8 is illustrated and discussed by Jung in "Concerning Mandala Symbolism" (see Note 1).

3. *The Tibetan Book of the Dead or the After-Death Experiences on the "Bardo" Plane,* according to Lama Kazi Dawa-Samdup's English Rendering, ed. W.Y. Evans-Wentz, London: Oxford University Press, 1927 and 1957. cf. also Jung's Commentary in *Psychology and Religion: West and East*, CW 11, §§831ff.

4. Quoted from Linda Fierz-David's summary of this material, which is included in Miss Foote's seminar notes.

5. The final vision of Part Three is given here more fully to clarify further discussion.

6. Trans. B.M. Hinkle, New York: Moffat Yard, 1916; London: Kegan Paul, 1917. Extensively revised and re-translated as *Symbols of Transformation*, CW 5.

7. cf. *The Archetypes and the Collective Unconscious*, CW 9, i.

8. cf. Jung's "Psychological Commentary on the Kundalini Yoga" (four lectures), *Spring 1975, Spring 1976.*

9. cf. Zeus Sosipolis in *Themis*, by Jane Harrison, Cleveland: Meridian Paperback, 1962, pp. 150ff.

10. *Stromata, III,* 13, 92.

11. A.F.A. Bandelier, *The Delight Makers*, New York, 1890 and 1918.

12. cf. also *Symbols of Transformation*, CW 5, Plate 10.

13. G.R.S. Mead, *Fragments of a Faith Forgotten*, London: Watkins, 1931, pp. 185ff.

14. *The Ten Principal Upanishads*, New York: Macmillan, 1937, p. 78.

15. cf. *Symbols of Transformation*, CW 5, §§574f.

ILLUSTRATIONS

Illustration 1
The Indian standing on the brink of the pool beside his dead horse.

Illustration 2
Supplicating hands raised to the Indian as redeemer.

Illustration 3
The cortege moving backward in time.

Illustration 4
The eyes of the animal.

Illustration 5

"A white bird . . . flew up beyond the reach of the flames."

Illustration 6
The green-eyed satyr God.

Illustration 7
The beautiful youth and the old man in a turban.

Illustration 8
On the lap of an ancient mother.

Illustration 9

"Then I knew that I had become a tree . . ."

Illustration 10

The white flame of enlightenment.

Illustration 11
The past world is the overwhelming giant.

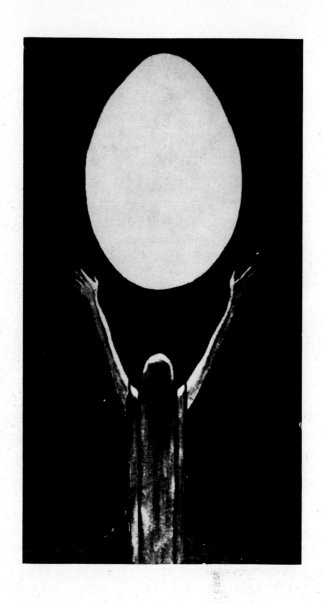

Illustration 12
"Open that I may know what is within you."

Illustration 13
The Negro as a God of vegetation.

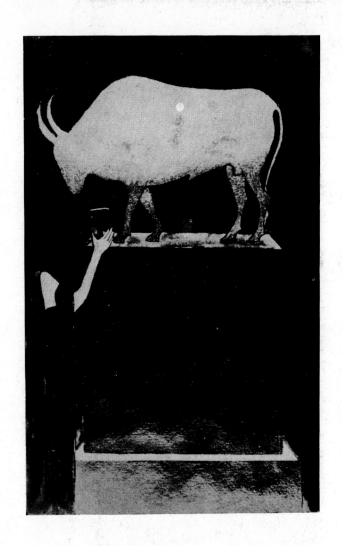

Illustration 14
"From that goblet you shall forever renew your strength."

Illustration 15
St. John with chalice and dragon.
(Detail of an altarpiece by Quentin Matsys.)

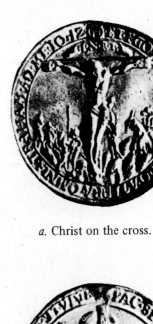

a. Christ on the cross.

b. The snake lifted up.

Illustration 16
"A snake . . . wound itself upon the cross."

Illustration 17
Two sides of a thaler
from the Ciba Archives in Basel.